New Ideas for Effective
School Improvement
Vision · Social Capital · Evaluation

New Ideas for Effective School Improvement Vision · Social Capital · Evaluation

William Ramsay and E. Eugene Clark

LIBRARY

 The Falmer Press

(A member of the Taylor & Francis Group)
London · New York · Philadelphia

UK   The Falmer Press, Rankine Road, Basingstoke, Hampshire RG24 OPR

USA   The Falmer Press, Taylor & Francis Inc., 1900 Frost Road, Suite 101, Bristol, PA 19007

First published 1990

British Library Cataloguing in Publication Data
Ramsay, William
  New ideas for effective school improvement: vision, social capital, evaluation.
  1. Australia. Young persons. Education
  I. Title II. Clark, E. Eugene
  371.00994

  ISBN 1-85000-696-2
  ISBN 1-85000-697-0 pbk

Library of Congress Cataloging-in-Publication Data
Ramsay, William.
  New ideas for effective school improvement: vision, social capital, evaluation/William Ramsay and E. Eugene Clark.
    p.   cm.
  Includes bibliographical references.
  ISBN 1-85000-696-2: — ISBN 1-85000-697-0 (pbk.):
  1. Catholic schools — Australia — Tasmania — Hobart — Evaluation. 2. Catholic schools — Australia — Tasmania — Hobart — Longitudinal studies. 3. St. Mary's College (Hobart, Tas.) — Evaluation.
  I. Clark, E. Eugene. II. Title.
LC509.3.H62R36 1990
377′.82′9461 — dc20   90-32216
                                             CIP

Jacket design by Caroline Archer

Typeset in 10.5/12pt Bembo × 28 picas Linotron 202 by Graphicraft Typesetters Ltd., Hong Kong

Table of Contents

v

Acknowledgments

We wish to record our thanks to Sr Barbara, the Principal of St Mary's College, for her friendship and support in making the school evaluation possible. We would also like to thank: colleagues at the University of Tasmania for their help and encouragement, especially Dr Brian Caldwell and Dr Paddy Lynch; Brother Reg Long, Principal of St Virgil's College, for permission to quote from the school's Mission Statement. Not least we express appreciation to the present and past students and staff of St Mary's College for their genuine cooperation with and interest in the project from which this book emanates. Finally, we would like to acknowledge our families for their patience and understanding in allowing us to become involved in this, our obsession to learn about the nature of school improvement.

List of Tables

List of Figures

List of Appendices

Preface

It was a joy for me to be invited to write a preface to this book. Its authors combine between them a range of qualifications and personal experience in academic life and professional educational practice and theory, both in Australia and the United States. The Catholic school, nine years of whose life is the subject and source of the book's empirical research, is one of the oldest and best loved in Tasmania. I found every chapter absorbing, and some of the material very challenging indeed.

Socrates, Plato and Aristotle were convinced that 'the unexamined life is not worth living'. They pursued that conviction with restless energy, and made it integral to the assumptions of Western cultural life. They devised a conceptual apparatus and a battery of philosophical techniques of astonishing power and fertility for the venture.

The authors of this book are driven by a very modern version of the same conviction. They bring it to bear on modern school-life. They confidently deploy the conceptual and dialectical resources of contemporary educational theory; one will not be surprised if their development of two key concepts contributes to research into aspects of the educational process far removed from their chosen focus. They also command the statistical rigour, and have devised the specific empirical techniques necessary, if their study is to transcend impressionistic generalizations. And they have been able to bring all this to bear on a particular school, especially suited to their purposes, which has entered into the inquiry with enlightened generosity.

Academic researchers are always addressing professional colleagues in their chosen field. I wish this book well with that readership, whose response will of course be the primary concern of the authors. But I anticipate that it will engage the active interest of two other types of reader.

Section 116 of the Australian Commonwealth Constitution was consciously, though neither exclusively nor mechanically, modelled on the First Amendment of the United States Constitution. But with regard to

the application of these to schools of religious character, the interpretations handed down by the respective supreme courts, and the practice followed by legislatures and governments, are very different in the two countries. Australian practice is quite positive. Both Federal and State Governments contribute significant funding to Catholic, Anglican (Episcopalian), Protestant, Jewish and Moslem schools.

In this matter, practice in Australia is considerably ahead of philosophy. Perhaps this is all to the good. There is a strongly pragmatic bent in the Australian mind-set and its popular culture, and a strongly empiricist tradition in professional philosophy here. Government funding of schools of religious inspiration arose from the pragmatics of politicking, far more than from dialogue of high principle about the Human Rights of parents to free and equal choice.

But now that the political dust has settled, there is a quickening appetite for enlightened inquiry into the intrinsic character, and the legitimately expected outcome, of the educational process. There are plenty of partial convictions, but little progress towards systematic overview of the desirable relationships between family, school, local community, wider society, and the national interest: all with regard to the individual student, who 'must always be treated as an end, never simply as a means'.

I believe that Ramsay and Clark's work will be of real value to those debates. The 'general educated public', outside schools and faculties of Education, is involved more vigorously than ever before; but they lack specific resources of vocabulary and concept. 'Social Capital' and 'Educational Vision' are not new terms invented by the authors, but they are lucidly and persuasively developed here in ways that will help the general reader to articulate judgments and arguments strongly felt, but not yet so well formulated as to contribute to the debate.

Catholic parents and pastors will be intensely interested in the 'School Evaluation'. The Catholic Church in Australia pours enormous human and financial resources into its schools. It is astonishing to think how miniscule is the fragment of these devoted to monitoring the success of the outcome: even to formulating criteria of such 'success'.

It is sometimes said with a somewhat haughty air of superiority, 'We are not in the numbers game', as if disdaining those involved in that 'game' as crass or unspiritual. Every diocesan Catholic Education Office has dedicated administrators who are, thank God, heart and soul into the 'numbers game' of staffing, funding, and every other aspect of the process. It is splendid that the research of Ramsay and Clark, and the liberal participation of the school, shows us how we may move towards building into our system a habitual practice of monitoring success and failure, and adjusting policies and methods in the light of the findings.

This book appears, providentially one may feel, at the very time that Particular Churches are preparing to capitalize to the full on the Catechism or Doctrinal Compendium being prepared by the Universal Church.

That preparation has been causing many people to re-discover the place of doctrinal education within the total effort of the Catholic school. Any sound education, especially at high school level, must involve the *whole* person. A sound Christian education must involve *all* the faith-powers: not only the affective and the conative, but also the cognitive: intellect, memory and imagination. Young Christians need to be empowered to discover for themselves that the doctrinal infrastructure of their faith is just as intellectually serious, just as incarnate in contemporary culture, as the other 'subjects' they are studying. Reading this book, I found myself re-formulating many such principles. I trust that it will have all sorts of similar effects on many a general reader, as well as engaging the authors' peers in fruitful professional dialogue.

+ Eric D'Arcy,
Archbishop of Hobart

Chapter 1

Introduction

Background to the Study

This book evolved from a school evaluation project at St Mary's College, an all girls school situated in Hobart, Tasmania, Australia. The Evaluation comprised a two-fold longitudinal study focussing on present and past students' perceptions of school and quality of school life.

As the work proceeded, however, elements of the broader context of school improvement increasingly began to intrude themselves into the design. Such elements — the perceptions of the school community (of parents/guardians and teachers, as well as students); the school's vision; the 'social capital' of this community — were like the insistent sounds and rhythms which at times enter the brain and will not go away without attention. This book is the result of our response to that essential music of school improvement, in the experience of which we would discover discord as well as harmony.

A Reflection on How the St Mary's College Study Began and an Introduction to Its Theoretical Context

There were a number of seemingly unintended motivations for the St Mary's College Evaluation Project. In the first place one of the authors, whilst on leave from the University, had joined the school staff full time for a term and as part of the arrangement would contribute to the work of the College's Curriculum Committee. During this period this 'consultant-staff member' and other staff members informally discussed the situation of contemporary Catholic schools. Questions emerged about the nature of the Catholic school's independence, its effectiveness in the current political climate, the possible future of Catholic education, etc. The St Mary's College Project was mounted partly in light of the concerns felt by teachers, as well as those recently expressed in the literature on Catholic schools and school improvement.

During the design phase of the study we began to look more closely at the literature on school evaluation, especially related to Catholic schools. This led to to our realization of the disparate nature of research into Catholic schools, and also to an awareness of some conceptual distinctions. For instance we noted Epstein's (1981) important distinction between research on the quality of school life and studies on the quality of schools.

> In most previous research, the quality of school has been defined in terms of school quantities. Schools with higher per-pupil expenditures; better teacher credentials; more library books, laboratories, or other facilities or equipment; and high average achievement scores have been considered schools of high quality. However, the presence of high achieving students and good school resources can be the result of family background and community conditions and may have little to with the quality of daily life in the school ... Many studies (Coleman *et al.*, 1966; Averch *et al.*, 1972; Jencks *et al.*, 1972; Rutter *et al.*, 1979) have pointed out that the quality of school life for students and teachers is more likely to be determined by social processes in schools and classrooms than by objective quantities of things and that school effects are more accurately assessed with attention to multiple student outcomes'. (p. 1)

In the process of organizing the design and building the methodology of the study we also recognized more clearly its basic purpose — that of school improvement. We conceded that in sending their children to Catholic school, the families had already made a strong, conscious commitment to a Catholic education (a point we found later expressed in Wehlage *et al.*, 1989). Thus we were constrained in a sense to temper our approach to evaluation with an understanding of what 'improvement' might or should mean. We knew that such school improvement could not be accomplished without a close analysis of what the Catholic school — in its real character as a community of parents/guardians as well as teachers and students — was already trying to achieve. In other words we were confronted with the necessity to understand the concept of a school's vision, what this meant for the Catholic school and how an evaluation might enable the vision to become reality.

Our understanding of the Catholic nature of the school community was considerably broadened by the work of Coleman and Hoffer, and Lesko, among others, who have interpreted this notion of community as social capital — the network of values, beliefs and norms of a Catholic community which include and influence the 'child in its midst'. Coleman and Hoffer's (1987) studies of Catholic schools in the USA presented empirical evidence of the greater effectiveness of these schools and con-

cluded that this was basically due to the strength of the network of norms and values — the social capital — which characterize Catholic schools. This concept along with that of school vision illuminated the meaning and potential of evaluation and we began to recognize their interrelatedness in an evaluative study of the identity of the Catholic school and how it could be improved. Our later discussion of these conceptual elements refers to other features which together formed a paradigm for what we consider constituted the most appropriate school evaluation process.

Finally, we have been able to reflect upon the nature and potential effectiveness of the St Mary's College Project through the appearance of some later research literature. We were much influenced by the recent research of Nancy Lesko (1988) into the special nature of Catholic schools. Lesko found that Catholic schools traditionally emphasize an ethos of 'community' and 'belonging' where all are equal in the eyes of God and expected and encouraged to develop and nurture their talents to the full. Such a philosophy is not mere doctrine, but pervades all aspects of the school curricula and structure and is celebrated in rituals, expounded upon in school literature, promoted in school newsletters, etc. Lesko concluded that this Catholic culture has a significant and positive impact upon students most at risk of dropping out (St Mary's College has a retention rate to grade 12 of approximately 80 per cent which is at least 20 per cent higher than the State school average). Lesko concludes by observing that Catholic schools today, however, are at risk. This is the result of a growing tension between the traditional notion of school as community and a more recent and competing vision of school as a place of competition.

Other concerns were raised by Sister Josephine Egan's (1988) survey of Catholic school senior students in Wales which noted the paucity of evaluative research on the effectiveness of Catholic schools. Archbishop of Cardiff, John Ward, in the foreward to Egan's book, *Opting Out: Catholic Schools Today* (1988), argues that there is an urgent need for a longitudinal study of Catholic school students 'to see what time has done to their perceptions of their Catholic schooling'. Archbishop Ward also calls for other Catholic school research projects which involve the views of teachers, parents and other members of the Catholic community in which the school is embedded. Sister Egan herself calls for more supportive qualitative research to validate and further elucidate the empirical findings of surveys such as her Wales study. Such recommendations find support in the Australian work of Flynn (1975 and 1985). They also validate the St Mary's design which involves quantitative and qualitative measures, is longitudinal in scope (1978–86) and incorporates the views of parents and teachers, as well as those of students.

We were heartened by the work of Wehlage *et al.* (1989) in a study of selected schools across the United States which were judged to be

particularly effective at providing school-community support to those students most at risk of dropping out. This research provides a useful synthesis of the macro/societal perspective of Coleman and Hoffer (1987) with their notion of social capital and the voluminous body of literature on effective schools. Coleman and Hoffer's finding that Catholic schools do a better job at retaining their at-risk students, argue Wehlage and colleagues, is only partially explained by the social structure *outside of school* — the social capital which derives from the Catholic community with its commonality of values, expectations, etc. The weakness of such an approach is that it ignores the impact of what goes on *inside* the Catholic school which makes it effective. It is here that the micro-level, school effects research complements the broader perspective of Coleman and Hoffer and others:

> Based on an extensive body of ethnographic data that now exists on the importance of the culture of schools, it would seem that any explanation for the differential success of schools that ignores the internal workings of the institution must almost certainly be inadequate. A theory of school effects ought to include factors arising outside the institution, as well as those resulting from the culture and relations inside it.

Accordingly, the St Mary's Evaluation has been an examination of the school — 'inside and out'. It considers not only the special nature of the Catholic community of faith, of which St Mary's is an integral part, but seeks further to discover how, in what ways, and with what effects, the day-to-day events and organization of St Mary's make a difference in the lives of its students.

Structure of this Book

Building upon the reports of findings presented to St Mary's College, this book further explores the nature and process of school evaluation, enlarges upon the concept of educational vision, and examines the idea and importance of the social capital of school communities. With reference to the study itself, particular attention is given to the comparative analysis of data from students, teachers and parents.

Chapter 2, *The Context of School Improvement*, highlights the need for a holistic view of school improvement which considers the interrelationship of school evaluation, educational vision, social capital and the effective implementation of change in bringing about school improvement. Also stressed is the appropriateness of a longitudinal study which can reflect these concepts in action over a period of years within the same school. This chapter provides a theoretical overview of the causal factors implicit to effective school improvement. It discusses the importance of

macro or social elements such as the epistemological foundations and the social, political and economic setting of which the school is a part.

Chapter 3 explores *The Nature of School Evaluation*. A brief history of evaluation theory and practices is presented. The relative advantages of quantitative and qualitative evaluation are discussed and examples given of popular evaluation models. Drawing on the previous theoretical discussion, a detailed rationale for the St Mary's College Evaluation paradigm is presented.

Chapter 4 describes the methodology for the *St Mary's School Improvement Project* and presents the major findings. These include findings from the students alone, a comparative analysis of results from students, teachers, and parents, together with the results of the analysis employing four psycho-social variables. Summary reports of follow-up student and teacher reaction discussions and summaries of interviews with past and present students are also included. While these findings will be of special interest to Catholic schools, we presume that they are nevertheless relevant to all schools and illustrate the kinds of information which can result from a comprehensive school evaluation.

Chapter 5 builds upon the work of Starratt, Caldwell and others which stresses the important of *Educational Vision*, a picture of a desired future state towards which all school improvement efforts are aimed. The chapter presents examples of school vision statements and explains how vision relates to other features of school improvement such as school management and leadership.

Chapter 6 is concerned with another vital aspect of school improvement, that of *Social Capital*. Social capital is the network of parents, staff and students who share common values, norms, beliefs and expectations. These groups have a collective vision of the nature of the educational good. The existence of such networks, most often a feature of religious schools, provides many educational benefits, especially for those students most at risk of dropping out of school. The chapter offers a number of examples of, and strategies by which, schools, parents and the wider community can enhance social capital and thereby provide greater educational benefits to the youth of the community.

Chapter 7 briefly considers the task of *School Management* and how a school's vision can be reflected in, and its social capital enhanced by, the day-to-day organization of school life. Special emphasis is given to the notion of 'collaborative management', a school management model popularized by Caldwell and Spinks in Australia, New Zealand, and England.

Chapter 8 turns from day-to-day realities of school management, to examine the process of *Educational Change* itself. School communities do not remain static — in many respects they evolve over time. Indeed, the very concept of improvement implies a 'change' for the better. The St Mary's College Project tells a story about the nature and experience of

educational change. Reflecting on that experience, we share our insights about how educational change may be facilitated.

Finally, the *Concluding Statement* addresses the broader implications of the St Mary's Project and what it says about the contribution effective schools can make to society as a whole.

Chapter 2

The Context of School Improvement

Introduction

While the overall purpose of the St Mary's College Evaluation was school improvement, this could not be accomplished without a consideration of what the school — the community of parents, teachers and students — was trying to achieve, its vision of education. For a Catholic school, that vision was inextricably bound up with the Catholic Faith. Thus, our exploration of school improvement led us to explore relatively new concepts like vision, school culture and social capital — the community network of values, beliefs and norms of which a child is a part — together with leadership, school management and the process of change itself.

In this chapter we chronicle the development of school improvement efforts from the 1950s to the 1980s. That development suggests that social, economic and political changes caused by the shift from industrial to post-industrial periods have left many schools in a state of crisis as they seek to adjust to the problems of operating in modern society. These problems include greater uncertainty, a new information environment, a changing family structure, greater interdependence between countries and greater pluralism within national borders. As a result of these social, economic and political factors, school improvement in the 1980s and 1990s is contextually different from school improvement in the preceding decades. Accordingly, previous theories which focussed individually on evaluation, change, leadership and other central features of school improvement must be replaced by more holistic approaches to school improvement which account for the new dynamics and interrelationships between schools and society and, at the same time, take into account the history, politics and key agents active within the local context. In the narrow sense, this chapter summarizes what the authors have learned about school improvement from the St Mary's Study. In a broader sense, however, the lessons learned from the St Mary's experience may prove to

be helpful to people in other schools, government and private, who seek a greater understanding of the dynamics of school improvement.

The Changing Face of School Improvement

Van Velzen *et al.* (1986) point out that school improvement for OECD countries in the 1950s and early 1960s consisted primarily of small scale curriculum improvement and the development of new learning materials. The individual teacher was the focus of improvement and the approach was a technical one involving the 'seeding' of various innovations coupled with the hope that other teachers in the same school, then other schools, would adopt the innovation. Outside consultants were often utilized as subject experts. Nevertheless, the actual process of change received little attention.

In the late 1960s and 1970s, however, many educators became disillusioned with this often simplistic and narrow approach. As a result, school improvement efforts increasingly took account of system-wide reform, whole school organization and related value and attitudinal changes. As Van Velzen *et al.* describe it:

> In many countries the accent lay on comprehensive school reform. The improvement was primarily focused on the whole faculty, or on key persons such as school leaders. The strategy was more process-oriented, taking normative changes into account. Nevertheless in many countries the strategy was general. All the participating schools got more or less the same treatment. There was little attention to the individual teacher, the classroom implications and the development of differential teaching material. Most curriculum development bore a general character, though more attention was paid to the mutual adaptation of the innovation and the local school with its own context and characteristics. (1986, p. 31)

In short, educators in the late 1960s and 1970s recognized the complexity of school improvement. They also emphasized the importance of process, as much as subject matter. Outside consultants were viewed as 'process helpers' in the implementation of change. There was in fact, as Stoel and Scheerens (1988) have pointed out, a shift in emphasis in school effectiveness research from 'input-output' to 'process-output' studies — a 'first and second phase' of this research. Coleman *et al.* (1966) and Jencks *et al.* (1972) represented the first phase, and Edmonds (1979) and Rutter *et al.* (1979) the second phase. Stoel and Scheerens explain that the latter phase ignored what became known as a '5 factor model' of school effectiveness which implied academic goal consensus, safe and orderly climate, strong instructional leadership, high expectations for student

achievement, and frequent evaluation of pupil progress. This was also a period of educational growth as the governments of most countries poured significant funds into improving their educational system.

By the 1980s, however, it had become clear that making widescale structural changes would not necessarily affect what went on in the individual classroom. As schools cope with changing economic, political and social realities there are signs of a convergence of the approaches of the last three decades (Van Velzen *et al.*, 1986). School improvement has taken on a much more holistic, yet individualized school-based approach which requires the collaborative efforts of school leaders, teachers, parents and students (Caldwell and Spinks, 1986 and 1988). This development has seen an enhanced view of teachers as professionals and the realization that school improvement is quintessentially concerned with the resolution of basic values and a consensus about the nature of the educational good (Holt, 1987). In addition there were certain questionable assumptions attending the '5 factor model'. These assumptions related to ethnic and socio-economic differences in school populations together with differences in organization. Essentially the important feature emerging was the evaluation of schools in terms of their cultural context.

The 1980s has also seen a continued emphasis on process and the institutionalization of change. Governments in many countries are putting into place structural mechanisms which aim to prepare schools to be more flexible and adaptable to local needs, yet take into account national and state guidelines and priorities (Marsh, 1988). As a result of these and other social forces, the approach to school improvement is changing and new theories are emerging which attempt to take into account new perspectives on the school-based focus, need for collaboration, greater national and international interdependence, the need to understand the process and nature of change, and how school improvement is actually brought about. Some of these emerging concepts are discussed below, but first we must consider the wider societal context from which these ideas spring.

A Time of Uncertainty and Transition

Alvin Toffler (1981), John Naisbitt (1982), and Daniel Bell (1984) are three among many popular writers who contend that society is in the midst of a major transition as the industrial age ends and is replaced by the information age. According to Toffler (1981), for example, civilization has experienced three major waves. The First Wave was led by developments in agriculture which made it possible for humankind to give up a nomadic hunter way of life and settle permanently in one location. The Second Wave ushered in the Industrial Revolution and a world of cities, specialization, nuclear family, mobility, individualization,

compulsory schooling and highly intricate social, political and economic networks. The Third Wave began in the mid 1950s, when for the first time in societies like the USA, white-collar workers in technical, managerial and clerical occupations outnumbered blue-collar workers. For the first time more people were employed in information linked occupations than with the production of material goods.

As this Third Wave moves inexorably towards its crest, society has struggled to maintain its balance amidst the shifting sands of cultural-value fluctuations, demographic changes, cultural diffusion, technological advancements and social innovation (McDaniel, 1982). Similarly, Naisbitt (1982) identifies ten 'megatrends' which are having a significant impact on the nature of schooling and therefore school improvement: 1) changing from an industrial society to an information society; 2) the increasing need for high technology combined with a corresponding high level of human interaction; 3) movement from a national to a world economy; 4) a shift of emphasis from short-term to long-term planning; 5) a move away from centralized government and towards decentralized government and social services; 6) more emphasis on self-help as opposed to government help; 7) trend from representative democracy to participatory democracy; 8) a shift from organizational hierarchies towards organizational networking; 9) a demographic shift to sun belt areas; and 10) fewer either/or choice situations and more situations characterized by multiple options and possibilities.

As a result of these and other developments, educators are beginning, and must continue, to adjust to a curriculum which emphasizes process more than subject matter content. Learning will have to be considered as a lifelong process with several major periods of re-learning necessary along the way. Schools are also likely to play a less important role in the lives of students as technology and other influences challenge roles traditionally relegated to schools. Greater participatory democracy will also mean a more active role in schools to be played by students, teachers, parents and local community. The computer and accompanying technology will also bring about more individualized learning and a classroom situation less dominated by the teacher. An increasing emphasis on cultural pluralism will also mean that schools will have to make adjustments to cater for such individual differences.

While popular writers explore 'megatrends' and prepare to ride society's 'Third Wave', other writers proclaim the need to explore less obvious and more contextually bound realities (Walker and Barton, 1989). They seek answers to such questions as: How do organizations, like schools, gain control? How are the activities of teachers structured and organized? What forms of legitimation support and 'naturalize' existing organizational structures? What and whose interests are promoted by the forms of control and structure which predominate? As Ball observes:

The workplace is a site of ongoing dialectic interaction between competing groups. But we should note that conflict in the organization is not limited to vertical relationships between leaders and workers. The complex structure of organizations, certainly schools, also fosters lateral internecine conflicts. These also need to be taken account of in the development of a coherent theory. (1989, p. 220)

In Ball's view, the improvement of education must be seen as involving predominantly political action. Dale (1989) and Morrell (1989) are among the writers who have traced the nature and effects of this political action by analyzing how political ideologies and initiatives have generated a particular agenda and accompanying problems and challenges for education:

The United States and British economies are in the midst of one of the most powerful structural crises they have experienced since the depression. In order to solve it on terms acceptable to dominant interests, as many aspects of the society as possible need to be pressured into conforming with the requirements of international competition, reindustrialization, and (in the words of the National Commission on Excellence in Education in the United States) 'rearmament' ... In the process, in the United States, Britain and Australia, the emphasis of public policy has materially changed from issues of employing the State to overcome disadvantage. Equality, no matter how limited or badly conceived, has become redefined. No longer is it seen as linked to past group oppression and disadvantagement. It is simply now a case of guaranteeing individual choice under the conditions of a 'free market'. (p. 4)

On an individual and micro level, too, new ideas are emerging as educators begin to recognize that intelligence is not comprised solely of cognitive faculties, but includes musical, artistic, spacial, kinesthetic and interpersonal domains (Gardner, 1987). Thus new teaching and learning strategies and curriculum changes will have to take these into account in order to develop all of an individual's talents. Major developments in learning theory have also pointed to the fact that teachers and students have different learning styles (Katz and Henry, 1989). Thus, school improvement effort will have to account for individual as well as societal needs. There will also be important attitudinal adjustments. As the knowledge explosion escalates in geometric proportions, today's answers will increasingly be proven wrong tomorrow. Thus, educators, in one sense, will have to show less reverence for the past, be prepared to re-socialize and be more future-looking (Cornstein and Hunkins, 1988). These are just a few of the possible changes which will be facing schools in the 1990s and beyond.

While these changes hail an age of great excitement and challenge, they also produce feelings of instability, anxiety, chaos and uncertainty. This atmosphere of crisis is exacerbated by the increasing rate of change. The shift from hunter-gatherer societies to agricultural communities took thousands of years. The shift from agricultural to industrial societies took several centuries in Europe and a century in the United States. In stark contrast, the shift form an industrial to an information society has occurred in only a few decades (Toffler, 1981).

Shift from Traditional to New Educational Paradigms

So rapid and monumental have been the changes in society that education appears to be in a state of crisis. Around the globe, school administrators, teachers, parents, industry and whole communities have at times expressed dismay at the inability of schools to solve a host of problems: how to design an appropriate curriculum; how to cope with change; how to get more support from parents and community; how to prepare children for a society with high unemployment; how to deal with increased conflict within families; how to determine the proper role of computers; how to educate children for more autonomy, and so on (Pusey, 1979). Thus Crozier (1975) wrote of the failing of the legitimacy of public education in Western Europe democracies:

> Education as a moral establishment ... is in trouble all over Western Europe. It has lost its former authority. Teachers cannot believe anymore in their sacred mission and their students do not accept their authority as easily as they did before. Along with the religious rationale for the social order, educational authority does not hold firm anymore. (1975, p. 137)

Pusey (1979) argues that another feature of this crisis is the blurring of demarcations between organizations and society. 'The boundaries of school principals dissolve as they struggle, amid mounting anxiety, to do the work of priest, marriage counsellor, social worker, career advisor, policeman and educationist' (Thomas, 1987, p. 34).

At the core of much of this anxiety, uncertainty, change, even chaos, in educational theory and practice has been the debate about the epistemological foundations of educational knowledge itself. Emerging from the management models of the 1930s and reaching its peak in the middle 1960s the predominant, and largely unchallenged, paradigm of education was that of empirical-analytical positivism. Claiming to be value free or neutral, this approach sought to apply the rigours of scientific predictive

empirical research to social phenomena. By the 1970s, however, it had become increasingly apparent that social realities could not always be adequately measured, predicted or understood by the application of scientific methodology. Thus alternative approaches emerged which have been given different names. Those writers following an interpretative (or hermeneutic) paradigm suggest that organizations have no ontological existence apart from the meanings given by the people who comprise them. The interpretivist sees education as a process based on the existential needs of participants. These participants come to a greater understanding of their universe by a systematic analysis of their different perspectives, and a decodification and consideration of possible solutions to their shared problems (Greenfield, 1986). A related, and often complementary paradigm is the critical perspective, which 'does not restrict itself to reflection and communication, but combines the reflexive operations of the interpretative cycle with the action-oriented steps of planning, execution and evaluation' (Lierman, 1987, p. 19).

These paradigm shifts are important because they depict the struggle of educators to determine the nature of educational knowledge. They suggest that there is much that we do not know about education and schooling. At the same time, emerging paradigms offer new ways of perceiving, examining, accounting for, predicting and even controlling the growing complexities of social reality. This point is made by Harmon (1976) who noted that a 'paradigm shift' was necessary before science was able to predict earthquakes. Scientists needed to challenge the traditional assumptions, to take off the perceptual blinkers of the existing paradigm, so that they could discover a new set of rules which enabled them to answer what was previously unanswerable (Thomas, 1987). On a larger scale paradigm shifts such as those of Copernicus, Galileo and Einstein often involve major and fundamental changes in, and challenges to, society's values and goals. In this respect such paradigm shifts also have a major impact on our ideas about school improvement.

An Emerging Paradigm for School Improvement: A Contextual Approach Uniting Global and Local Perspectives

In the remaining sections we survey the implications of social, economic and political changes which are having a profound impact on schools. These changes mean that school improvement in the 1990s and beyond will be different from school improvement efforts in the past. They also mean that educators will require a new paradigm of school improvement which will provide new ways of analyzing and coming to grip with these changes and the problems, opportunities and challenges they bring.

The Importance of Context Generally

A recent United Nations publication, appropriately entitled Our Common Future, emphasizes the interrelationship between the world economy and the planet's ecology and calls for local, state, national and international action to deal with problems which have transcended national borders. Coincidentally with the world becoming a 'global village' there is another world-wide trend in an apparently opposite direction. In education, it is characterized by the actions of national education bodies which are providing greater autonomy to local schools to manage their own affairs (Caldwell, 1988). At the same time education generally is coming under increasing centralized control. Responses of schools to change are therefore complex and demanding.

This paradoxical development highlights the need for school improvement theorists and practitioners, to understand the context of their activities. Leadership, culture, parental involvement, evaluation, change, curriculum design, teaching strategies etc cannot be considered in a vacuum. Effective school improvement in the 1990s will require more holistic approaches which consider local as well as global realities. This new paradigm for school improvement will be characterized by the need to 'think globally, but act locally' Dubos (1981). As Dubos points out, we need to to be aware of the wider world and our inter-connectedness with our fellow human beings, but, at the same time, we must begin to solve global problems by acting locally.

> Most of human life since the Old Stone Age has been spent in small, fairly stable communities, consisting of either moving bands of nomads or small stable villages, which were organized to satisfy the invariants of humankind out of the resources locally available. There have been countless political revolutions and other upheavals in the course of history but their final outcome has always been to recreate communities of a few hundred or thousand people in which everyone knew his or her place in the social order of things and accepted, willingly, or under duress, the local rules of the game. Surprising as it may seem, this pattern of social structure still prevails to a large extent in most of the world today. The word 'community' or its equivalents in other languages has everywhere a deep sentimental appeal. (Dubos, 1981, p. 87)

Dubos' analysis suggests why school 'communities' working out their own problems can be such a powerful force in achieving real school improvement. As Cuban (1988, p. 241) concludes:

> With all of the criticism of the effective schools movement and its research from both academics and practitioners, one fact has

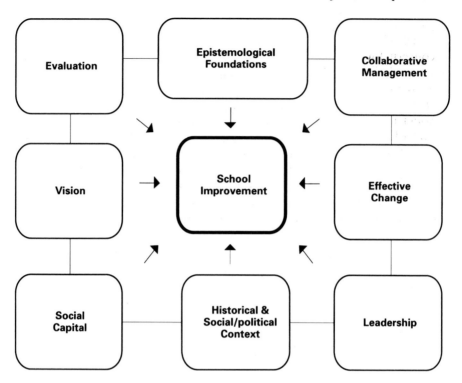

Figure 1   *Significant factors in the context of school improvement*

stubbornly emerged: Substantial changes that touch the inner core of classroom activities occur at the school site where principal and teachers work together with students to achieve common aims. The literature on effective schools, reinforcing the folk wisdom of practitioners, has underscored the importance of building com- mitment to the goals among those who do the daily work and holding them responsible for outcomes.

The diagram above highlights some of the major contextual factors which which must be accounted for in a paradigm of school improve- ment followed by a brief discussion of the relationship of these factors to the process of school improvement.

Importance of Historical Context

In book three of their trilogy, *Anatomy of Educational Innovation: A Mid to Long Term Re-study and Reconstrual,* Smith *et al.* (1988) emphasize the roles of history and political science in understanding how educa- tional innovation comes about in a particular school. Educationists of the

past, however, have tended to be either historians or contemporaneous social scientists. 'The former tend toward narrative orientations with less concern for formalizing their theoretical insights. The latter tend to be more applied social scientists — organizational theorists and sociologists — with less concern for the history of their substantive concerns' (Smith *et al.*, 1988, p. 282). These writers argue the case for more intimate contact between the two. This means that on a macro/theoretical level, one cannot ignore the global societal, political and economic changes which are impacting upon schools. At the same time, neither can educationists truly grasp the nature of school improvement without an understanding of the historical development and background within which those improvements operate. Thus Smith *et al.* (1988) advocate the value of longitudinal studies such as their study of the Kensington School and Milford School District over a period of sixty years:

> In our view, now, anyone who attempts to talk about school innovation ahistorically, without an understanding of the kind that an historical case such as the Milford chronicle gives, is seriously limiting their perspective. (p. 259)

Accordingly, in the spirit of Smith and colleagues, we portray the St Mary's school improvement story within the broader context of Catholic schooling in Australia and against the backdrop of the local historical context as it has evolved over 120 years.

Importance of Political Context

Another important and useful concept in understanding school improvement is that of politics and power. Who runs the school, the nature of conflict within the organization and the underlying values of various political interests are crucial elements underlying the reality of any school. Indeed, Smith and colleagues contend that their realization of the importance of understanding organizational politics in school improvement to be one of the most important findings of their longitudinal study (1988, p. 316). Quoting Bruner, the authors describe the interplay between politics, social theory and educational innovation:

> In his usual provocative style, Bruner (1983) ... comments: 'I suppose my hopes for a clarification (or even a taxonomy) of the nature of human values grew from a conviction that psychology could not live healthily in isolation from the normative or policy disciplines — jurisprudence, literary criticism, legal and moral philosophy, political science. Like many anthropologists and like "conceptual pragmatists" generally, I believe that we constitute and negotiate our own social reality and that meaning is finally

"settled" by these constitutive and negotiatory processes' (1983, p. 281). He seems to be arguing for psychology what we have been arguing for education in general and for educational innovation in particular. As we have indicated these issues run much deeper in philosophy and the social sciences. Bernstein (1978) speaks of 'the restructuring of social and political theory' and Fay (1975) speaks of the reconceptualization of 'social theory and political practice.' Their positions seem important for 'the many faces of democracy in innovation and schooling'. (Smith *et al.*, 1988, p. 336)

A recent example of a school evaluation which takes into account political, as well as social and historical contexts, is Angus' (1988) study of a Catholic, Christian Brothers school in Australia. Drawing upon the work of Bourdieu, Giroux and others, Angus analyzed the tensions between those Christian Brothers who seek to reaffirm the traditional mission of school as offering a radical, Catholic and spiritual alternative to the dominant Anglo-Protestant ruling class model, and those Brothers for whom 'Catholic resistance to Ango-Protestant domination took the form of a bid for comparable Catholic social and economic power' (p. 152).

Educational Vision and School Improvement

We noted earlier that schools increasingly will also have to be more concerned with the future. Long term planning, vision, a focus on looking forward, will become increasingly important. For this reason, a paradigm for school improvement in the 1990s must concern itself with educational vision (Bennis and Nanus, 1985; Starratt, 1986; T. Greenfield, 1986; W. Greenfield, 1987; Caldwell and Spinks 1986 and 1988; Beare, Caldwell and Millikan, 1988). An effective vision is founded upon values which permeate all aspects of the school, from curriculum policies to day-to-day operations. Effective schools have leaders who articulate a compelling vision which is shared and fostered by the wider school community (Roueche and Baker, 1986). Finally, it is important to realize that a vision is founded upon a set of values and beliefs concerning the nature of the educational good. As Holt (1987) observes, many recent school improvement efforts have failed to produce long-term benefits because they focussed exclusively on the procedures involved in the management of change. To achieve significant educational change we must be aware of a wider context which recognizes that school improvement is integrally involved with the solving of moral problems, that is, value judgments about the nature of the educational good (Etzioni, 1988).

The Role of Evaluation in School Improvement

Another important concept in the new context of school improvement for the 1980s and beyond is that of evaluation (see Chapter 3). Many schools have unfortunately viewed evaluation as a luxury to be afforded on rare occasions. In these schools evaluation has accordingly been a one-time event which has produced little school improvement and only resulted in a printed report sitting on a shelf, neatly bound and gathering dust. In order to be effective, however, evaluation must be an aid to decision making, a regular component of the management cycle of the school. Properly employed, evaluation is the mechanism by which a school community can measure the extent to which its educational vision has become school reality. Evaluation therefore serves a multitude of purposes: accountability, management, school improvement and more informed decision making.

Parents and School Improvement: The Importance of Social Capital

An often ignored, yet vital component in school improvement is parents. In their recent study of the effectiveness of public, Catholic and non-religious private schools, Coleman and Hoffer (1987) have demonstrated the vital importance of social capital — the network of parents and the wider community of adults of which children and the school are a part. A paradigm of school improvement must therefore consider parents and the importance of social capital in the education of children. That is, the more this understanding of social capital is reflected in the school's examination of its life, the more clearly may the school's effectiveness be crystalized; and the greater the likelihood for improvement to occur in reality. It will be very interesting, in the final results of the St Mary's Study, to compare parental, student and staff responses regarding their expectations of the school and their respective views regarding how well the school has fulfilled those expectations. Chapter 6 explores this concept of social capital in detail.

Collaborative Management: A General Strategy for School Improvement

Another vital ingredient to effective local action is collaboration, especially between the participants of school communities. The work of Caldwell and Spinks (1986 and 1988) offers a blueprint for the ways in which school communities can work together toward school improvement. The

St Mary's College School Improvement Project provides a logical, case-study ,accompaniment and a Catholic complement, to the Caldwell and Spinks study which involved a state school and was described in The Self Managing School (1988). The theoretical framework of collaborative management is discussed in detail in Chapter 7.

The St Mary's College Project demonstrates the experience of a school engaged in a struggle to maintain its unique ethos and autonomy at a time of change, of general contraction and a scarcity of resources. Importantly, its self-evaluation was a collaborative effort of students, parents, school leaders and staff. Moreover the study was designed not simply to help the school be accountable, but to be accountable with integrity in the face of potential threats to its educational autonomy. The school has attempted to establish its own educational vision, to re-cognize the significance of its social capital in its development and out-comes, and to find collaborative ways for transforming its vision into reality.

Effective Implementation of Educational Change

While the process of change cannot be the sole focus for school improve-ment it does play a vital role. Indeed, in practice one of the most widespread difficulties in school evaluation and school improvement efforts has been the failure to implement the desired change. Caldwell and Spinks (1988) outline a general strategy for guiding a school from over-arching vision through to contextual reality. The seminal work of Miles (1987) provides a theoretical yet practical framework of how to get from what is to what should be. Miles identifies four essential preconditions for the successful implementation of change:

a) the existence of a principal who has leadership and management skills;
b) the existence of school autonomy;
c) a staff environment that is characterized by relatively low con-flict and high trust and an overall cohesiveness;
d) good programme design in training, technical support, planning and monitoring procedures.

Chapter 8 highlights the existence of many causal factors which are important in bringing about effective educational change. Miles and others have noted the absence of and need for longitudinal studies on a specific school in which school improvement in its full context may be studied. The authors feel that, when completed, the St Mary's College Study will fulfil that requirement.

Bridging the Gulf Between Theory and Practice in School Improvement

Bennis, Benne and Chin (1961) relate a delightful parable which aptly describes the gulf which has traditionally existed between educational research and practice.

> There is an old parable that has made the rounds about the grasshopper who decided to consult the hoary consultant of the animal kingdom, the owl, about a personal problem. The problem concerned the fact that the grasshopper suffered each winter from severe pains due to the savage temperature. After a number of these painful winters, in which all of the grasshopper's known remedies were of no avail, he presented his case to the venerable and wise owl. The owl, after patiently listening to the grasshopper's misery, so the story goes, prescribed a simple solution. 'Simply turn yourself into a cricket and hibernate during the winter'. The grasshopper jumped joyously away, profusely thanking the owl for his advice. Later however, after discovering that this important knowledge could not be transformed into action, the grasshopper returned to the owl and asked him how he could perform this metamorphosis. The owl replied rather curtly, 'Look, I gave you the principle. It's up to you to work out the details!' (Bennis *et al.*, 1961, p. 3)

A school improvement paradigm which does not consider the elements described above, may be only as helpful as the owl's advice to the grasshopper. In fact, Miles *et al.* (1986) submits that this has often been the case. In contrast, the approach adopted in the St Mary's Study represents an integration of empirical–analytical and interpretative–critical paradigms to form a more contextual approach to school improvement. By the use of such a holistic approach within the context of a longitudinal study, we hope to bridge the gulf between research and practice. Thus, in the St Mary's Study, the researchers have not been distant, value-neutral observers. Rather, the authors have been and remain involved from within the organization. Gene Clark was the Deputy Principal of St Mary's and Bill Ramsay, while on study leave, spent a full term at the College as a full-time classroom teacher. The St Mary's College Study was not imposed upon the College from the outside. Rather it grew, evolved, from a consensus of the school community. This is why the results of the Study have, we believe, so much practical implication and interest to other schools and scholars. The importance of bridging this gulf between research and practice is beautifully illustrated by Lierman (1987, p. 21) who adds the following sequel to the parable cited above in Bennis *et al.*:

At the end of the next winter, a group of grasshoppers came back to see master owl. He was delighted to notice that they looked rather well, and he asked them: 'Well, did you apply my principle?' One grasshopper, apparently the leader of the group replied: 'No sir. We held a long discussion, and then decided to build a shelter with the means at hand.' 'That may well be,' said the owl, 'but I do not see the principle behind all this.' The leader smilingly replied: 'To understand this, you will have to come down off your branch, and to share out grassroots experience. Good principles are learned from good practice...'

Conclusion

The traditional empirical-analytical tradition of educational theory is increasingly viewed as inadequate to describe the rich and intricate realities of social life. This is not to say, however, that education has gained little from traditional empirical research. As Leirman (1987, p. 21) points out: 'Our insight into dimensions and phases of the educative process, into psychological and social conditions of learning, into the illusion of quick attitude change, into the nature of systems and subsystems of education, into leadership styles and their effects into the diffusion of knowledge, into the effects of new technologies, etc has largely been acquired thanks to this tradition'. Also, scientific positivism and its rich heritage of quantifiable, highly verifiable methodologies continues to play a major role in developing educational knowledge. At the same time, however, a growing number of educators are of the view that there exist many qualitative social realities which are better accounted for by the interpretive-critical paradigms. These emerging paradigms more accurately gauge the subtle human intricacies at play in a holistic context of individual, group and institutional actions. Such actions can transcend the bounds of the classroom, the school or even education itself, and take into their kin the whole intricate network of a wider society of which education is but a part.

The St Mary's Study has been an attempt to think globally, but act locally, in bringing about school improvement. Globally, we have attempted to consider the 'megatrends' operating in society and their impact upon schools. Had we stopped there, however, we would probably have despaired at the magnitude and complexity of the task. The key to action is to start in your own backyard, your own community, your own environment, your own school. That community, for the authors, is St Mary's College. It is here that the we have come down off the theoretical branch and share the grassroots experience of the teachers, parents and students who comprise St Mary's College. The early results

of that experience are chronicled in this book. Through reflection upon those rich experiences and the implementation of policies which take them into account, we, the community which is St Mary's, hope to find, as did the grasshoppers, that good principles are indeed learned from good practice.

Chapter 3

The Nature of School Evaluation

Evaluation in Context

In its neophyte stages the St Mary's College Study focussed primarily on school evaluation. In fact, it is common for school improvement efforts as well as the collaborative form of school management (which involves principal, teachers and students in shared and long term policy-making, evaluation and management of the school) to begin with an evaluation. However, out of such beginnings, we discovered that an evaluation, in and of itself, would not bring about school improvement. As argued in Chapter 2, the central point emerging from the St Mary's Project is that an evaluation which actually results in school improvement is one which is inextricably bound up with a school's vision, its social capital, leadership, school culture and collaborative management (which involves principal, staff, parents and students in shared and long-term evaluative and management activity), each contributing to the successful implementation of change. These are all pieces of the puzzle which must be in place before a clear picture of school improvement emerges.

In this chapter we define and trace the history of school evaluation. However, unlike other works, evaluation here is viewed not as an end it itself, but as an invaluable means to determine the extent to which a school's vision has become reality. Evaluation is a vehicle by which schools can commence the voyage of self-discovery leading to significant development. In different forms, evaluation is also a mechanism by which the school can find answers to important questions such as: How is the school performing? What is working well? What needs more attention? Are we, as a school community, moving towards the fulfilment of our vision?

Evaluation: The State-of-the-Art

Anyone coming into educational evaluation for the first time would likely confess to some feelings of confusion and bewilderment when faced with

a plethora of evaluation models and theories, each employing its own vocabulary, paradigm, assumptions and methodology. Even those who are experienced in the field often feel like the person in Plato's cave, trying to make sense out of evaluation shadows hoping to discern some idea of the educational reality outside. Even after decades of research and theorizing about the subject of educational evaluation, the extent to which the educational shadows actually reflect their objects is uncertain (Marsh and Stafford, 1988, p. 59). However, there is at least some comfort in the realization that one is not alone in the educational cave. Indeed, writers and thinkers around the globe continue to address the nature of evaluation. As a result, considerable progress has been, and is being, made as different perspectives, different ways of looking at the educational shadows, emerge. Below is one description of the shadows which the present authors perceive on the educational cave wall. Initially this chapter examines the central definitions involving educational evaluation. Next, the chapter traces the evolution of the recent field of educational evaluation and analyzes the different epistemological bases underlying various evaluation models. Also provided is a brief summary of the major evaluation models together with a weighing of the advantages and disadvantages of each. The chapter also summarizes and critiques the practice of educational evaluation in Australia. Finally, the chapter presents a justification of the evaluation paradigm employed in the St Mary's College Study and comments upon the role of evaluation within the broader scope of school improvement.

Definitions and Basic Concepts

It is beyond the scope of this Report to present a 'dictionary' of terms employed in educational evaluation. Indeed, Popham (1975) and Rose and Nyre (1977), among others, suggest that such a task would be impossible because of the amorphous nature of the field. Popham characterizes educational evaluation as an 'immature specialization' with confused terminology, a large number of models and an incomplete technology. Nevertheless, a few basic definitions are proffered in order to delineate the outer limits of the present debate in this rapidly expanding field.

Evaluation for Different Purposes

Evaluation has been variously defined by numerous scholars. Scriven (1967), for example, defines evaluation as 'an observed value compared to some standard'. In contrast to this very general and rather vague definition, Alkin (1980), Cronbach (1975), Stufflebeam (1971) and others define

educational evaluation as the collection and use of information to make decisions about an educational programme. The latter definition obviously emphasizes evaluation as a tool for decision making, yet other types of evaluation have little or nothing to do with decision making. Different definitions thus emerge dependent upon the writer's conception of the purposes of evaluation, as well as epistemological assumptions inherent in various models. Some of these models emphasize either qualitative or quantitative approaches. Yet other models emphasize both qualitative and quantitative methodologies. Moreover, some evaluators focus on evaluating the goals of the institution, while others, like Scriven (1973), advocate 'goal free' evaluation. Consequently, the parameters of what constitutes evaluation are amorphous and still evolving. Finally, although the definitional debate continues, some writers detect the emergence of a consensus regarding basic definitions of evaluation and appropriate evaluation methodologies.

Educational Evaluation as a Study

Ralph Tyler (1942 and 1949), generally regarded as the 'father' of modern evaluation theory, first coined the term 'educational evaluation'. He defined it as a study which is designed and conducted to assist an audience to judge and improve the worth of some educational object (Tyler, 1942). Today, this definition is being challenged as education finds itself bogged down in an epistemological quagmire with positivists, interpretivists and critical theorists struggling to gain the philosophical high ground (Coomer, 1986). Thus a pure definition of an educational evaluation study remains unattained as theorists continue to discuss and debate the answers to more fundamental questions: What is education? What is evaluation? What purpose(s) does evaluation serve? What should an evaluator do? What assumptions are inherent in the process of evaluation?

Perhaps the flavour of this epistemological debate is best explained by an example. Tyler, as seen above, would view the purpose of evaluation as the measuring of the intended outcomes of a programme against actual outcomes. In contrast, writers like Stake (1976) would see an evaluation study more as a 'portrayal'. Referring to his theory of 'responsive' evaluation, Stake writes that 'an educational evaluation is responsive evaluation if it orients more directly to programme activities than to programme intents' (1975a, p. 14). In a responsive evaluation study, the design will focus on educational issues rather than objectives or hypotheses, and on the plurality of value standards held by various groups and not just those of the programme staff. Responsive evaluation as 'portrayal' is therefore quite unlike the Tylerian measurement of objectives against outcomes (Stake 1976, pp. 19–22). Yet both are seen as educational evaluation studies.

The Evaluation 'Model'

Another term which is important in educational evaluation is that of 'model'. A seemingly endless number of different evaluation models confront the educational practitioner, but few of these actually define the term 'model' (Antonoplos, 1977). Gephart (1978) proposes the following definition:

> A model is defined as a representation that displays the component of the item being represented, the relationship between these components, and how those components function either independently or together. (pp. 6–7)

Gephart submits that evaluators need to reach a consensus regarding the criteria upon which the analysis and synthesis of existing models should be based. He suggests a six-fold set of criteria which might be used to form such a synthesis. Moreover, Worthen (1977a, p. 7) argues that most 'models' of evaluation are neither models nor theories in a scientific sense. Rather they are merely attempts to 'order the content of a new and partial field into some kind of logical structure'. He further suggests that educational evaluation is a relatively new field of inquiry that is only gradually evolving towards a science. At this point in time there is an absence of a solid empirical base, testing and verifying the relative efficacy of various evaluation techniques (Apple, Subkoviak and Lufler, 1974). A clarion call is therefore now being sounded for 'meta-evaluation' — an evaluation of evaluation itself. This call is being made in regard to both the conceptual and technical development of evaluation models. To date, this call remains largely unanswered. Employing the metaphor of a musical band, while there exists many evaluation players with different instruments, they continue to play solo and have yet to organize themselves into a harmonious musical group.

Evaluation and Accountability

It is to be noted that evaluation can serve many purposes — one of which is accountability. Accountability usually means the demonstration that money allocated for a specific purpose has been effectively spent towards that purpose. Thus, an educational evaluation might be conducted for the purpose of accountability. However, it can also be employed for the purpose of school improvement, for public relations purposes and so on (Beare, 1987).

In Australia there has been a distinct move towards educational evaluation for the purpose of accountability, as education dollars must increasingly compete against moneys needed for other national purposes

— defence, welfare and so on. Although the bulk of educational evaluation to date has been for the major purpose of school improvement (Foon, 1986), recent government imperatives in the form of standardized curricula, increased retention rates and so on, will make accountability a focus of more attention in the future. Indeed, the St Mary's Study is a case in point where the results of the evaluation will provide a mass of data which is able to be used for many purposes, including school improvement, decision making and accountability.

Evaluating School Effectiveness

Today, one hears much talk of educational excellence. It is important to note that 'excellence' assumes some standard by which one can determine what is 'good' or 'excellent' about a particular school. Rutter *et al.*, for example, in the book *Fifteen Thousand Hours* (1979) demonstrated that the correlations between many factors describing excellent schools was not high. They found, for instance, that 'the second best school on the academic measure was the worst for behaviour' (Sterne, 1979, p. 198). The important point is that evaluators, in measuring educational excellence, must clearly articulate the criteria employed in determining what 'excellence' or 'effectiveness' means and by what criteria excellence and effectiveness are measured (Erickson, 1977). Finally, as mentioned above, it is crucial that evaluation and school effectiveness be seen as interrelated parts of the much larger whole issue of school improvement, that is movement of a school towards the fulfilment of its educational vision (Clark, Lotto and Astuto, 1989; Goldberg, 1971).

A Brief History of Educational Evaluation

Beginnings

Madaus, Scriven and Stufflebeam (1983, pp. 3–6) claim that although the art or science of evaluation is quite ancient the number of evaluation studies in education, though increasing, is noticeably small. They trace the origin of educational evaluation practices from the public examinations of nineteenth-century England and the study of spelling practices by J.M. Rice in America. Evaluation was further developed by the testing and efficiency measures of researchers like Binet, Thorndyke and Dalton during the first thirty years of the twentieth century. Though these evaluations were for the most part local rather than national in scope, they nevertheless formed the intellectual foundation for a scientific management approach which was to come in the 1930s and 1940s.

Tyler and Modern Evaluation

Ralph Tyler (1942, 1949 and 1951) is generally regarded as the 'father' of modern evaluation theory and his eight year study in 1942 is a landmark in the educational evaluation field. Tyler viewed an educational curriculum as a broadly planned set of school experiences designed and implemented to help students achieve specified behavioural outcomes. Evaluation was to measure such intended outcomes against actual outcomes (Madaus, Scriven and Stufflebeam 1983, pp. 8–9). Tyler is also credited with being one of the first theorists to employ a wide range of measures to evaluate a programme, including pupil performances, sociograms, pupil diaries and case studies.

Extending Tyler's seminal work, Bloom (1981), Krathwohl (1980) and others developed the concept of evaluation objectives. They sought to make evaluation more precise by specifying the behavioural objectives to be achieved. Their hierarchies were often criticized in recent years because of their failure to come to grips with the complex realities of the educational world. However, the behavioural objectives approach continues to be a valuable analytic tool still employed by educational evaluators today (Popham, 1975; Maling-Keepes, 1976).

1960s and 1970s

The Tylerian concept of evaluation remains influential. However, several writers have commented that a plethora of new models emerged in the 1960s and 1970s as Tylerian approaches were increasingly seen as inadequate to the task of evaluating the large scale social programmes, particularly those emanating from the initiatives of the Kennedy and Johnson administrations in the United States (Caro, 1977; Case, 1969). Tylerian approaches were also viewed as more suited to summative or end-product evaluation, rather than to formative or ongoing evaluation, which would provide more feedback during the various stages of programme development (Cronbach, 1963; Harlen, 1975; Madaus, Scriven and Stufflebeam, 1983; Fraser, 1984).

The large sums of public money spent on education in the 1960s and 1970s also led to a demand for greater accountability. Thus influenced by the cost-analysis methods of business, many evaluators adopted systems approaches to evaluation in order to determine the extent to which educational plans proceeded as formulated (Simon, 1965; Hoy and Miskel, 1982; Gronn and Greenway, 1982; Watkins, 1983). Stufflebeam's popular and highly influential decision-making model for evaluation was and remains prominent among those evaluators who have gone in that direction (Stufflebeam, 1974; Popham, 1975).

The literal explosion of evaluation theory began with the publication

of Scriven's (1967) 'The Methodology of Evaluation' and Stake's (1967) 'The Countenance of Educational Evaluation'. Indeed Fraser's (1982) *Annotated Bibliography of Curriculum Literature* found that all thirty-nine books and 167 of 174 individual papers annotated were published after 1967. Scriven distinguished between formative (ongoing) and summative (end-product) evaluation. He also observed that too many theorists had simply accepted curriculum goals and assumed they were worthwhile. Scriven in contrast argued that goals themselves should be evaluated — an idea which led to his development of a goal-free model of evaluation (Scriven, 1973; Hamilton, 1976 and 1977).

Stake (1975a), in his evaluation theory, retained the emphasis on outcomes, but expanded the nature of what is to be evaluated to encompass transactions, antecedents and contingencies. These were complex realities of human social existence ignored by behavioural objective approaches to evaluation. Referring to what he called 'responsive evaluation' Stake suggested that:

> An educational evaluation is responsive if it correlates more directly to programme activities than to programme intents, if it responds to audience requirements for information, and if the different value perspectives of the people at hand are referred to in reporting the success or failure of the programme. (Stake, 1975a, p. 14)

Epistemological Crises Underlying New Models

Contributing to this explosion of evaluation models was the underlying epistemological crisis of recent decades (Burrell and Morgan, 1979; Hamilton *et al.*, 1977). Increasingly, educational theorists challenged the traditional scientific positivistic approaches to gaining knowledge about education. Spearheaded by writers like Greenfield (1985), a new interpretive paradigm has emerged. It rejects the validity of scientific positivism and argues that the only organizational reality is that created in the minds of the people who have certain perceptions and act according to various assumptions regarding that organization. As Greenfield (1982) puts it: 'Organizations have no ontological reality: they do not exist in the "real world" or in any other world except as individuals act them out' (pp. 18–19). This interpretive or phenomenological paradigm has provided the philosophical underpinning for new educational evaluation models like Parlett and Hamilton's (1972) model as well as various ethnographic and naturalistic models which will be discussed later in this chapter.

Another challenge to traditional evaluation approaches is found in the critical social theory which developed from the organizational theorizing of Jurgen Habermas (1975). Bredo and Feinberg (1982, pp. 273–4)

succinctly summarize the relation of critical theory to positivism and intrepretivism:

> In critical theory [various] types of action are seen as closely related to three types of knowledge that are also hierarchically related. The need for instrumental adaptation is related to an interest in that kind of knowledge that allows for the prediction and control of events. Habermas terms this a 'technical' cognitive interest. Second, the need for social integration creates a related interest in knowledge that facilitates the understanding and the reaching of understandings with others. This is termed a 'practical' cognitive interest. Finally, the need to resolve contradictions between the first two types of action, in the direction of greater autonomy, creates an interest in knowledge that facilitates this resolution. This third interest is termed an 'emancipatory' cognitive interest. Each of these three cognitive interests is seen as constituting a different type of knowledge...

Critical theory focusses on the evaluator as a facilitator of communication who helps those involved reach a shared understanding of the inferences, potentials and limitations of various modes of communication, in specific social contexts (Bates, 1988). Through this process it becomes possible for agreement to be reached on future courses of action (Coomer, 1986).

Influenced by these recent developments, a number of evaluation theorists have branched out in different directions. They have borrowed from other disciplines — literature, law, journalism, art, etc — to enable audiences appropriately to evaluate the educational realities of their specific contexts. This has led to the connoisseurship model (Eisner, 1972); the adversarial model (Owens, 1973), the journalistic model (Guba, 1979) and the literary criticism model (Kelly, 1975) to mention but a few.

Emergence of Evaluation as a Distinct Discipline

As a result of all this intense activity since the 1970s, evaluation has emerged as a separate discipline distinct from traditional social science research (Macdonald, 1976). This development is reflected in the emergence of a number of journals devoted solely to evaluation. Also, universities have begun to offer courses in evaluation methodology (Madaus, Scriven and Stufflebeam, 1983, pp. 15–16).

Where is the field of educational evaluation headed? Presently, there appears to be, on the one hand, a growing polarization between theorists emphasizing positivistic, quantitatively-based approaches to evaluation and those writers who stress interpretivistic-qualitatively based methodologies. On the other hand, there is also some movement, especially in the United States, towards establishing standards for programme evaluation

— a movement toward consensus (Hawkbridge, 1978; Harlen, 1976). Similarly, other writers argue that the quantitative versus qualitative debate represents a false dichotomy as the best evaluators utilize a combination of approaches, both quantitative and qualitative, and worry little about remaining true to the epistemological foundations inherent in any particular paradigm (Walker and Evers, 1988). As will be explained below, this was the approach adopted by the authors in designing the St Mary's College evaluation.

Combining Quantitative and Qualitative Evaluation Methodologies

A number of scholars are now suggesting that an over-emphasis on particular evaluative paradigms is unwarranted and tends to exaggerate the incompatibility between quantitative and qualitative approaches (Smith, 1987; Patton, 1980; Smith, and Fraser, 1980). It is contended that the choice of evaluation methodology should depend upon the specific context at hand and that a combination of quantitative and qualitative methods is often desirable (Cook and Reichardt, 1979; Rist, 1977). For example, an evaluation conducted for a multiplicity of purposes (e.g., accountability, school improvement, public relations) is usually better accomplished by using a variety of evaluation methods. Indeed the two methodologies can complement each other and give deeper insights than would be possible using solely quantitative or qualitative methods. Qualitative methods can help the evaluator understand the significance of statistical associations (Fetterman and Pittman, 1986). As Cook and Reichardt suggest:

> ... a researcher need not adhere blindly to one or the other extreme paradigms that have been labelled 'qualitative' or 'quantitative' but can freely choose a mix of attributes from both paradigms so as to best fit the demands of the research problem at hand. (1979, p. 19)

Cronbach and his colleagues in the Stanford Evaluation Consortium espouse a similar view in submitting that most evaluations should include both quantitative and qualitative methods (Eisner, 1979a and 1979b; Cronbach *et al.*, 1980; Smith and Fraser, 1980; Madey, 1982). House (1977) adds that the best researchers and evaluators, whether they admit it or not, employ both quantitative and qualitative methods. He stresses that quantitative methods always involve considerable intuitive judgment. In particular the processes of formulation and interpretation are subjective processes. Although good insights are often derived from quantitative studies, they usually result from the analyst making the right

intuitive judgments rather than the right calculations (Eisner, 1967, 1972, 1976 and 1981).

Finally, Harlen (1976) suggests that whether the evaluator elects to use predominantly quantitative or qualitative methods will depend upon three broad considerations. First, the evaluator must decide whether to gather a restricted variety of data from a large sample (scale) or a wide range of data from a smaller sample (scope). Scale is important where measurement is regarded as central, but scope is critical where the purpose is to explain different effects and conditions associated with a curriculum. Second is the issue regarding whether the evaluation should focus on intended outcomes (goal based) or attempt to monitor all outcomes, intended or not (goal free). A third and related issue concerns the particular emphasis which focusses on process or product. Qualitative evaluation methods are more suited to monitoring all outcomes and focussing on processes (Willis, 1978). Quantitative evaluation methods, however, will be better suited to goal-based studies seeking to measure end-products (Rossi and Wright, 1977).

Some Popular Models Employed in Educational Evaluation

Earlier sections of this chapter have defined key terms, outlined the history of evaluation, and described and critically appraised the various epistemological foundations underlying the various approaches to evaluation. It was noted that evaluators, depending upon their specific circumstances, should be rather eclectic in approach. They should utilize a variety or combination of models and methods as they suit the particular context and needs of the community being evaluated (Lewy, 1977a; Tawney, 1976). Below is a description of some of the major evaluation models. While not comprehensive (it has been estimated that there are over 40 different evaluation models e.g., Stufflebeam, 1971; House, 1978; Gephart, 1977; Jenkins, 1976), this description should suggest the available variety of approaches to evaluation. Traditional approaches discussed include goal attainment models, decision-making models, and productivity/investment models. These models are founded upon traditional scientific positivism and emphasize outcomes as measured by highly controlled and quantifiable data. In contrast, naturalistic models are also described, including responsive evaluation, illuminative evaluation, goal-free evaluation and the connoisseurship model of evaluation. The naturalistic models have been highly influenced by interpretivism and critical theory. The boundaries of evaluation in these latter models are much less controlled and there is much greater emphasis on process rather than outcomes, and on qualitative data as opposed to quantitative data.

Goal Attainment Models

Goal attainment evaluation models have long been, and remain, a very important and popular method of evaluation. Goal attainment models involve the statement of defined objectives. Against these objectives school life and student performance in their various aspects are measured and evaluated. As stated by Tyler (1949):

> The process of evaluation is essentially the process of determining to what extent the educational objectives are actually being realised by the programme of curriculum and instruction. However, since education objectives are essentially changes in human beings, that is, that the objectives aimed at are to produce certain desirable changes in the behavior patterns of the students, then evaluation is the process for determining the degree to which these changes in behavior are actually taking place. (pp. 105–6)

To the extent that the objectives are very broadly defined, goal attainment models tend to produce results which are difficult to quantify, and therefore this approach tends to be used more for internal evaluation aimed at school improvement, as opposed to school accountability. When the goals are stated with precision, however, goal attainment approaches can be quite successful whether one's purpose is school improvement or accountability (Caro, 1977). Although criticized by those preferring qualitative approaches, this model pioneered by Tyler remains highly influential today.

Productivity and Investment Models

With the great expenditures on education in the 1960s and 1970s came the need for public accountability to demonstrate that the large investment of public funds was actually producing results. Thus a number of productivity and investment models evolved. Basically, these models suggest that productivity can be measured by comparing output with input. Inputs include many elements such as educational expenditure, capital, facilities and management skills. Outputs include gains in knowledge as well as emotional and social development (Dressel, 1976).

Investment evaluation models provide yet another framework from which the evaluator tries to measure educational achievement so as to gain accountability. The investment model views educational expenditure as an investment in people which beneficially affects the economy (Department of Education, Queensland School-based Evaluation, Vols 1–10, 1982).

The productivity model places emphasis on the cost of education and

tends to ignore societal benefits in favour of individual benefits. Invest-ment models, on the other hand, suggest that careful management of the investment in education should increase the social returns. Both models are concerned with manpower and the development of human resources to meet government and economic needs. These models, however, with their emphasis on efficiency and effectiveness, fail to account for the qualitative and non-operational aspects of education. Reliance, therefore, purely on productivity and investment models tend to provide a very narrow focus and consequently fails to achieve fundamental change in an educational institution (Foon, 1986).

Stufflebeam's CIPP Evaluation Model

Stufflebeam, in this widely used evaluation model, defines evaluation as 'the process of delineating, obtaining, and providing useful information for judging decision alternatives' (1971, p. 19) or, more simply as 'the science of providing information for decision making' (1969, p. 53).

The CIPP (content, input, process, product) model indicates that there are planning decisions which determine objectives, structuring deci-sions which project procedural designs for achieving objectives, im-plementing decisions which involve the execution of chosen designs and recycling decisions which determine whether to continue, terminate or modify the project. These decision types are facilitated by four types of evaluation. Context evaluation provides information about needs, prob-lems and opportunities in order to identify objectives. Input evaluation provides information about the strengths and weaknesses of alternative strategies for achieving given objectives. Process evaluation provides information about the strengths and weaknesses of the strategy during implementation so that either the strategy or its implementation might be strengthened. Product evaluation provides information for determining whether objectives are being achieved and whether the procedure em-ployed to achieve them should be continued, modified or terminated. The CIPP model helps answer questions regarding what objectives should be accomplished, what procedures should be followed, whether procedures are working properly, and whether objectives are being achieved.

Stufflebeam's (1971) CIPP model does take into account the qualita-tive equation of economics. Moreover it provides more accountability than either the goal attainment or the goal free models. This model is intended to guide both improvement efforts within a particular school as well as serving accountability needs in a specific and general sense. Stufflebeam argues that evaluation can be characterized as either a decision-making or an accountability experience. When evaluation serves a formative role, it is assisting decision makers. However, when evalua-

tion serves a summative role it constitutes the basis for accountability. The CIPP model is very strong in that goal attainment is seen to be meaningful only in so far as the goals meet the needs of the people they are intended to serve. Foon (1986) argues that if the identification of inputs, contexts, processes and products is made a continuing aspect of school management, this evaluative process could provide the feedback which can produce just the accountability that is being demanded by governments. In addition, it can also meet the needs stressed by other models which seek to improve the quality of school life.

Goal Free Evaluation

Michael Scriven is the major proponent of goal free evaluation which is a radical alternative to goal based approaches. Scriven argues that, although goals are necessary for effective programme planning and implementation, they are not necessary for evaluation. According to Scriven:

> The goal free evaluator (GFE) is a hunter out alone and goes over the ground carefully, looking for signs of any kind of game, setting speculative snares when in doubt. The goal based evaluator, given a map that, supposedly, shows the main game trails, finds it hard to work quite so hard in the rest of the jungle (1973, p. 327).

The goal free approach involves the evaluation of actual effects against a profile of demonstrated needs. Scriven suggests that it is improper to use the goals of either the evaluated or the evaluator as the standard of merit for an evaluation unless these can be proven to be appropriate and morally defensible. Thus, goal free conditions, where the evaluator can focus on school effects, rather than preconceived goals, will enhance the objectivity and independence of an external evaluator. Goal free evaluation reflects the fact that educators often come closer to the truth when looking in unexpected directions than intended ones (Gardner, 1977). A goal free evaluation, therefore, is more likely to lead to something which everyone has overlooked or to the production of a novel overall perspective. Critics of the goal free approach to evaluation refer to this model as 'aimless evaluation' and argue that, like goal based models, goal free evaluators often have difficulty in securing precise quantification of outcome variables.

Naturalistic Evaluation

Pioneered by such theorists as Guba (1978) and Alkin (1980), the naturalistic mode of inquiry provides an approach to educational evaluation

with roots in ethnography and phenomenology. Naturalistic studies are characterized by such factors as large expenditure of time within school settings, the absence of formal hypotheses, an exploratory search for questions, and an attempt to be unobtrusive (Alkin, Daillak and White, 1979; Alkin and Daillak, 1979). 'The naturalistic observer, in contrast with the more traditional experimenter, spends more time looking over the lay of the land before he decides on the direction in which to move' (Apple, Subkoviak and Lufler, 1974, p. 84). A number of models including Stake's responsive model and Parlett and Hamiltons' illuminative model encompass the spirit of the naturalistic approach.

Naturalistic models of evaluation, in the spirit of Scriven's goal free approach, are much less concerned about goals and quantifiable outcomes. Instead, the emphasis is on portrayal, process and qualitative data. Guba (1978) acknowledges that a definitive, fully explained methodology of naturalistic inquiry is not yet developed. Three methodological problems confront naturalistic inquirers. They are boundary problems, focus problems and authenticity problems. Guba indicates that boundary problems relate to the scope of the inquiry and involve questions of how to set limits and decide what is to be included and excluded in a particular evaluation study. Focussing problems involve how to derive a set of categories to include as many data items and perspectives as are relevant. Frequently in naturalistic studies the set of categories which the naturalistic evaluator derives tends to be too large to be manageable. The problem of authenticity relates to the establishment of bases for trust in the outcomes of an inquiry and involves well known classical criteria like validity, reliability and objectivity. These classical concepts require some reinterpretation in regard to naturalistic inquiry. Thus Guba develops such concepts as openness and fairness as relevant qualitative criteria for obtaining neutrality in naturalistic studies.

While naturalistic inquiries are helpful and enlightening, especially in regard to school improvement, they tend to be far less useful if the purpose of the evaluation is accountability. Also, such studies, because of their uniqueness, produce little or no comparable data by which one can evaluate other schools and similar settings.

Stake's Responsive Evaluation Model

A specific example of a naturalistic evaluation is Stake's model of responsive evaluation which has had an enormous impact in the field of educational evaluation. Stake defines responsive evaluation as follows:

> An educational evaluation is responsive evaluation if it orients more directly to programme activities than to programme intent; responds to audience requirements for information; and if the

different value perspectives present are referred to in reporting the success or failure of the programme. (1975, p. 14)

Stake distinguishes what he calls preordinate evaluation approaches from those which are responsive. Stake (1976) maintains that most pre-ordinate evaluation designs emphasize a formal statement of goals, stand-ardized tests of student performance, value standards held by programme staff and a 'research-journal' type of report (Scheyer and Stake, 1976). In contrast, the responsive design will usually involve educational issues more than objectives or hypotheses. It will incorporate direct and indirect observation of programme participation, the pluralism of value standards held by various groups (not just those of the programme staff) and continuous attention to audience information needs and media for report-ing. In responsive evaluation the role of the evaluator is to facilitate the school personnel's efforts to understand and remedy their programme. The responsive approach to evaluation can assist in this role by providing vicarious experience through portrayal of what is happening somewhere outside the programme personnel's view (Hall, 1979). In this way, the responsive approach attempts to respond to the natural ways in which people assimilate information and arrive at understanding. Moreover, in preparing portrayals, 'the evaluator will find that case studies of several students may more interestingly and faithfully represent the educational programme than a few measurements of all the students' (Stake, 1975a, p. 25; Kemmis, 1977; Lewy, 1977b).

In outlining the various steps which might be involved in responsive evaluation, Stake (1976) highlights twelve events which can occur at numerous times during the evaluation. These events include: 1) identify-ing the programme scope; 2) overviewing programme activities; 3) discovering purposes, concerns; 4) conceptualizing issues, problems; 5) identifying data needs regarding issues; 6) selecting observers, judges, instruments (if any); 7) observing designated antecedents, transactions, outcomes; 8) thematizing, preparing portrayals, case studies; 9) matching issues to audiences; 10) formating for audience use; 11) assembling formal reports (if any); and 12) talking with clients, programme staff, audiences.

Evaluation as Illumination

Yet another evaluation model, and one which has many similarities to Stakes' responsive evaluation, is found in the illumination theory of Parlett and Hamilton (1972). These writers propose an anthropologically-based alternative to educational evaluation (Parlett and Dearden, 1977). At the same time, they offer a critique of the traditional paradigm which is referred to as the agricultural-botany approach. It is characterized as follows:

> Students — rather like plant crops — are given pre tests (the
> seedlings are weighed and measured); and then submitted to
> different experiences (treatment conditions). Subsequently, after a
> period of time, their attainment (growth or yield) is measured to
> indicate the relative efficiency of the methods (fertilizers) used.
> (Parlett and Hamilton, 1972, p. 4)

In short, the traditional approach to evaluation is seen as a paradigm for
plants rather than for people. Furthermore, the traditional approach is
seen as too expensive. It is unable to strictly control all the extraneous
factors involved, for the real world, unlike the science laboratory, tends
to be untidy. Also, traditional evaluation approaches assume that the
programme undergoes little or no change during the period of study.
Traditional approaches tend to over-emphasize quantitative data and neglect subjective or impressionistic information. Finally, traditional evaluation approaches seldom acknowledge the information needs of different
audiences. Thus, attention is too easily diverted away from educational
practice and focusses instead on more centralized and bureaucratic concerns (Marsh and Stafford, 1988, chapter 3).

Parlett and Hamilton submit that illuminative evaluation is primarily
concerned with description and interpretation rather than measurement
and prediction:

> The aims of illuminative evaluation are to study the innovative
> programme: how it operates; how it is influenced by the various
> school situations in which it is is applied; what those directly
> concerned regard as its advantages and disadvantages; and how
> students' intellectual tasks and academic experiences are most
> effective. It attempts to discover and document what it is like to
> be participating in the scheme, whether as teacher or pupil; and in
> addition to discern and discuss the innovation's most significant
> features, recurring concomitants, and critical processes. (Parlett
> and Hamilton, 1972, p. 9)

This approach is analogous to that of a social anthropologist in that no
attempt is made to manipulate or control variables. The illuminative
evaluator simply tries to unravel the complex reality which it is seeking
to evaluate.

Parlett and Hamilton identify three stages which characteristically are
present in illuminative evaluation. These are observation in order to
become knowledgeable about the system and its milieu; further inquiry to
focus on the study; and explanation observed patterns of cause and effect.
Within this three stage framework it is suggested that data are collected
from the four areas of observation, interviews, questionnaires and tests,
and documentary and background sources.

Another important feature of the illuminative strategy is that the eva-

luator does not pass judgment. The evaluator's task rather is to 'illuminate' or provide a comprehensive understanding of the complex realities surrounding the programme. The evaluator aims to 'sharpen discussion, disentangle complexities, isolate the significant from the trivial, and to raise the level of sophistication of the debate' (Parlett and Hamilton, 1972, p. 30).

The illuminative model of evaluation has not been without its critics (Parsons, 1976). Crittenden (1978) discusses a number of its weaknesses. First, by stressing the uniqueness of each setting, illuminative models do not produce findings which have any generalizability. Second, relying on the 'perceptions' of the observer introduces problems of subjectivity. Third, the desirability, or even possibility of the evaluator remaining 'judgment free' is questionable. Fourth, the scale of illuminative models is limited to one school. Finally, by focussing on schools in action the illuminative model tends to ignore the underlying objectives and structure of the organization itself.

Evaluation Models Derived from Other Disciplines

Finally, a number of evaluation models have recently emerged which employ methodologies derived from other disciplines. Wolf's (1975, 1979a and 1979b) and Thurston's (1978) judicial models, Rippey's (1973) transactional model, and Eisner's (1972) connoisseurship model are some of the more well known. Other models have developed an evaluation model borrowed from anthropology (Dobbert and Dobbert, 1976), journalism (Guba, 1979; Denny, 1978), literary criticism (Kelly, 1975), art (Donmoyer, 1976), artistic criticism generally (Eisner, 1976), communication theory (Eggleston and Galton, 1976) and others (Fraser, 1982).

School Evaluation Practices in Australia

In the early stages of the St Mary's College Project we wrote to every state department of education and Catholic Education Office in Australia requesting information regarding evaluation practices in those states. This section presents a summary of the wider context of evaluation practices in Australia so that the local St Mary's context, which is discussed in the next section, may be better understood.

School evaluation in Australia reflected similar developments in the United States and England with a great surge of activity coming in the mid 1970s. The Curriculum Development Centre (Canberra) in 1976 extensively investigated school-based curriculum evaluation, an approach which remains prevalent today in both state and private schools around

Australia. The result of these investigations was the Teachers as Evaluators Project (1981) which aimed to develop materials and resources to assist teachers in curriculum evaluations.

Also in the mid 1970s, in the private school sector, the Headmasters' Conference of Australia invited leading United States theorists to conduct a number of seminars on school-based evaluation. This led to the production of the School Evaluation Manual for Australian Schools and Guidelines for School Evaluation (Foon, 1986). In general terms most models of school evaluation have been, and remain, school based. They are participatory and goal oriented, and often involve the use of facilitators or outside experts (Hogben, 1977).

From 1980 to 1985, the Australian Commonwealth Schools Commission has promoted the concept of school-based evaluation as inherent in school improvement. Accordingly, projects have been funded involving schools in evaluating their own activities in light of their objectives. Under the present 'Hawke' government, however, the Commission has lost responsibility for administering most of its programmes. It has been stripped down to a policy advisory role (Durston, 1987). Nevertheless, school evaluation activity among independent schools, both private and Catholic, continues to grow.

School-based evaluation also appears to be firmly entrenched in the structure of most state education departments. Moreover, with the move to more local autonomy, the trend towards school-based evaluation (in contrast to departmental evaluation) in which schools are evaluated in terms of their own statements and goals, seems certain to continue. The Victorian School Improvement Plan is a notable example.

Among Catholic Schools around Australia, school-based evaluation also continues to grow and develop, perhaps accelerated by recent government demands for more accountability. Most dioceses either have adopted or are investigating the possibility of adopting evaluation policies for the schools within their system. Also, various Order schools, for example the Christian Brothers, have adopted school-based evaluations for their schools situated throughout Australia. These approaches usually involve facilitators who assist the individual school in conducting its evaluation and the creation of its 'mission statement'.

The School Evaluation Manual for Australian Schools, referred to above, has also led to many school evaluations among non-Catholic private schools. The National Council of Independent Schools provides a school evaluation programme as a service to schools (Marsh, 1988). This programme adopts a structure whereby a school defines its aims and and objectives and evaluates itself against these aims and objectives. The evaluation suggests improvements, and the school invites an external committee to validate these internal findings before implementing the recommendations.

The Rationale for the St Mary's College Evaluation

A number of criteria emerged to form the basis of the rationale for the St Mary's College Evaluation (Figure 2). These were based upon the history of educational evaluation, discussion of epistemological foundations and analysis of the various evaluation models utilized in Australia and elsewhere.

First, it was seen that a school evaluation should be holistic (Anderson and Ball, 1978). It should consider both the formal and informal aspects of the curriculum. Moreover, the perceptions of all segments of the school community should be considered. This includes students, staff and parents (Cumming, 1985).

Second, following from the holistic nature of an evaluation, the best approach would employ methodologies providing a wide range of quantitative and qualitative data. In the St Mary's Project, the researchers, in conjunction with staff, designed a Perception of School Survey instrument in such terms. Also a highly reliable Quality of School Life instrument was employed so that both formal and informal aspects of the curriculum were taken into account. In addition to the extensive general survey, the researchers utilized student records. From these records mechanisms were constructed for controlling the variables of age or grade level, level of academic achievement, the year of leaving St Mary's and geographic locality. The researchers also conducted numerous personal interviews involving individuals, small groups and class groups (see Fehrenbacher, Owens and Haenn, 1976, for verification of this approach). Finally, staff and parents were surveyed as well as students. The study has yielded a vast amount of data, both quantitative and qualitative, which provide a detailed portrayal of the school and its community.

Third, the SMC (St Mary's College) Project design recognized that evaluators should be aware of the underlying assumptions, prevailing ideology, and strengths and weaknesses inherent in the chosen model of evaluation (Kemmis, 1986). Furthermore, it was acknowledged that evaluators should also be aware of their ethical responsibilities (Madaus *et al.*, 1983; Straton, 1977; Elliott, 1978). Thus, evaluators should strive, among other things, to make the process open; information should not be released to others until cleared with the informant; and there should be a commitment to be conscious of and responsive to the full range of people's concerns (Brennan and Hoadley, 1984, p. 29). It is important that evaluators appreciate the wider context of the evaluation. This entails knowing about the history of school evaluation, the range of possible evaluation approaches, and the evaluations utilized by similar schools in related contexts. All of these considerations will help ensure that the evaluation method chosen is fully understood and that there is a good programme fit between the evaluation model and the particular school.

These aspects of the study are covered in depth in later chapters; it suffices to say that in the context of the St Mary's Study such factors needed conscious and continual response.

Fourth, past evaluation studies have rightly been criticized for being single-shot, one-off events. As a result it has been difficult, if not impossible, to compare evaluations of the same school over a period of time or to compare one school with another. Accordingly, we thought it vital that the SMC Study be longitudinal (Tamir, 1981). Present students were surveyed, using the Quality of School Life instrument, not only once, but twice, involving the same population over consecutive years and at different times during the year. Also, in order to measure the school's performance and students' attitudes over time, the Perception of School Survey involved present students and past students from the previous eight years between 1978–86. A standard Quality of School Life (QSL) instrument was employed so that the St Mary's results could be compared with results from other studies which have utilized the QSL instrument. The study was designed so that comparisons could be made with Flynn's study of more than twenty NSW Catholic schools between 1972 and 1982. Finally, the SMC Study was designed so that it could also serve as a paradigm for the evaluation of other schools, and especially for Catholic schools. For this reason, too, the Perceptions of School instrument focussed in depth on the central issue for Catholic schools — the spiritual and personal development of students.

Fifth, related to the idea that an evaluation is neither a one-shot picture nor an end in itself, is the finding from the best regarded literature and practice, that evaluation be cyclical. Accordingly, the long-term plan of this study is that evaluation becomes a regular event and feature of school life. The SMC Study may result in the adoption of new policies. These policies, however, will themselves have to be evaluated so that the school community may know if the new policies made a difference. Did they work? If not, why not? Also, as a result of this study, a larger investigation involving all Catholic schools in Tasmania is contemplated. It is the researchers' hope that this will lead to regular, systematic and cyclical evaluation as an integral component of school improvement.

Sixth, the literature indicates that evaluation can have many purposes (King and Thompson, 1983; Leviton and Hughes, 1981). The St Mary's Study, therefore, was designed to accommodate multi-faceted aims. The combination of both qualitative and quantitative methodologies ensured that the evaluation was able to be utilized for both school improvement and accountability as well as for other purposes. These included identification of problems, basis for decision making, public relations, better use of resources, school renewal and so on.

Seventh, Stufflebeam (1971) and others have demonstrated the importance of evaluation as an integral part of decision making. With this view in mind, the researchers were careful to have staff and administra-

tion input into the design of the survey. Only if the questions asked were relevant to real and ongoing concerns would the evaluation be addressing areas which were deemed important by the school community. Also, the researchers, the administration, staff, students and parents were all involved in the processes of data collection and interpretation. From the beginning, both researchers and staff saw the development of a large data bank of valuable information as a major benefit of the study. This data source would serve as a resource and reference for the study of future school problems and the formulation of policy. As stated in the document *Curriculum Evaluation: How It Can Be Done* (1982, prepared by the Curriculum Development Centre, Canberra):

> The value of evaluation lies in its ability to help clarify the issues facing a school and to help teachers make informed decisions. These decisions are often made on an informal intuitive basis, rather than a more formal manner. While there is no denying the value of this approach, it can be usefully supplemented by more systematic procedures. (p. 7)

Eighth, as a corollary to the role of evaluation in decision making, it is also important that evaluation, though vital, be seen not as an end in itself. Rather, evaluation is a process which is inextricably linked to other school processes, including school vision, decision making, curriculum design, financial planning, policy formation, all involved in the life of the school and wider community (Holt, 1981). Accordingly, the focus of the SMC Study was based upon key questions gathered from staff and discussed by them. They helped determine the major categories to be studied, contributed questions and were involved in the interpretation of results. Indeed, the researchers have at all times been cognizant of the significance of the sustained support of the school's leaders. This meant their time, their help in giving focus to the study, providing resources, protecting key staff from additional responsibilities, etc. Coupled with continuous, hands-on, practical classroom support, all these factors together would make an evaluation work and result in real improvement in the school (Lieberman and Miller, 1984; Cox, 1983). The evaluation was action-oriented, concentrating on how the evaluation would affect actual educational practice (Brennan and Hoadley, 1984, p. 29).

Ninth, a common thread running through the evaluation procedure in many states of Australia was the combination of local autonomy guided and assisted by outside expertise. This pattern also became part of our rationale as the university consultant-researcher combined with the local school (St Mary's) in helping the school community conduct its own evaluation. It was important that the evaluation not be something imposed from outside. Accordingly, Dr Ramsay, while on study leave from the university, taught full-time at the College, became a known member of staff and worked closely with the whole school community.

Importantly, too, as indicated earlier, the whole approach to evaluation — areas to be examined, specific questions to be asked, etc — was drawn from the staff with the assistance and guidance of the consultant-researcher. Moreover, staff, parents and students all played a role in commenting on the results of the analysis. This process aided the researchers and gave the whole community a role and stake in the outcome of the evaluation. It will also have the effect of enhancing the likelihood of definite and constructive policies for the future. It is also significant that the Catholic Education Office has provided part of the funding for this study. The role and value of a central body providing financial and educational resources in helping schools evaluate themselves has thus been demonstrated.

Finally, another important aspect of the rationale behind the St Mary's Study was that it demonstrated how the university theorist may combine with a school community significantly to aid the process of school introspection and improvement. Currently many people are calling for much closer links between the university and society. What better demonstration of such cooperation than an evaluation made possible by bringing together the research expertise and insights of the university with the practical reality of a school setting in order to bring about a more effective school. As Schon (1983, p. 290) concludes, 'It is inefficient to expect one group of teachers to independently re-invent a wider range of educational wheels'. The contact with tertiary institutions allows classroom experiences to be placed in a wider context. This will improve the analysis and interpretation of those experiences. And, it is a two way street. Teachers' experiences will have broadened and deepened the understandings of academics who will see their academic ideas tested and tempered in real classrooms. Finally, as noted by Duignan (1986), concept must keep pace with the growth of theory and practice in the field. Our knowledge about educational evaluation therefore must continue to grow and expand. Also both theorists and educational practitioners must regard evaluation as an integral part of the ongoing organization, growth and development of the school community (Madaus, Scriven and Stufflebeam, 1983).

Figure 2 depicts and summarizes the major elements in the design of the St Mary's Study.

The Growing Importance of School Evaluation

In the late 1980s schools are in a transition period — adapting to new information technology, changing social functions and a shifting position of education in society. Many schools are in a period of non-growth, perhaps even contraction. At the same time, there is today greater emphasis on individualism and multiple options in school curricula. We also

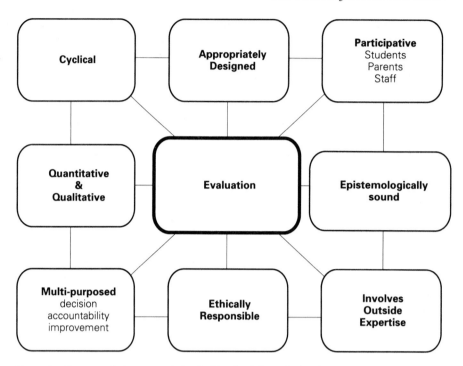

Figure 2   Conceptual elements of the St Mary's College Evaluation

live in a society which is becoming increasingly pluralistic, thus creating more consumer-demand pressures on the school.

In this context school evaluation is gaining in importance and becoming more formalized and embedded as a regular and necessary part of school administration. Also, as education dollars increasingly compete against defence, social welfare and other programmes, there is mounting pressure for school evaluations which demonstrate accountability for the expenditure of public funds. This pressure has resulted in moves towards a central curriculum which threatens the autonomy of schools to be truly active in governing their own affairs. As Duignan (1988) argues:

> ... in order to counterbalance arguments for central curriculum control, they [schools] will have to mount their own arguments based on defensible criteria. To combat corporate managerialist thinking (top-down control and vertical accountability), they will need to develop participative and democratic structures for the development and evaluation of their curricula. They need to demonstrate that they have a large measure of horizontal accountability (peer and community evaluation), or they are likely to be subjected to an uncompromising vertical variety. (p. 70)

Accordingly, evaluation will be absolutely essential in order for schools to demonstrate the extent to which they are actually making a difference in the lives of their students. Moreover, in a society in which change and the rate of change are increasingly apparent, there is a growing demand for planned change based upon informed decisions as opposed to ad hoc hunches founded upon mere intuition. Thus, schools have a real need to formulate a base of quantitative and qualitative data to aid them in their decision making and in their ability to show, both to the school community and governmental authorities, the actual effects of schooling.

There is little doubt that we are moving toward the establishment of evaluation standards and ethics based upon paradigms of evaluation encompassing both quantitative and qualitative measurements of social reality. At the same time, however, we need to be realistic in recognizing that the normative nature of schools, and concepts like 'school improvement' and evaluation make the task difficult indeed. Too often, 'researchers have ridden off in all directions armed with different conceptual and methodological trappings, and have returned with formulae that often appeared incompatible and incommensurate' (Huberman and Miles, 1986, p. 61).

Despite these limitations it is clear that the university and other tertiary level institutions, as well as departments of education, will be instrumental in helping schools, teachers, parents and students piece together the educational shadows so that a clearer picture of the true nature of education, school improvement and the role of schools in society will thus emerge.

Chapter 4

St Mary's College:
A Case Study of School Evaluation

Introduction

In Chapter 2 we argued the case for a contextual approach to school improvement. By context we referred specifically to the school community of teachers, students and parents. The previous chapter demonstrated the growing importance of school evaluation in such school improvement. There we also advanced a paradigm for a multi-dimensional approach encompassing both quantitative and qualitative measurements of the social reality of the school.

We now present a descriptive account of a 'live' evaluation case study of St Mary's College. Our purpose in doing so is four fold. First, as an intensive study of all aspects of the school programme, the results of this evaluation provide for a comprehensive and detailed overview of one school such as to constitute a foundation for appropriate change. Second, the study being longitudinal in design, enables us to examine the processes of change, and stability, which contribute to the purposes of school improvement. Third, because the study encompasses the perceptions of teachers and parents, as well as students, its parameters are derived from and reflect the surrounding social, as well as school, context. Finally, since the best theories and the best practice are inexorably linked, the case study is intended to illuminate and confirm the theoretical propositions presented.

The St Mary's College Evaluation focusses on a Catholic school and will be of particular interest to Catholic and other religiously-based schools. However, the questions considered — the role of evaluation in education, importance of school vision and the social capital of the school community, the ideological bases for school improvement, and the management of change — we submit, are of universal application.

Methodology

Basis for the Design

There was an essential pragmatic element in preparation for the project. After discussion with the Principal and senior staff the researchers sought from all the teachers their opinions as to what kind of questions should form the basis of such an evaluation. Finally one question was chosen and despite its daunting comprehensiveness it was agreed that it should be the starting point for the design. The question in the form presented to the researcher was as follows:

> To gain a full evaluation of the total effects of the curriculum it is suggested that a study be made of a cross section of students two to five years after leaving grade 12 at St Mary's with particular emphasis on their spiritual, social, academic and community involvements (including sporting activities).

The design and methodology of the study were based on this question, the parameters of which were broadened to include a teachers and parents sample.

Sample

For this phase of the evaluation, the research sample included students at St Mary's College of grades 10, 11 and 12 who were either present at the College in 1986 or who had left the school between 1978 and 1984. The 1985 group was omitted from the sample in order to provide a clarity of separation between the past and present student groups. There were a total of 120 past students in the sample for data analysis.

Table 1 shows the distribution of the sample in the Perceptions of School Study.

For Quality of School Life dimension of the evaluation the sample included all students in the Senior School at St Mary's College in 1986 — grades 10, 11, and 12 — a total of 402 students in 1986. Data were again obtained from these students in 1987. Table 2 shows the sample for the Quality of School Life study.

The teacher sample included a total of 30 teachers, representative of all classes in the Senior School for 1986. Table 3 shows the sample of parents.

The research design incorporated psycho-social variables. Tables 4 to 6 show distributions of the student sample in terms of year of leaving, level of academic performance, and residential locality. Distribution for age and grade level is incorporated in the Perception of School and Quality of School Life Samples.

Table 1   Sample for perceptions of school dimension (N = 249)

Grade	Past Students	Present Students	Total
10	31	50	81
11	20	41	61
12	69	38	107
Total	120	149	249

Note: The figure of 120 past students, obviously is far less than the original number listed. Many of these students could not be contacted, having moved away or lost association with the school. Given the sliding scale of school numbers over the period of the study, the sample of past students was considered adequate for comparisons to be made.

Table 2   Sample for quality of school life dimension (N = 402)

Grade	1986
7	86
8	75
9	75
10	72
11	54
12	40
Total	402

Note on Distribution: In 1987, 7 per cent of the student population at St Mary's College senior school were non-Catholic. This figure diminishes slightly when past students are included in the sample.

Table 3   Showing sample of parents

Grade No.	
7	34
8	38
9	38
10	33
11	25
12	24
Total	192

Table 4   Showing distribution of student sample for year of leaving

Year of leaving	No.	Grouped Total
1978	5	
1979	8	
1980	18	
		31
1981	17	
1982	16	
1983	14	
1984	12	
		59
1986	159	159
Total	249	249

Table 5   Showing distribution of student sample for levels of academic achievement

Achievement Level	No.
1	59
2	130
3	60

Table 6   Showing residential locality of students

Locality	Student Number
Hobart	98
Glenorchy	18
Clarence	90
Brighton	4
Kingborough	14
New Norfolk	7
Sorell	4
Huon	3
Oatlands	1
Port Cygnet	3
Richmond	5
Country	2
Total	249

Instruments

The *Perceptions of School* questionnaire [Appendix 1] firstly provided background information from the students, including involvement in school activities, Church, Sporting, non Sporting etc. Past students were asked to indicate the year and grade in which they left College, and their current occupation. The remainder of the instrument was divided into lists of items for seven categories of information:

1   What is the School For — which asked students for their perceptions of the importance of certain goals of school and also how well they thought their school had achieved those goals (20 items).
2   Academic — in which students gave their opinion about their choices of 'HSC' subjects (16 items).
3   Vocational — where students gave opinions about various aspects of the vocational programme of the College (leisure, work, experience, craft, home economics, sewing) (8 items).
4   Personal and Spiritual Development — Here the students responded to a number of statements about the contribution St Mary's College might make to their personal or spiritual development. The statements included aspects of religious and moral issues, religious education and religious practice (24 items).

5 Leadership and Sporting — As the name implies, this category asked for student comment about the aspects of leadership and physical education which they experienced at St Mary's College (13 items).

6 The Q-line — This category was designed to gain information from students about their experience with the optional alternatives to the academic subjects (12 items).

7 Teachers — Here students were asked to give their perceptions of their experience of classroom teaching (16 items).

In addition to responding in the above categories the students were asked to comment additionally, if they wished, in respect of any or all of the categories. Validity and reliability of this instrument was determined by reference to the ten year study of Flynn (1985) in which factor analyses for similar instruments were done. The SPSS programme reliability test was employed there.

The *Quality of School Life* dimension [Appendix 2] of the study employed the ACER Quality of School Life questionnaire instrument. This has 71 item statements each preceded by the descriptor, 'School is a Place where (I have good friends etc)'. Students were asked to express agreement or disagreement with the item statements in terms of a four point scale — from definitely agree, mostly agree, mostly disagree to definitely disagree. The responses were clustered into seven domains (after the developmental work in Australia by Hunt and Fordham, 1983). The domains were as follows:

1 General Affect (or general satisfaction with school);

2 Status (or a student's perception of the relative degree of prestige afforded to her by significant others);

2a Identity (feelings of self worth, acceptance of self);

3 Teachers (or students' perception of the actions of teachers in relation to their work, and personally);

4 Positive Affect (or positive feelings about school and as a place where such feelings are engendered);

5 Negative Affect (or perceptions of a sense of alienation felt at school);

6 Adventure (the sense that learning is self-motivating, and provides feelings of adequacy and the ability to cope with its demands);

7 Opportunity (the felt degree of relevance of school life in terms of a sense of security in learning).

Data were collected employing the same instrument for all the groups (except the 1986 grade 12) a year apart. This enabled a comparative analysis to be achieved, together with information about any variations in the responses over the year's data collection period. Reliability of

the QSL instrument was provided from the testing procedures of the ACER (Willmott, 1988).

The *Teachers and Parents questionnaires* contained the same items as those presented to the students. For some categories and for the domains they were designed to ensure the teachers' and parents' views as to what the students' perceptions would be. Background information and opinions on school administration were sought, but are not reported here. The questionnaires are included in the appendices (Appendices 3,4 and 5 respectively).

Collection of Data

For the *Perceptions of School* dimension of the evaluation, data were gathered by means of a survey questionnaire and by interviews with a sample of both past and present students between the years 1979 and 1986. The questionnaire was piloted with a sample of senior students in 1986. In September 1986, the revised questionnaire was sent to all past students who could be contacted. A second round was completed within two months of the first distribution.

For the *Quality of School Life* dimension of the evaluation students in all grades of the senior school at St Mary's College were asked to respond to a questionnaire. The instrument was piloted in July 1986 in order to check for validity and reliability. No statistical analysis was applied in view of the fact that much of the structure of the categories was drawn from instruments previously validated (Collins and Hughes, 1978 and 1982). The instrument was implemented late in 1986 and again about mid year 1987.

The *Teachers and Parents questionnaires* were distributed to teachers via the Principal in April 1988, and in the same period to parents during a series of Parent-Teacher evenings. The researcher outlined and discussed the nature and purpose of the questionnaire with the parents for each grade level. The distribution of the instruments to both teachers and parents followed a letter of request to each teacher and parent involved.

Interviews. A sample of 29 students was selected for interviews, which were held at St Mary's College following the distribution and 'collection' of the POSSTUDY questionnaires. Students, about half in number from both past and present student groups, were selected according to a range of characteristics. These included age or grade level, academic level, locality of residence and, in the case of the past students, year of exit from the college [Appendix 6].

The interviews were carefully designed to gain further insight as to the meanings of responses to the questionnaire items and so interview questions were directed at the categories of the Perception of School instrument. Each interview was recorded and was conducted for at least

fifteen minutes, with both individuals and groups of two or three students. In some cases, especially with the past students, the interviews ran for a much longer period. This partly confirmed the expectation that the subjects (students) chosen were those who would be able to give fairly full, clear and insightful comment and opinion. The interviews formed a valuable complement to the information gained from the questionnaire and also had the function of a check on the reliability of the item statements and questions.

Teachers and students reaction sessions. Following presentation of results to Principal and staff via the Interim Report in February 1988, formal sessions were arranged for teachers in which their reactions to the results in general, and in terms of specific categories, were recorded. The procedure for these sessions is described in this chapter where the sessions are reported. Similar sessions were held with students in all the senior grades (10, 11 and 12) and these too are described and reported in this chapter.

Analyses

Student data
Perceptions of School — The analyses of data from this questionnaire to students involved counts of frequency distributions for the sample on each of the categories. Cross tabulations were calculated and a chi square test for significance at .05 or .01 levels applied for each item in relation to the psycho-social variables.

Quality of School Life — The approach to the analysis of data from the Quality of School Life Questionnaire is described in the findings related to these data.

Interviews — Interview data for the 'perceptions of school' dimension were typed and bound in a printed collection under the category headings.

Following collection and preliminary analysis of the data, the interim results were presented both to the staff and to each of the current grades of senior students. The staff wrote written responses according to their groupings for each of the categories. The researcher held hour long discussions with each grade in order to gauge the students' interpretation of the results. In addition meetings were held with parents from all grade levels at which the research as a whole was introduced and their part carefully explained.

Teacher and parent data
Frequency distributions were counted for each sample relating to all categories and domains as for the student instruments. Data were listed in terms of percentages of agreement with the item statements.

Summary of Major Findings

Students' Perceptions

Expectations of school

1   The first major result was that in general the students regarded the affective area of the school's objectives as of greater importance but less well achieved than those of the cognitive area. In other words, feelings of well being at school were generally more important to students than formal academic achievements, yet were less well obtained by the school on their behalf.

2   Consistent with Flynn's Australian research on Catholic schools (1985), employment was found to be of great concern to students who regarded employment related goals as of great importance. Yet, the majority of students considered that the school's objectives in this area had not been well achieved.

3   In terms of formal academic subject areas generally, the majority of students considered the school's task of enabling them to understand the traditional academic subjects in depth to be both important and well achieved.

4   St Mary's is perceived by the students as being generally more successful in the traditional academic role than in providing effective counselling about specific employment when they leave school.

5   However, looking at specific subject areas, the students made some important qualifications. First, less than half of the students considered the objective of knowing and appreciating the major works of English literature to be important. Second, the students considered the objectives of understanding mathematics to be of only moderate importance and not well achieved by the school. On the other hand in the broader area of the sciences, the students considered an understanding of the basic ideas of the sciences to be important and generally well achieved by the school. Third, most students perceived an understanding of the fine arts to be an relatively unimportant objective of the school and one not well achieved. Indeed, throughout the period of study (1978–86) an appreciation of beauty declined in importance in the minds of students, both as a goal of the school and in terms of their view of the school's achievement of this goal.

Students' academic world

6   Students' choices of subjects for study at senior level (grades 10–12) were related quite highly to the need of those subjects for gaining the employment of their choice or less directly for qualification to enter a university or other tertiary institution. However, the factor rated highest by students as a reason for subject choice was their intrinsic interest in the

subjects chosen. Further, they appear to be making such important decisions with negligible influence from their parents or friends.

Vocational

7 A majority of students favoured an increase in vocational studies if they were to be prepared for life after school. However, in their consideration of the appropriateness of their vocational subjects to their choice of career, the majority of students focussed narrowly on employment as opposed to vocation as a life-calling. In addition, the majority of students did not consider that leisure education was useful in opening up a possible career.

Personal and spiritual development

8 In the area of social morality the students appeared to be clear about the issues and strongly committed to high moral standards, but in the area of sexual morality, the most deeply personal area of their lives, they expressed considerable uncertainty.

9 Overwhelmingly, the greatest influence on students' religious development is the instruction/example of their parents or guardians. Of other influences — including, teachers, friends, parish priest — the least influential is the religious education provided by the school.

10 Less than half the students indicate they attended Mass or worship on Sunday and almost half the students attended Reconciliation 'practically never'. Less than a quarter of students prayed daily and a quarter only prayed several times a week. Participation in religious practice declines once students leave school.

Leadership and sporting life in school

11 Students perceive the school to be successful in helping them understand what leadership is. Nevertheless, almost half the students neither consider teachers to be good models of leadership, nor that their experience at school actually helps them to develop the ability to be leaders. It was at grade 10 that most students felt that inadequate opportunities are provided for them to develop skills in leadership.

12 Students approve of the physical education classes provided at school and, in fact, two thirds of the students consider that more classes in this area should be offered. Student approval of physical education at St Mary's increased over the eight year span of the Study.

13 While most students considered the physical education programme to be comprehensive and worthwhile, less than half consider the value of physical activity to be emphasized sufficiently in school for them to continue such activity after leaving school.

14 A majority of students feel that physical education and sport are 'directed mainly at the gifted and talented students'.

The Q-line
15 Almost all the students considered that the Q-line is a feature of St Mary's which should be continued and two-thirds of the students agreed that it should be compulsory.

Teachers and teaching
16 From the students' viewpoint most teachers at St Mary's College clearly organize their classwork, cover a great deal of material in the time allowed, try to make their classes useful rather than entertaining and set homework regularly.

17 On the other hand, less than half the students consider that teachers make their teaching material relevant to student needs, extend students to the limit of their abilities, or stimulate them to think or work creatively.

18 Less than a third of the students consider that teachers understand students' study problems and less than a quarter that teachers succeed in making their classes interesting.

19 When comparing groups of students (in terms of varying levels of academic performance, age or grade levels or socio-economic difference) for most questions there was no significant difference in the results.

Quality of school life
20 In general, students at St Mary's College perceive the quality of their school life in very positive terms.

21 The data indicate that St Mary's College generally appears to be successful at providing experiences and environments which enhance students' general satisfaction with school, the extent to which they are looked up to by significant others, and their sense of self-esteem.

22 Students tend to disagree with statements such as: 'School is a place where I feel depressed'. They suggest that they have relatively few negative feelings about school.

Comparison of Viewpoints of Students, Teachers and Parents

Expectations of school
23 There was considerable discordance between students on the one hand and teachers and parents on the other.

24 [As stated above, students considered cognitive and affective areas as objectives of the school to be extremely important but *not* well achieved.] In contrast with students, the teachers and parents considered the cognitive areas generally to be important and well achieved. Similarly, teachers and parents perceived the affective areas to be generally important and well achieved by the school on the students' behalf.

25   In the specific areas of work and careers all three groups (students, teachers and parents) considered this area to contain important objectives by the school. Yet, whilst teachers and parents considered the objectives to be well achieved, students do not perceive it to be so.

Academic life of the school

26   In this aspect of the Study also there was discordance between the three groups.

27   Teachers considered that academic choices of students are strongly influenced by the parents, though this was the least important reason given by students and parents.

28   Teachers, much more strongly than parents or students, perceived that students choose subjects primarily for gaining entrance to a tertiary institution. About a third of the teachers consider that students choose their subjects because their friends have done so in contrast to 8 per cent of students and 14 per cent of parents who hold this view.

Vocational aspects

29   In this area, there was a generally high level of agreement between teachers, students and parents — mostly in a positive direction. However, about twenty per cent of teachers and a third of students, compared with half the parents regarded leisure education as useful in opening up a potential career.

Personal and spiritual aspects of school

30   There is high agreement by teachers and parents with the students' view that in students' religious development, the instruction and example of parents is the most significant influence. However, the students' religious practice presents a generally depressing picture as indicated in the Mass attendance and other faith practices.

31   The religious education programme does not seem to be working for the students and the teachers largely agree with this. The parents, however, appear to view the students' opinions to be otherwise.

Leadership and sporting aspects of the students' experience at school

32   There is a strong concordance of views among parents, teachers and students that students' experience at school helps them to understand what leadership is, and that there are sufficient opportunities to develop leadership in the senior grades (11 and 12). (Note there is a contrasting result for grade 10 in the 'leadership' area as listed in the results and discussed in the psycho–social variables summary.)

33   However, there was significant discordance of views as well. Almost all teachers and parents considered students to regard teachers as

good leadership models and physical education classes as comprehensive and worthwhile. In contrast, less than 60 per cent of the students regarded teachers as good models of leadership and only two thirds of the students saw their physical education classes as comprehensive and worthwhile.

34   A strong majority of parents and teachers viewed the students as perceiving there are sufficient number of classes in physical education; experience in school physical education encourages students to continue such activity in after-school life; and that students develop the ability to be a leader as a result of their school experience. Yet, less than half of the students actually held this view of these aspects of their school experience in leadership and sport.

Teachers
35   There was strong concordance between teachers, students and parents that: teachers clearly outline and organize their work; cover a great deal of material in the time allowed; give students a broad general understanding of subjects; and succeed in making their classes useful rather than entertaining.

36   In other instances the strength of perception of teachers and/or parents is greater than is the case of students. Less than half the students view teachers as attempting to make their teaching material relevant to their needs, but more than three quarters of teachers and parents perceive students as holding this view. Half of the students consider the teachers as allowing what they perceived to be 'classroom discussion', whereas an overwhelming majority of teachers and parents perceive students as in accord with this view.

37   Approximately half of the teachers and a majority of parents perceive teachers as making their classes interesting. Yet less than a quarter of the students have this perception.

38   Almost all of the parents and students consider that teachers set homework regularly. In contrast, less than two-thirds of teachers consider this to be the students' perception.

Quality of school life
39   Overall, there is a strong general separation between the views of teachers and those of students and parents as to how students perceive the quality of their experience at school. Relatively, the teachers' perceptions reflect a less positive view of such experience for students than do students themselves or parents.

40   Where there is a variation between students' and parents' perceptions, it is the students who appear more positive about the quality of their school life.

St Mary's College Study: Findings in Detail

Introduction

The picture of the findings is drawn first as a presentation of student perceptions of school (i.e., over a span of eight years from 1978 to 1986). In addition the perceptions of students, teachers and parents have been compared. Next the students' perceptions of the quality of their school life are presented. The perceptions of students, teachers and parents concerning the students' quality of school life also are compared. The students' perceptions are also explained in terms of selected psycho-social variables, including variations in perceptions of students in terms of their differing age/grade levels, differing academic achievement levels, and differing years of exit from the school. The interpretations then are illuminated by extracts from interviews with students and the reactions of both teachers and students to the results of the Study are presented.

Students' Perceptions of School

Students' expectations of school (Table 7)
As described earlier, in this category students' responses indicated their view of how important certain objectives of the school were and also how well they considered the school to have achieved these objectives. That is, there was an indication of the students' views of the ideal and the real school according to a number of agreed school tasks. Such concordance can be measured in terms of a comparison of fifteen 'cognitive' and 'affective' responses. 'Cognitive' refers to the things to be known; the more intellectual learning aspects, 'affective' refers to the things students would 'feel about' as distinct from 'know about'; the attitudes rather than the things known.

The first major result emerging was that in general the students regarded the 'affective' area of the school's objectives as of greater importance, but less well achieved, than those of the cognitive area. In other words, feelings of well being at school were generally more important to the students than formal academic achievements, yet were less well attained by the school on their behalf. Such well being included the students' sense of understanding themselves and how others see them, feelings of self-confidence, feeling able to respond to large social issues, and to accept others who think and act differently. Formal academic achievements included an understanding of the traditional academic subjects, appreciation of English literature, the ability to read, understanding of the sciences and the fine arts, and possession of specific skills for a chosen field of work.

Table 7   Results of student responses for expectations of school category

A = Affective C = Cognitive It's The School's Task to Make Sure that you	How Important %	Rank of Item	How Well Achieved %	Rank of Item
1. Know about a wide range of possible jobs (C)	89	5	31	14
2. Understand in considerable depth one or more traditional academic subjects (e.g., English, chemistry) (C)	76	12	64	3
3. Have a reasonable understanding of yourself and the way others see you (A)	73	15	28	15
4. Know and appreciate a number of the major works of English Literature (C)	43	19	55	4
5. Can organize your own time and work independently (A)	89	6	28	15
6. Can listen sensitively and with understanding to others (A)	81	7	41	9
7. Understand some of the abstract principles of mathematical reasoning (e.g. algebra, set theory) (C)	44	18	38	10
8. Are an individual developing as you wish (A)	74	14	23	19
9. Are able to read with understanding (C)	99	1	81	1
10. Accept those who think and act differently (e.g., those of different race, dress, life-style) (A)	94	3	50	6
11. Understand the world of work—its routines, demands, responsibilities (C)	79	9	28	15
12. Have specific skills you need for a chosen field of work (C)	76	13	42	8
13. Understand some of the basic ideas in sciences (e.g., biology, physics) (C)	67	16	52	5
14. Have some understanding of one or more of the fine arts (e.g., painting, classical music) (C)	41	20	33	13
15. Are generally obedient to parents, teachers and all in authority (A)	81	8	68	2
16. Work hard at things you find difficult and do not like (A)	77	11	43	7
17. Are self-confident and possess self-respect (A)	94	2	35	12
18. Know of and are concerned to respond justly to major social issues (e.g., unemployment, the future of Aboriginal society) (A)	79	9	21	20
19. Have developed an appreciation of beauty (A)	49	17	23	18
20. Can form a considered opinion and act on it even if this means going against what most people think (C)	90	4	36	11

The students also considered each of the other affective aspects of the school's task to be highly important. But in every case, except one, the objectives were considered to have been inadequately achieved. These affective items mainly had to do with the students' perceptions of the school's task in helping them grow and develop as individuals and as persons in the community, that is: understanding themselves and how others see them; listening with understanding; developing freely as individuals; accepting those who think and act differently; developing self-confidence and self-respect; knowing of and responding to major social issues; and acting obediently to those in authority.

In the attainment of all but the last item — which has to do as much with functional responding in a particular and corporate situation as with self-growth — the students generally regarded the school as unsuccessful. Objectives having to do with their self-esteem were among the most important but the least well achieved, according to the students. In terms of the area of personal development and relationships the younger, that is grade 10 students, were again more critical of (less satisfied with) the school's achievement. The school appears to have been more successful in helping the students of earlier years (1978–84) to become secure in terms of their personal development and the development of relationships than for present students. The school thus appears always to have had difficulty in achieving success for students in this area. It has obviously become a significant matter of concern to students currently. Similarly past and present students all considered the school to have achieved little success in helping them respond to major social issues, though present students are less disapproving than are past students of the school's achievement in this. Flynn (1985) in his study of year 12 students in NSW, over a period of ten years, found similarly that the affective areas of the school's task were more significant but less well achieved than those of the cognitive domain. The real school for such students appears not to match the ideal presented to them by the school.

In this affective area there is a clear discordance between the ideal and the real school in the minds of the students. The responses of students in this area and in many of the cognitive aspects emphasize the distinct possibility that the social and cultural context of the school is highly significant to the degree of success which students may achieve in terms of the school's academic objectives.

Students' Expectations for the World of Work   Responses in the 'cognitive' area generally referred to the students' perceptions of the world of work and to academic subject areas. Though students regarded the affective area to be more important, the cognitive area and concerns about the world of work were still important to them. As in Flynn's research, the St Mary's College Study found that employment was a great concern of students especially, if not entirely, at the senior years. This was so for all

students, though in fact the high achievers regarded their development in school of specific skills for a chosen field of work as far more important than did middle or low achievers. More gifted students are perhaps more likely to have a specific career in mind and therefore stress the importance of learning specific skills. In contrast, those students likely to end their formal education soon are facing a much more general and limited range of employment prospects with less concentration on specific skills.

Most recent students of the College were more approving of the school's efforts in ensuring that students understand the world of work. This is a reasonable interpretation in light of the significant difficulties of current school leavers in finding employment. Less attention was given to the subject of career education a decade ago. Yet noticeably the majority of students, including the present ones, considered that the school's objectives in this area had not been well achieved.

Knowing about a wide range of jobs, understanding the world of work and having specific skills needed for chosen areas of work, were all regarded as important expectations of school. However, the majority of students found that the 'real' situation sharply contrasted with their 'ideal'. This general perception was reflected in the interviews when, for instance, students commented favourably on the value of work experience, but felt there should be more opportunities for this in the earlier years of their secondary education.

Students' Academic Expectations   In terms of the 'formal' academic subject areas, the majority of students considered the school's task of enabling them to understand the traditional academic subjects 'in depth' to be both important and well achieved. However there were significant differences between the groups of students in terms of their age and grade levels, particularly between the younger grade 10 group and those of grades 11 and 12 (see section on psycho-social variables later in this chapter). In the traditional academic areas the grade 11 and 12 group regarded the school's task as being of greater importance than did the grade 10s. Also, they regarded the school as more successful in this area than did the grade 10 group. The academically weaker students themselves stated in interviews that the academic areas became more significant to them as they reached the final years. (The grade 10s also regarded the school as having less well achieved other 'academic' objectives — in terms of reading with understanding, organizing time and work independently, etc. Their responses were stronger for these items than for the more substantive academic subject areas.)

If we look to specific academic subjects, the picture varies. Dealing firstly with a subject representative somewhat of the humanities, we find that less than half the students (who are in the senior levels — grades 10 to 12) considered the objective of knowing and appreciating the works of English literature to be important. Noticeably the younger (grade 10)

students, who are at the first point of exit from the school considered this area to be of lesser importance than did the more senior years.

The point worth considering here is the hint of decline in what is perhaps the most significant of all subjects — the students' own language and literature. Of course a number of possible explanations, or dimensions of explanation, may be advanced for these results. One view is that there has been a decline in English teaching and learning in and from the primary school years. Then there are the difficulties faced by an increasing number of students for whom English is not their first or native language, the students evidently discriminating between the importance of and their needs in English language learning and those in English literature. Another explanation, simpler perhaps, is that the grade 11 and 12 students regarded the subject of English as more important than did the grade 10 students simply because they are more cognizant of the goal in this area and of the need of it for success in their chosen fields. Whatever the explanations to this point, the results in terms of students' perceptions across the span of eight years show a diminishing in the importance which students attach to the subject of English.

When the cultural significance of literature is considered such perceptions on the part of the young bear pondering. Surely growth in people's understanding of their literature contributes to the nourishment and elegance of their culture. Lack of such growth diminishes the potentially civilizing character of the growing society.

In relation to the specific subject area of mathematics, partly representative of the scientific areas of study, St Mary's College students considered this objective of the school as only of moderate importance. The students also perceived the school as not having achieved this objective well. It is intriguing that the area of mathematical understanding perceived as a significant goal of the school and perceived by the community as being so essential to children's later success, is held in such low regard by the students. The explanation will not be simple, but since St Mary's College is an all-girls school, the possibility is that these results reinforce a common view that girls hold generally negative attitudes towards mathematics, the subject having been regarded as the traditional domain of males.

Student perceptions in the broader area of the sciences revealed a somewhat different pattern of response. Generally the students considered the school's objective — enabling them to understand basic ideas of the sciences — to be important and generally to be well achieved by the school. Thus the traditional perception of mathematics does not apply to the general area of science. Looking at students of differing achievement levels, the pattern changes again. The 'lower' achieving students rated the objective in relation to the sciences as of much less importance than did 'middle' or 'higher' achievers. Notably, the 'higher' achievers were much less satisfied that the school had achieved such an objective than were

the other students. Of course a 'chicken or egg' possibility occurs here. The lower achieving students may perform less well because they do not perceive the sciences to be important enough or hold this perception because their achievement in the sciences is low. The school cannot risk assuming that students' perceptions of what is important in their school learning does not significantly affect their performance. The school must address both the cultural significance of students' perceptions of such subjects as the sciences and its own task in relation to raising the stature of such subjects, especially for low achieving students.

Finally, in the 'academic' subject of fine arts, the students' expectations of school were similar to those for English and mathematics. That is, most students perceived an understanding of fine arts to be a relatively unimportant objective for the school. Also they considered that this objective had not been well achieved by the school. Indeed the students' ranked the fine arts as lowest in importance of all the items concerning their expectations of school. When the students considered the 'school's task' of development of an appreciation of beauty the result was similar. Less than half of the students, that is across the eight year span, perceived beauty to be an important school objective. In fact throughout this period an appreciation of beauty declined in importance in the minds of students — both as a goal of the school and in terms of their view of the school's achievement of this goal. In terms of differing groups of students, high achievers, together with middle achievers, regarded the goal of an appreciation of beauty as more important than did low achievers. Also the grade 10s and grade 11s were less satisfied than the grade 12s with the school's success in the achievement of this objective. Yet generally, less than a quarter of the students regarded the school as having achieved its objective well in this area. Of course we might wish to dismiss the item entirely on the grounds that adolescents could not appreciate beauty except in a fairly functional or pragmatic sense. Yet there were variations in the perceptions of differing groups of the whole sample. Also there is a clearly diminishing proportion of students from 1978 to 1986 who regard this objective as important.

The results again accord with those of the Flynn (1985) ten year study in which the students regarded matters of employment as of much greater significance than those of the fine arts. In other words, the rounded education, education of the whole person, has a diminished perception in the eyes of the senior students. This result relates to others in which there are implications for the cultural upbringing of the young — the cultural context or significance of English and the students' perceptions about mathematics, for instance.

Expectations of School: Academic versus Employment   The results showed that the goal of 'academic' achievement was better attained than the goal of assisting students in knowing about the range of possible jobs. St

Mary's is thus perceived by students as being generally more successful in the traditional academic role of teaching particular disciplines than in providing effective counselling about specific employment for students when they leave the school. Yet more students are staying on at school for longer periods and more employers are demanding more education, even for the low skill employment sector. It appears therefore that for students the school needs to be more effective in assisting students towards the successful transition from school to workplace. The 'academic' school also needs to guide students in making appropriate job choices by providing them with more knowledge of the world of work. Here again the students' perception of concordance and discordance between the real and ideal school is exemplified. The school's role in the academic areas is considered by students to be important and well achieved. But in terms of developing in them certain understandings and abilities which they feel are vital when they enter the uncertain world of work, the school, in their eyes, has achieved far less well. To the students, though they consider there has been some late recognition of the problem by the school, the real does not yet match the ideal.

Academic aspects (Table 8)
It seems clear in most countries that it is the academic aspects which claim most attention in modern secondary schooling. This tends to be true for parents who are concerned to be assured that their children are likely to 'succeed', and academic 'results' most clearly indicate such success. Similarly, employers often judge the best prospects for industry, commerce, and even the arts, by academic results. And since the schools are in a sense both guided and judged by community criteria, academic outcomes are the key to the school's as well as their students' performance. On the other hand, the means by which students get on the track to academic success are not always clear. Intellectual talent is not the only criterion. Access to performance information in terms of academic results, mainly through formal tests and examination, is relatively easy to accomplish. But it is clear that other important indices of academic success exist which, however, are more difficult to ascertain. Students are not passive receptacles of learning. Their own perceptions and active 'cognitive' and 'affective' involvement in learning will also be critical to academic success. Nevertheless little appeared to be known as to what St Mary's College students themselves perceived as the effective and important means of, and timing for, to 'making it' on to that 'track'. Hence it seemed useful for the school to know something of the reasons for students' choices of their subjects which was their prerogative in the senior years.

The students were asked which were the most significant reasons for their choice of subjects at their senior level (that is, for the matriculation examination which in Australia is the Higher School Certificate). Second-

Table 8   Results of student responses for academic category

Item No.	Choosing HSC Subjects		
	Reason for choice	% Agreed	% Disagreed
4.	You were intrinsically interested	93	7
1.	You needed particular subjects to to qualify for university or other tertiary institutions	91	9
2.	Needed subjects to gain immediate employment of your choice	85	15
5.	Had achieved good results in that subject in year 10	80	20
10.	Appropriate information was available regarding prerequisites for tertiary study	61	39
11.	Appropriate information was available regarding specific subjects required for specific fields of employment	58	42
6.	You knew nothing of subject and wanted to fill gap in your knowledge	51	49
8.	Choices were largely determined by organization of subjects into lines	34	66
9.	The sciences appeared to be more important than the humanities	18	82
7.	Parents strongly influenced choice	17	83
3.	Your friends were doing that subject	8	92
Item No.	Benefits from Choice of HSC Subjects		
	Your Choice of HSC subject assisted you:	% Agreed	% Disagreed
13.	In gaining entrance to a tertiary institution	89	11
14.	Providing sound introduction and foundation for further study	87	13
15.	Providing basis for continuing personal interest in an area or discipline	85	15
16.	Opening up new areas of study for you	84	16
12.	In gaining immediate employment	72	28

ly, students were asked to judge the benefits derived from these choices. Given the strength of expectations from external forces, so to speak, especially from parents and employers, it might be assumed that students would respond fairly directly to these influences. On the other hand, since their responses were the judgments of youth, we might expect that friends and/or the ways in which the students were functionally organized by timetabling, for instance, would be strong forces of choice.

In fact the results confounded these logical assumptions. The students appeared to have been making individual and relatively mature judgments in the realm of their academic experience in school. Of course they had been aware of the strength of the demands of the employment market. Their choices of subjects were related highly to the need of subjects for gaining the employment of their choice, or less directly for qualification to enter a university or other tertiary institution. However, in terms of the results here, the factor rated highest by students in their

choice of subjects was that their intrinsic interest in those subjects. More than 90 per cent of the students regarded this as a reason for their choice. Furthermore they appeared to be making such important decision largely without the influence of their parents (less than 17 per cent of the students regarded their parents as influencing their choice of subjects). Among differing groups of students, it was the higher achieving students rather than the middle or lower achievers who regarded parents as having influenced their choice of subjects. Also, it was the most recent students of the College rather than those of the earlier years (eight years before) who were more likely to be influenced by parents in making their subject choices (see discussion of psycho-social variables later in this chapter).

In terms of the simpler, perhaps more pragmatic reasons, students regarded the organization of subjects within the timetable as one of the least significant reasons. They rated the influence, and especially the example, of their friends as the very least of the categories of reasons. Less than 10 per cent of the student sample across the span of the eight 'leaving' years gave friends as a reason for their subject choice.

The students obviously were aware of the significance of subject choices for employment, benefits or purposes. Hence they rated, 'gaining entrance to a tertiary institution' very highly as an assumed, if indirect, means to gaining employment. However, 'opening up new areas of study', and 'providing a basis for continuing personal interest in an area or discipline' were rated about equal to the 'employment' benefits, as reasons for the choice of subjects. Of course it might be argued that it is simply logical that students are likely to focus on the subjects which they were interested in and did well at, and that they would choose these for their employment purposes. Nevertheless the point of these results surely is that the students were not prepared to sacrifice their intrinsic interest in subjects to expedite their successful entrance to the employment market. In fact the least rated of all the statements about the benefits to be derived from students' choice of subjects was the benefit, or purpose, of 'gaining immediate employment'. In terms of the grouping of students according to their academic levels, we found that less than half the lower achievers agreed that their choice of subjects would be likely to assist in their gaining immediate employment. The point echoes the students' perceptions about the purposes of school. That is, matters of their own confidence, and confidence in the outcomes of what they did at school, were as important to most students as the functional and formal routines in which they engaged. This was notwithstanding that those routines aimed at the vital objectives of achieving jobs and careers.

Vocational aspects (Table 9)
There is little doubting the recent increased significance of vocational subjects to this and many other school systems in recent years throughout the world. Nevertheless teachers and parents certainly have been aware

Table 9   Results of student responses for vocational category (N = 249)

Item No.	Vocational Education	% Agreed	% Disagreed
1.	The subjects I (study) studied suit (ed) my career choice	85	15
2.	Leisure education was (is) useful in opening up to me a potential career	36	64
3.	Because of my craft studies I am now able to do simple repairs at home	46	54
4.	My skills in cooking, dressmaking have carried over into other areas	67	33
5.	Work experience has helped me in deciding upon my career	69	31
6.	More vocational studies are required at HSC if students are to be prepared for life after school	77	23
7.	Work experience helped me understand the world of work.	73	27
8.	Vocational studies have proven beneficial in my life outside school		
	Cooking	89	11
	Dressmaking	68	32
	Craft	48	52

that the vocational area has been part of schooling for a long time, in Australia, for example, at least since secondary education became compulsory in 1947. There have been vocational classes in upper primary levels of school in a number of States before and since World War Two. Therefore the nature of the recent revival of vocational awareness in secondary schooling needs to be examined. Partly, of course, the field of employment has narrowed. For instance, the common apprenticeship schemes in Australia diminished from the end of the 1950s, in concert almost with the increasing academic emphasis and the establishment of the matriculation or higher school certificate — grades 11 and 12 (in some countries grade 13) — levels as the assumed targets of schooling achievement. Indeed the increasing academic emphases of secondary schooling in recent decades was accompanied in the early stages by a considerable proportion of students moving into the matriculation or higher school certificate areas without a real prospect of succeeding academically. There were a number of school principals who considered that 30–40 per cent of their students who were going on to senior levels had no prospect of success. In the view of some educators this retention was at least partly a political attempt to hold down the unemployment figures among the young. These changes, bolstered by the lessening employment prospects for school leavers, has meant that secondary school systems began to enlarge the vocational offerings in their syllabuses. Students could now find some vocational preparation in secondary school and not be forced to go on to matriculation simply in the hope of gaining the more marketable academic qualifications.

But the most serious part of the question as for the rising significance of systems of vocational education is whether this has worked, and achieved the results they had hoped for. The experience of St Mary's College data may make a useful comment on this question.

The vocational area of schooling at St Mary's included activities and classes associated with the dimensions of leisure, work and home-crafts, which include 'home economics' (mainly cooking), 'crafts' (mainly woodworking), 'dressmaking' and typing/shorthand. Computer classes operated as a separate though not strictly vocationally designed activity of the syllabus. Results are not presented for the areas of typing, shorthand or computer skills. This is an area which will require investigation in the future.

The leisure section of the area was designed to assist students in actually exploring a variety of work-related activities in such a way as would help open to them potential jobs and careers. In addition the course was designed to assist students in using their leisure time creative-ly. The work aspect mainly focussed on a period of work experience in which students spent a week in an occupational area of their choosing. The work experience was confined to the final year of secondary school (grade 10). The leisure and 'homecrafts' aspects were experienced by students throughout their first four secondary years (grades 7–10).

Although the students largely endorsed the vocational subjects they studied as appropriate to whatever career choices they felt able to make, only in terms of one aspect did they consider their study/activity helpful in deciding upon their career. This was the aspect of work. In this aspect a little over two-thirds of the students agreed that it was helpful. The majority of students did not consider leisure aspects of their vocational courses to be useful in opening up for them a potential career. Neither were the homecraft courses, with the understandable exception of cook-ing, considered beneficial to their life after school. Indeed, when com-paring the perceptions of students over the eight year period there was diminishing endorsement for this homecraft aspect in terms of its benefit for 'life after school'.

Given the students' recognition of the fresh relevance of the voca-tional area to their schooling, what was the reason for its relative lack of impact? There was virtually no evidence to suggest that the courses in themselves were inadequate. Also such was the variety in activity and presentation that there was little chance for the student perception of 'boredom'. Beyond this the students clearly were in favour of an 'increase in vocational studies' if they were to be 'prepared for life after school'. One possible interpretation is in the students' perception of the nature of the vocational courses. In the work aspect, the study and activity were directly related to the real world of work. Students experienced a im-mediate and pragmatic transfer to that real world. But the leisure and homecraft activities appeared not to make that transfer. It is possible that

if the courses and activities in these two vocational areas were given more time and status, their vocational significance would more readily rise in the minds of some students at least.

The vocational area of the school syllabus has been undergoing many changes and has yet to occupy a solid position in a well defined sense in the school curriculum. It should not escape the notice of educators that for more than half the students in secondary school it is the vocational rather than the academic track they will take in after school life.

The personal and spiritual world experienced by students (Table 10, a–c)
St Mary's College is a Catholic school and thereby its curriculum is imbued with a spiritual and moral dimension. This is not to say that personal, moral and spiritual concerns do not exist or are not significant to schools in general. Society generally is much aware of the personal, moral and spiritual needs of the young in a very stressed modern world. Perhaps it is because St Mary's is a school whose curriculum has this ideological commitment that the perception of its students in the personal, moral and spiritual area are likely to be of interest generally.

In terms of a respect for truth and social responsibility the responses were unequivocal. The students greatly endorsed a respect for truth as a fundamental element in the stability of society and expressed a deep concern for community and world social problems such as poverty and war and illicit drug consumption.

In the area of sexual morality, as confirmed by interviews, and in discussion with the most recent classes of students, clearly they did not

Table 10 (a)   Results of student responses for personal and spiritual category

Item No.	Moral and Religious Issues	% Agree	% Disagree
1.	A respect for truth is a fundamental element in the stability of any society	99	1
2.	At times I am afraid of losing my faith	54	46
3.	The great world problems such as poverty and war don't worry me particularly	9	91
4.	It is all right for people who are not married to live together	50	50
5.	To drive a car when unsteady after drinking is not only foolish but morally wrong	78	22
6.	Trying out drugs (e.g. Marijuana) is all right so long as you don't go too far	22	78
7.	I feel concerned that many people tell untruths lightly, that is, without serious reason	73	27
8.	Religion has helped me answer the real questions about the meaning of life	60	40
9/10.	My education at SMC (has) helped in preparing for such things as:		
	Marriage	46	54
	Pregnancy	38	62
11.	Being a Catholic is very important to me	79	21

Table 10 (b)   Results of student responses showing influences on religious development

Item No.	Influence	% Important	% Unimportant
12.	Instruction of parents and their example	73	8
13.	Example and personal guidance of teachers	44	18
14.	Example of friends at school	41	19
15.	Guidance and influence of some Religious, Priest, or Minister	40	28
17.	Religious education provided by the school	31	33
16.	Religious instruction provided by Parish or church	35	35

Table 10(c)   Results of student responses showing 'religious belief/practice'

		% Response
23.	*Performance of Apostolic Action or good deeds for others (I normally perform...)*	
	Weekly	58
	About once or twice a month	22
	About once in two months	3
	About once in three months	4
	About once or twice a year	3
	Practically never or never	1
24.	*Prayer. I normally pray*	
	At least once or twice daily	23
	Several times a week	25
	Every week approximately	18
	Every month approximately	4
	Occasionally during the year	17
	Practically never or never	11
19.	*RE Classes at School*	
	Strengthened commitment to God	12
	They were related to real life to my needs	16
	I found them quite interesting	45
	Were irrelevant to my life	13
	Were boring/uninteresting	13
20.	*Mass Worship attendance*	
	Very or rarely/never	17
	Sundays at least	41
	Attend daily or	4
	About once per month	6
	About 4 or 5 times a year	21
21.	*Receiving Holy Communion*	
	Daily or several times a week	4
	At least on Sunday's	40
	About two or three times a month	8
	About once a month	6
	About four or five times a year	19
	Very rarely or never	21
22.	*Confession/Reconciliation*	
	Weekly	0
	About once or twice a month	1
	About once in two months	5
	About once in three months	13
	About once or twice a year	39
	Practically never	43

endorse the sexual promiscuity commonly portrayed in the media. On the other hand in some areas they expressed ambivalence or confusion. For instance, half the students considered it allowable for couples who are not married to live together. In another sense the students felt ill prepared at school for decision making in the area of sexual morality. Less than half the sample considered that they were adequately prepared for such things as marriage and pregnancy. In terms of a comparison with earlier years, this concern was expressed to a greater degree by the present students and least by students leaving school seven or eight years ago.

Summarily, in the area of social morality the students appeared to be clear about the issues and strongly committed to high moral standards. But in the area of sexual morality, the most deeply personal area of their lives, they expressed considerable uncertainty and need.

The spiritual dimension of this aspect incorporated the religious education and religious practice which were associated with and affected by their school experiences. A prior issue put to students concerned the set of influences upon their religious development in general. Students were asked to rate the importance of various influences, including parents, teachers, the example of school friends, the influence of priests or ministers or other religious, their religious education at school and religious instruction provided in their church or parish. The results were surprisingly unequivocal. Only the parents' influence was regarded as significant. All other listed 'influences' received a very low rating.

More specifically regarding the students' religious beliefs and practices, the students, firstly, considered their religious education classes to be virtually insignificant to the strengthening of their commitment to God or in relating to their real life and needs. Secondly, less than half the students indicated they attended Mass or Worship at least on Sunday. Almost half the students attended Reconciliation (Confession) 'practically never'. Less than a quarter of the students prayed daily; and a quarter of the students prayed several times a week.

There were interesting differences when groups of students were compared according to their levels of academic performance, and the various periods (between 1978 and 1986) when they left school. For instance whilst less than half the students generally declared that they attended Mass or worship at least on Sunday, the lower achievers recorded the highest church attendance of all groups followed by the middle achievers and high achievers. Though attendances were still low in percentage a greater proportion of present students reported attending Mass at least on Sunday than did students five years or so previously.

In respect of attendance at Reconciliation (Confession), whilst nearly half of all the students attended 'rarely or never', the proportion of present students represented was far less compared with students of five years or eight years previously. The fall in attendance has been from more than 80 per cent to about 50 per cent.

This picture of demonstration of religious faith especially for a Catholic school — in terms of the students' practice and apparent growth — is far from positive. There has been considerable debate, however, as to whether such apparent decline in faith and practice among the young is to be regarded with alarm. For St Mary's College, whilst being Catholic was 'very important' to the great majority of students and God was seen almost exclusively as a loving Father rather than as a mighty Creator or Spirit apart from their lives, more than half of them expressed 'fear at times' of losing their faith. This latter expression might be interpreted as simply an acknowledgement of doubt and that this, together with the low level of religious belief and practice, was for the young a part of the natural process of faith development. Flynn (1985) makes the following observation:

> The opposite of faith is not *doubt*. Substantive, honest doubt is often a sign that a genuine faith is alive and well. The opposite of faith, as James Fowler, points out, is *nihilism* — the inability to contemplate any transcendent dimension to one's life. It is increasingly common today for people to experience times of questioning and confusion regarding faith. Through this process, earlier images of faith, often developed in childhood, can give way to more mature expressions of faith. (p. 236)

Flynn's study is consistent with the St Mary's Study which shows a decline in Mass attendance amongst students. Probing further, Flynn also had students rank six reasons for not attending Mass (p. 210). Three reasons ranked well above the rest: 1) the Mass is boring and always the same; 2) young people are too lazy to go, and; 3) young people do not feel involved or part of the celebration. Considerably lower ratings were given to the remaining reasons: 4) young people are going through a searching or questioning time of their faith; 5) young people do not understand the Mass, and; 6) the Mass liturgy is poorly performed. Flynn postulates that the boredom with the Mass is 'not so much a rejection of the Church as much as a beginning of a search for personal identity' (p. 211). He adds that at a time when youth desperately need assurance they receive conflicting messages from media, peers, school, parent. As a way of coping they 'frequently put their values into some kind of a 'deep freeze'. It is therefore little wonder that they see the opposite sex, cars, sports, windsurfing etc as more attractive at this time. Thus students appear to be going through a period of 'time-out' while they find their identity. As the identity crisis is resolved, Mass attendance would be likely to rise again. As to the laziness, Flynn cites the work of Hornsby-Smith in England suggesting that it is not physical but mental energy which is lacking and that without adequate home support, lapsed Mass attendance appears to be more a matter of drift than decision. Regarding the alienation factor, Flynn argues that youth particularly have a need to

feel welcomed and as a part of a community — a need often not satisfied in many parish communities. Thus young people will travel long distances to attend a parish Mass where they do find this sense of belonging.

Nevertheless there could be another perspective. The statistics of Mass/worship attendance for past students interestingly do not appear to support the hypothesis that the low level of religious faith and practice among youth is necessarily and simply a temporary 'time-out' period. There is no available evidence to show that the recovery of faith and practice after school life takes place in the same proportions as the decline in school years. Two factors at least are clear. One is that in their religious practice the students' need to feel welcomed and valuable within a community is very strong. The second is that it is the parents who play the most significant role in the development of the children's faith. These two factors indicate the necessity for the leaders of the school and the community of the school, specifically parents, to be alert to the requirements of their own religious faith. For the parents, they must understand that their expression of faith and practice is crucial for the future of their children's faith and moral welfare. For other adults in the community, their personal, spiritual and moral lives may lead to and constitute a building up of social capital. The future religious welfare as well as the education of the young in society generally will depend on the success of such building.

Leadership and sporting life (Table 11)
'Extra curricular' activities are a substantial part of virtually all non-state schools, especially in Australia. Moreover such activities have become significant to the education of girls for whom, particularly in the areas of leadership and sport, their role has been a traditionally passive one. This Study attempted to gauge the students' (all girls) perceptions of their experience over time in these two areas of leadership and sport.

The aspect of leadership in St Mary's College involved an agreed upon but unwritten tradition of action. It was also assumed that in a non-government or non-state girls' school, opportunities existed and needed to be encouraged, for all to develop qualities of leadership. These took the form of acceptance of various responsibilities and particular appointments to tasks as Prefects, House Captains or deputies, and class and year representatives. The quality of leadership was also implied in the opportunities taken to represent and support the school in debating, public speaking and sporting activity and to to represent and support classes or years in the variety of intra- and inter-school sporting and social activities which arose during the school year. The notion of leadership, in this context, was understood by the students and their responses were therefore significant for judging something of the school's achievement in this area.

Considering the school's investment of time and energy in providing

Table 11 Results of student responses for leadership and sporting category

Item No.	Aspects of Leadership/Sport	% Agreed	% Disagreed
1.	The teachers were good models of leadership	59	41
2.	School helped me to understand what leadership is	73	27
3.	The physical education classes at SMC provided a comprehensive and worthwhile programme	65	35
4.	Physical education and sport were directed mainly at the gifted and talented students	56	44
5.	Teachers encouraged students to join outside clubs when they leave school	23	77
6.	The value of physical activity was emphasized at SMC sufficiently for me to continue sport and leisure activities after leaving school (or outside school)	49	51
7.	I developed the ability to be a leader because of my experience at SMC	47	53
8.	I enjoyed activities at SMC other than study and sport, which I will continue (have continued) after leaving school	55	45
9.	At SMC there were sufficient opportunities to develop leadership in grade 10	44	56
10.	At SMC there were sufficient opportunities for me to develop leadership in grade 11	61	39
11.	At SMC there were sufficient opportunities for me for leadership in grade 12	76	24
12.	At SMC I feel (felt) free to make mistakes and learn from them (in areas other than class subjects)	56	44
13.	There is (were) a sufficient number physical education classes	39	61

opportunities for students to develop qualities of leadership, the results in fact were disappointing. Certainly the students perceived the school to be successful in helping them understand what leadership is. Nevertheless, nearly half the students neither considered the teachers to be good models of leadership nor that their own experience at St Mary's actually helped them develop the ability to be leaders. These results stood whether they were present or past students or high, low or middle achievers. However, one important point emerged when we compared the year levels (i.e., grades 10, 11 and 12 of the senior classes). It was at grade 10 that most students felt that inadequate opportunities had been provided for them to develop their skills in leadership. This was important because of the fact that students in grade 10 reached the point where they could leave school and go into the market place for social experience as well as employment in the community. If they decided to stay on at school, as most St Mary's students do, then they felt they must wait until then before actually developing the qualities of leadership which they considered legitimate.

The question of a developed sense of responsibility and the experience of what is required in leadership is an important social as well as

place teachers alone as responsible for the difficulties involved in achieving success in teaching for most students. Responsibility must be assumed also by parents and by social (including business) and political authorities who together influence the perceptions — and the fate — of the young, and whose influence being so powerful is also educative.

Summary of Findings from Comparisons in Viewpoints of Students, Teachers and Parents

Expectations of school (Tables 14 and 15, Figures 3 and 4)

As can be seen from the graphic representations of the data (Figures 3 and 4) there was considerable discordance between students, on the one hand, and both teachers and parents on the other. The comparison can be described in two ways. Firstly, the items may be grouped in terms of a roughly equal number of cognitive and affective responses. These items are marked on the listed data of responses. Secondly, the items may more specifically be referred to in terms of those regarding career or work, academic aspects, approaches to academic work and personal attributes.

It will be remembered that in general students considered (as objectives of the school) the cognitive areas to be extremely important, but not well achieved. The exceptions were in the areas of literature and the fine arts, where students considered these neither important nor well achieved. By comparison the teachers and parents considered the cognitive areas generally to be important and well achieved — including the aspects of literature and the fine arts. There were exceptions to this generality for teachers and parents, however. Teachers considered an understanding of the world of work to be neither important nor well achieved. Parents considered understanding of the world of work not to be important but fairly well achieved by the school.

In the affective areas, whilst students considered these to be extremely important, but not well achieved by the school, teachers and parents perceived these areas to be generally important and well achieved. There has been growing evidence in Australia and in the UK (e.g., Power Hughes *et al.*, 1982) that the most significant areas of dissatisfaction among students about school are the environmental areas (or affective aspects) where relationships, personal confidence, acceptance, a sense of self-worth, appear to have been neglected for many students. The St Mary's evidence simply endorses this. The point to emphasize is that this view of students is often not understood by teachers or parents.

Regarding the specific cognitive areas, another factor emerges relating to work or careers. All three groups considered this area to contain important objectives for the school. Yet, whilst both teachers and parents considered the objectives to have been well achieved, the students did not perceive it to be so. In terms of the academic aspects, only an understand-

Table 14 Results comparison of students', teachers' and parents' responses: Expectations of school — importance of school objectives

Item	Its the school's task to make sure that you (they)	Item No. *	Students % Importance	Item No.	Teachers % Importance	Item No.	Parents % Importance
1.	Know about a wide range of possible jobs	1	89	32	32	32	33
2.	Understand in considerable depth one or more traditional academic subjects (e.g., English, chemistry, maths)	2	76	3	96	3	100
3.	Have a reasonable understanding of yourself and the way others see you	3	73	1	96	1	100
4.	Know and appreciate a number of the major works of English Literature	4	43	23	95	23	83
5.	Can organize your own time and work independently	5	89	7	77	7	70
6.	Can listen sensitively and with understanding to others	6	81	37	65	37	60
7.	Are an individual developing as you wish	8	74	1	96	1	100
8.	Accept those who think and act differently (e.g., those of different race, dress, life-style)	10	94	11	68	11	63
9.	Understand the world of work — its routines, demands, responsibilities	11	79	32	32	32	33
10.	Have specific skills you need for a chosen field of work	12	76	27	91	27	97
11.	Have some understanding of one or more of the fine arts (e.g., painting, classical music)	14	41	23	95	23	83
12.	Work hard at things you find difficult and do not like	16	77	29	92	29	90
13.	Are self-confident and possess self-respect	17	94	21	71	21	77
14.	Know of and are concerned to respond justly to major social issues (e.g., unemployment, the future of Aboriginal society)	18	79	28	96	28	90
15.	Can form a considered opinion and act on it even if this means going against what most people think	20	90	6	96	6	100

* Some 'student' items omitted for sake of direct comparison

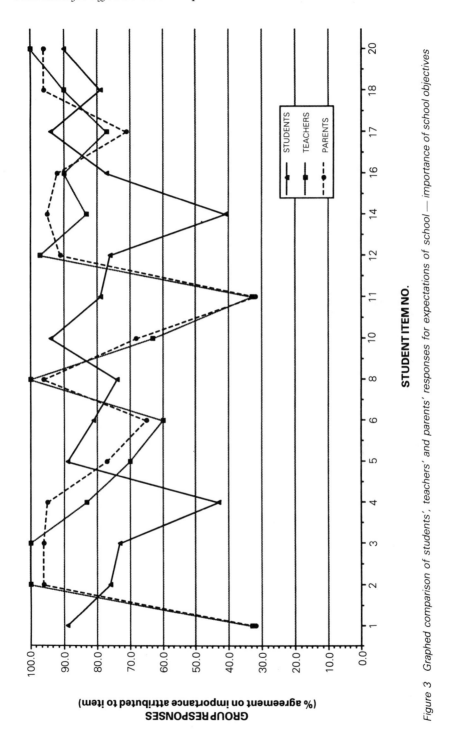

STUDENT ITEM NO.

GROUP RESPONSES
(% agreement on importance attributed to item)

Figure 3   Graphed comparison of students', teachers' and parents' responses for expectations of school — importance of school objectives

Table 15 *Results comparison of students', teachers' and parents' responses: Expectations of school — achievement of objectives*

Item	Its the school's task to make sure that you (they)	Item No.	Students % How well achieved	Item No.	Teachers % How well achieved	Item No.	Parents % How well achieved
1.	Know about a wide range of possible jobs	1	31	32	43	32	63
2.	Understand in considerable depth one or more traditional academic subjects (e.g., English, chemistry)	2	64	3	100	3	97
3.	Have a reasonable understanding of yourself and the way others see you	3	28	1	90	1	85
4.	Know and appreciate a number of the major works of English Literature	4	55	23	97	23	89
5.	Can organize your own time and work independently	5	28	7	87	7	87
6.	Can listen sensitively and with understanding to others	6	41	37	67	37	65
7.	Are an individual developing as you wish	8	23	1	90	1	85
8.	Accept those who think and act differently (e.g., those of different race, dress, life-style)	10	50	11	40	11	59
9.	Understand the world of work — its routines, demands, responsibilities	11	28	32	43	32	63
10.	Have specific skills you need for a chosen field of work	12	42	27	97	27	80
11.	Have some understanding of one or more of the fine arts (e.g., painting, classical music)	14	33	23	97	23	89
12.	Work hard at things you find difficult and do not like	16	43	29	67	29	92
13.	Are self-confident and possess self-respect	17	35	21	90	21	73
14.	Know of and are concerned to respond justly to major social issues (e.g., unemployment, the future of Aboriginal society)	18	21	28	97	28	99
15.	Can form a considered opinion and act on it even if this means going against what most people think	20	36	6	87	6	98

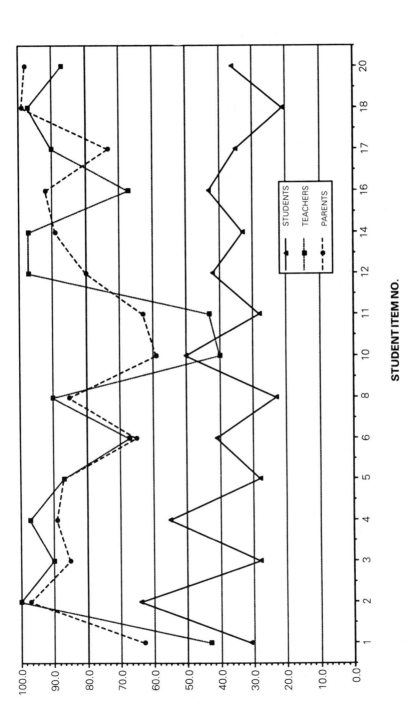

STUDENT ITEM NO.

GROUP RESPONSES

Figure 4   Graphed comparison of students', teachers' and parents' responses for expectations of school category — achievement of school objectives

ing of the traditional academic subjects was perceived to be an important objective of the school and to be relatively well achieved by the school. As mentioned above, in the aspects of literature and the fine arts, students considered these to be unimportant as school objectives and not at all well achieved. This directly contrasted with teachers and parents both of whom most positively regarded these to be important and perceived these as having been extremely well achieved. Concerning the school's efforts in assisting students in their approaches to academic work in working and in organizing their work independently, the skill of listening with under-standing, working with persistence at difficult tasks, and so on — the results again show contrasts. Whilst the students, teachers and parents all agree as to the importance of these as school objectives, only the students consider these not to have been well achieved.

For the areas of personal (affective) attributes — acceptance of others, understanding of self and how others 'see you', developing personally with confidence and self-worth, responsiveness to the surrounding social issues — again the contrasts were striking. In general all three groups agreed to their importance as objectives for the school. Generally, whilst the students regarded these aspects as not being well achieved on their behalf, the teachers and parents did. One exception is revealing. Whilst students considered the acceptance of others who think and act differently as being of extreme importance as an aim of the school, teachers and parents were not nearly as strong in this regard (though two thirds of the groups did consider it to be an important objective). In terms of how well achieved this aspect was perceived to be, only the parents regarded this positively (and again only two-thirds of the group). Both students and teachers considered the development of an acceptance of those who are 'different' not to have been well achieved.

In the above areas there is obviously a considerable discordance between the perceptions of students and those of teachers and parents. That such discordance applies in academic areas as well as in matters of personal attributes of students must be not only cause for reflection. There is a claim for a reviewing of agreement between the school, the students and the families as to what constitutes the significant aims of the school and how these may be achieved to the satisfaction of all.

Comparison of students', teachers' and parents' views on the
academic life of school (Table 16 and Figure 5)
As explained earlier, in this aspect the Study focussed on the reasons for the students' choices of academic subjects. These choices were related to student goals and expectations upon completion of their education at St Mary's College. All three groups agreed in the perception that students chose their academic subjects in accordance with the need for those subjects in gaining entrance to a tertiary institution, because the students were intrinsically interested in the subjects; or because the students had

Table 16   Results comparison of students', teachers' and parents' responses for the academic category

Item	Item No.	Students % Agreement	Teachers % Agreement	Parents % Agreement
Needed particular subjects to qualify for tertiary institution	1	91	100	88
Needed particular subjects to gain immediate employment of choice	2	85	84	73
Friend was doing the subject	3	8	32	14
She was intrinsically interested in the subject	4	93	84	90
She had achieved good results in that subject in year 10	5	80	95	81
She knew nothing of the subject and wanted to fill gap in her knowledge	6	51	5	29
Her parents strongly influenced her choice of subject	7	17	47	20
Choices were largely determined by organization of subjects into lines	8	34	21	54
The sciences (maths, science etc) appeared to be more important than the humanities (English, soc psych etc)	9	18	26	41

achieved good results in those subjects previously (at grade 10 level). Noticeably the teachers were convinced that students also regarded their performances at grade 10 level as a very important reason for choice, much more so than did the students or parents. However, teachers were much more likely to consider that academic choices were strongly influenced by the students' parents. This was the least important reason given by the students and indeed the parents themselves. Nearly half the teachers perceived that the parents influenced the students' choice whereas the view applied to only 17 per cent of students and 20 per cent of parents.

Close inspection of the results indicates that the teachers' perception is much more strongly (than either parents or students) that the students' choice of subjects is for gaining entrance to a tertiary institution. A little over half the students expressed the view that their choice of subjects pertained to their desire to fill gaps in their knowledge of those subjects Only 5 per cent of the teachers and 30 per cent of parents held this perception of the students' attitudes. On the other hand about a third of the teachers perceived that the students chose their subjects because friends had done so. This perception was held by only 8 per cent of students and 14 per cent of parents.

Comparison of students', teachers', and parents' perceptions on vocational aspects of school curriculum (Table 17 and Figure 6)
In this area there was a generally high level of agreement between students, teachers and parents, all in a positive direction. All three groups

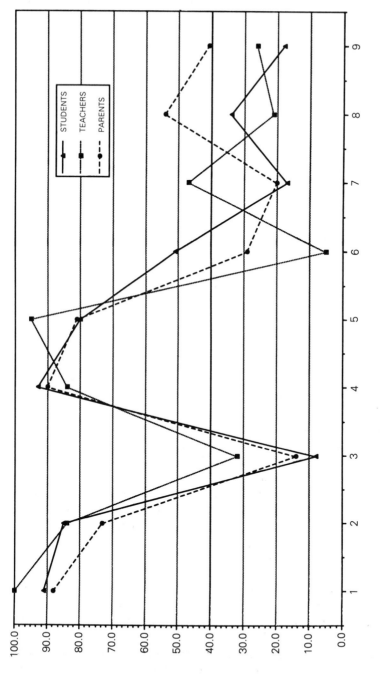

ITEM NO.

% AGREEMENT

Figure 5 Graphed comparison of students', teachers' and parents' responses for academic aspects

Table 17 Results comparison of students', teachers' and parents' responses for the vocational category

Item	Item No.	Students % Agreement	Teachers % Agreement	Parents % Agreement
		% Agreement		
Subjects studied suited career choice	1	85	84	91
Leisure education useful in opening up a potential career	2	36	21	51
Because of craft studies am now able to do simple repairs at home	3	46	63	55
Skills in cooking, dressmaking have carried into other areas	4	67	73	68
Work experience has helped in deciding on a career	5	69	89	79
More vocational studies required if HSC students to be prepared for life after school	6	77	73	73
Work experience helped in understanding the world of work	7	73	84	89
Vocational studies have proven beneficial in life after school — re cooking	8	89	89	86
Vocational studies have proven beneficial in life after school — re dressmaking	9	68	68	67
Vocational studies have proven beneficial in life after school — re craft	10	48	79	70

considered that the subjects studied in this area were appropriate to the students, that the students were helped by work experience in deciding on a career. Teachers and parents also concurred with the students' perception that an increase in vocational studies at HSC (senior) level was necessary if students were to be adequately prepared for life after school. Only at one point did the teachers' and parents' views not tally with the students' perception. Less than half the students were confident that their craft (e.g., woodworking) skills were beneficial to them or effective in their use after school life. On this point, the teachers and parents positively agreed that the students' perception was otherwise.

Comparison of students' teachers' and parents' views regarding personal/spiritual aspects of school (Table 18 and Figure 7)
These comparisons are related to the religious education aspect, an area of most obvious concern to the Catholic school community. The items in this comparison specifically address the importance placed by students upon various influences in their religious development.

There is high agreement by teachers and parents with the students' view that in their religious development the instruction and example of parents is the most significant influence. But there is wide disagreement between the students' perception and that of teachers and parents, both of

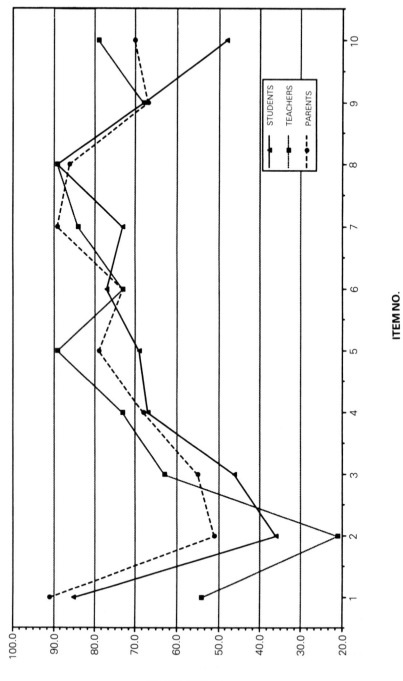

ITEM NO.

% AGREEMENT

Figure 6 Graphed comparison of students', teachers' and parents' responses for vocational aspects

Table 18   *Results comparison for students', teachers' and parents' responses for the personal and spiritual category*

Item statements (importance placed on the following influences)	% Agreement					
	Students		Teachers		Parents	
	Item No *	%	Item No.	%	Item No.	%
The instruction of parents and their example	1(12)	73	1	90	1	88
The example and personal guidance of teachers	2(13)	44	2	74	2	77
Religious education provided by the school	3(17)	31	3	74	3	75
The example of friends at the school	4(14)	41	4	74	4	57
Religious instruction provided by parish or church	5(16)	35	5	47	5	57
The guidance and influence of some religious, priest, minister	6(15)	40	6	37	6	45
I am very concerned about the opinion of teaching RE in this school	7		7	32	7	23
I am concerned about the teaching of RE in this school	8		8	37	8	27
I am satisfied about how RE is taught in this school	9		9	5	9	68
I am happy with the teaching of RE in this school	10		10	21	10	72
I am very happy about the teaching of RE in this school	11		11	16	11	66

* Numbers in brackets represent items for students. Non-bracketed numbers represent items for both teachers and parents

whom perceive that the religious education provided by the school and the example and guidance of teachers are significant influences upon the students. Also less than half the students considered their friends at school to be a significant influence whereas more than half the parents and three quarters of the teachers considered the students' friends were a significant influence.

In questions directed precisely to the teachers and parents regarding their opinion of the teaching of religious education in the school, the comparison is striking. Neither teachers nor parents registered much concern about the teaching of religious education. The parents in fact were generally happy with this teaching. However, despite such moderate 'concern', the teachers were considerably dissatisfied both with the teaching of religious education and how it was taught. In this, a most important aspect of the Catholic school's life, two major factors emerge. The first is that whilst teachers and parents agree with the view that students regard the parents, not the school, as the most significant influence upon their religious development, the students' religious practice (as seen in the section on specifically student views) is generally a depressing picture. Thus the parents' responsibility and significance in this area is pronounced. Secondly, the religious education programme is not seen

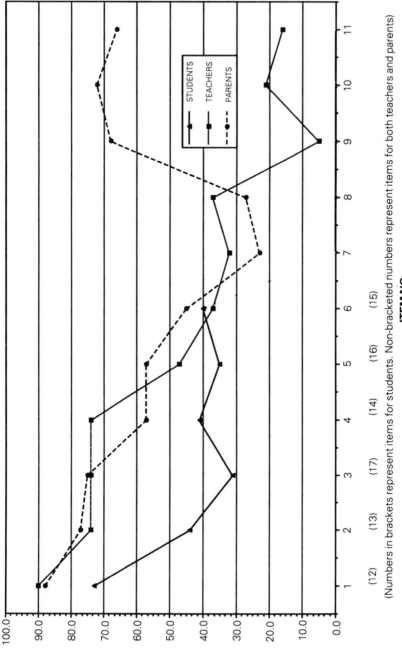

(Numbers in brackets represent items for students. Non-bracketed numbers represent items for both teachers and parents)

ITEM NO.

Figure 7   Graphed comparison of students', teachers' and parents' responses for personal and spiritual aspects

to be working for the students, and the teachers agree with this. The parents, however, appear to view the students' opinions to be otherwise. This area of religious faith and practice among the youth has been discussed earlier in the examination of students' perceptions. The point remains as to whether the school sees its role as having to change in this area — particularly in its relations to both students and parents.

Comparison of student', teachers' and parents' perceptions of leadership and sporting aspects of the students' experience at school
(Table 19 and Figure 8)
There were relatively high instances of disagreement by students with the perceptions of teachers and parents in the areas of leadership and sport. The disagreements ranged from moderate to relatively extreme. For instance 80–90 per cent of teachers and parents viewed students as considering teachers to be good models of leadership, and that physical education classes were comprehensive and worthwhile. Only half to two thirds of the students actually held this view. More extremely, from less than 40 per cent to less than 50 per cent of students considered that there were sufficient classes in physical education at school; that their experience of physical education at school encouraged them to continue such physical activity after school life; or that they developed the ability to be a leader because of their experience at school. In contrast two thirds to more than three quarters of teachers and parents considered these to held true for the students.

In some instances there was concordance between the perceptions of teachers, parents and the students themselves. There was (as to the students' views) a fair measure of agreement that sport and physical education classes were directed mainly at the gifted and talented students or that their experience at school helped students to understand what leadership is; or that there were sufficient opportunities to develop leadership in the senior grades. However, teachers and students concurred in the perception that there were not sufficient opportunities to develop leadership qualities at grade 10 (the end of high school, or the last year before the senior or matriculation years). In this respect more than three quarters of the parents considered that their student children had sufficient opportunities for this development.

The results here point up elements of the leadership and sporting programme pertinent to the interest and attention of both teachers and parents, specifically in the students frequent lack of agreement with their perceptions. Students appear to demand recognition of: the inadequacy of their leadership experience at grade 10; their questioning of the adequacy of the physical education programme; and that whilst students felt that they gained in understanding of leadership, they lacked a sense of development in this area.

Table 19   Results comparison of students', teachers' and parents' responses for the leadership and sporting category

Item statements	Students		Teachers		Parents	
	Item No.	% Agreement	Item No.	% Agreement	Item No.	% Agreement
The teachers are (were) good models of leadership	1	59	1	84	1	91
School help(ed) me understand what leadership is	2	73	2	90	2	91
The PE classes at SMC provide (provided) a comprehensive and worthwhile programme	3	65	3	90	3	81
PE and sport are (were) directed mainly at gifted and talented students	4	56	4	53	4	43
Teachers encourage(d) students to join outside clubs etc when they leave school	5	23	5	53	5	58
The value of physical activity is (was) emphasized sufficiently at SMC for me to continue sport and leisure activities after leaving school (or outside school)	6	49	6	68	6	71
I develop(ed) the activity to be a leader because of my experience at SMC	7	47	7	74	7	65
I enjoyed activities at SMC other than study and sport, which I will continue (have continued) after leaving school	8	55	8	68	8	67
At SMC there are (were) sufficient opportunities to develop leadership at grade 10	9	44	9	32	9	70
At SMC there are (were) sufficient opportunities to develop leadership at grade 11	10	61	10	74	10	81
At SMC there are (were) sufficient opportunities to develop leadership at grade 12	11	76	11	89	11	85
At SMC I feel (felt) free to make mistakes and learn from them (in areas other than class subjects)	12	56	12	58	12	78
There is (were) a sufficient number of physical education classes	13	39	13	68	13	78

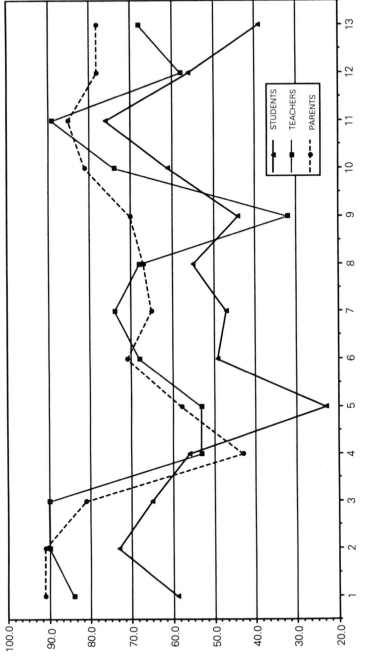

ITEM NO.

Figure 8   Graphed comparison of students', teachers' and parents' responses for leadership and sporting aspects

Concordance and discordance between students', teachers' and parents' perceptions of teachers (Table 20 and Figure 9)

The results for responses of students, teachers and parents in this category are listed in Table 20 and are presented graphically as a comparison in Figure 9. Students have some positive things to say about teachers, views which teachers and parents in general also perceived the students to be holding. The students generally consider that teachers clearly outline and organize their classwork, cover a great deal of material in the time allowed, give students a broad general understanding of the subjects and succeed in making their classes useful rather than entertaining.

In some instances the strength of perception of teachers and/or parents is greater than is actually the case for students. Less than half the students view teachers as attempting to make their teaching material relevant to the students' (perceived) needs but three quarters to 80 per cent of teachers and parents perceive students as holding such a view. Only half of the students consider the teachers as allowing (what they perceive to be) classroom discussion, whereas around 80 per cent of teachers and parents perceive students as having this view. Whilst teachers and parents generally agree with the students' perception that teachers provide 'friendly' help to students having problems with class-work, the two adult groups incorrectly perceive the students as seeing teachers having an understanding of students' problems generally. In-terestingly the teachers group who met to discuss the data in this category concluded that this question of understanding students' problems is one they needed to address.

There are other comparisons reflecting both concordance and dis-cordance among the perceptions of the three groups. Less than a quarter of the students perceive teachers as making their classes interesting. This view of students' perceptions is actually shared by more than 40 per cent of teachers and more than half the parents. Ninety per cent or more of students and parents perceive teachers as setting homework regularly, but only about two thirds of teachers consider this to be the students' percep-tion. On the other hand, both teachers and parents strongly (80–84 per cent agreement) consider students' to believe that teachers correct home-work regularly. The students' perception is obviously much weaker than those of the adult groups. Finally less than half of the students perceive teachers as extending students to the limits of their abilities, whereas just over half of parents and about 60 per cent of teachers consider students to have such a view. Thus the three groups vary in their perception, the teachers being slightly more detached from the other two groups.

In general there are both positive and negative perceptions of teaching behaviours in the classroom, in the perceptions of students. There is no doubting the students' and parents' concurring view that teachers act professionally in their teaching approach. Yet students perceive a lack in interest and relevance in their classes, and a lack of

Table 20   *Results comparison of students', teachers' and parents' responses for the 'teachers' category*

Item	Its the school's task to make sure that you (they)	Item No.	Students % How True	Item No.	Teachers % How True	Item No.	Parents % How True
1.	Teachers clearly outline and organize their class work	1	74	1	74	1	83
2.	Teachers allow classroom discussion	2	50	2	84	2	79
3.	Teachers try to make their teaching materials relevant to current trends and student's needs	3	44	3	74	3	79
4.	Teachers give friendly help to any student having problems with classwork	4	67	4	90	4	74
5.	Teachers try to be sure that student understand the work that is done in class	5	62	5	95	5	71
6.	Teachers cover a great deal of material in the time that is allowed	6	75	6	79	6	77
7.	Teachers place too much emphasis on detailed facts and memorization	7	43	7	16	7	25
8.	Teachers give students a broad, general understanding of their subjects	8	72	8	79	8	81
9.	Teachers extend students to the limits of their abilities	9	47	9	53	9	60
10.	Teachers encourage students to do independent work on their own	10	57	10	58	10	68
11.	Teachers are understanding of students' study problems	11	33	11	63	11	58
12.	Teachers stimulate students to think and be creative	12	40	12	53	12	63
13.	Teachers succeed in making their classes interesting	13	22	13	42	13	58
14.	Teachers try to make their classes entertaining rather than useful	14	3	14	0	14	13
15.	Teachers set homework regularly	15	92	15	63	15	89
16.	Teachers correct students' work regularly	16	65	16	79	16	84

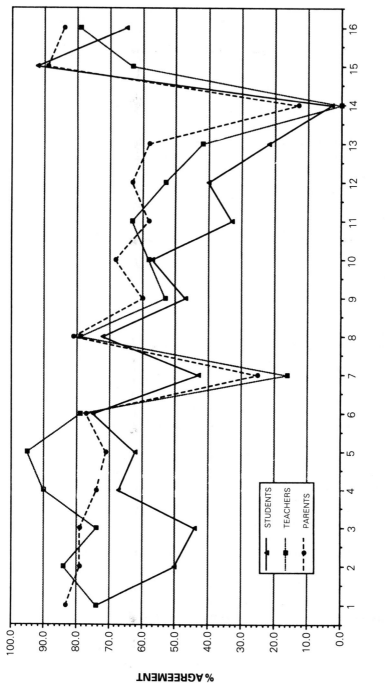

STUDENT ITEM NO.

Figure 9   Graphed comparison of students', teachers' and parents' responses for the 'teachers' category

understanding of their study problems (these factors may go together). Both of these perceptions are misapprehended by a considerable proportion of parents and teachers. There is also a question as to how well certain teachers are extending students 'to the limits of their abilities'.

Such responses are not straightforward matters which can be dismissed by simple labelling of teachers' inadequacies. The students live in a world which is anti-educational in the historic sense. For example, the power of the media, and what they present, define for children that education is to be only entertaining and fun. Addressing questions of student disenchantment and teacher inadequacy, so-called, must coincide with recognition of the fact that students and teachers face a series of social obstacles to effectiveness in the educational process. In this they need the greatest support and input from parents and community together. Indeed a re-definition of the nature and purpose of education for the young is warranted in the face of such obstacles. The results of this case study, at the least, argue for a new definition of partnership between the school and its community.

The Quality of School Life

Introduction

A most cogent overview and example of research into the quality of school life was presented by Willmot (1988). He reviewed the European and North American applications of the Epstein and McPartland (1976) Quality of School Life instrument and derivatives from it. The review centred mainly on the investigation of background and school variables which affect student perceptions of their school life. Willmot also referred to problems which had emerged from these quality of school life studies. Firstly, he said, they show up the limitations of quantitative studies. They helped 'chart the independent variables' related to quality of school life, but left the central questions of explanation 'unanswered'. Secondly, the Epstein and McPartland instrument and its derivatives such as the International Quality of School Life (IQSL) provided only limited data about the students' affective responses to the expressive and informal aspects of school experience. Instead they tended to emphasize student responses to the formal curriculum and classroom experience. Thirdly, in contrast to the more recent Williams and Batten (1981) instrument the theoretical analysis underpinning the scales needed further development.

Australian research on the quality of school life for some time was limited to the developmental work undertaken on the Australian Council of Educational Research (ACER) 'School Life' instrument and its application in a study of school life in the Australian Capital Territory schools by Hunt and Fordham (1983). Hunt and Fordham administered an

adaptation of the Williams and Batten (1981) instrument in ten high schools in the ACT Study and found that schools in the study were relatively successful in performing the function of generating social integration and developing technical competency, but appeared less successful in developing social responsibility and personal development.

Willmot's (1988) research was an advance on the Hunt and Fordham study. It represented an application of the Australian quality of school life instrumentation, and provided at least tentative empirical support for the Spady and Mitchell (1977) model as a theoretical framework against which to explain levels of student satisfaction with school. However, the precise links between the model and the dimensions of the quality of school life construct enunciated by Williams and Batten (1981) were not so readily 'thrown up' by the research findings. The Willmot study went beyond the sole reliance on quantitative data to describe the structures and processes evident in schools. It included observational case studies of some schools on the basis of an hypothesis, which the results supported, that differences in student perceptions of quality of school life would be found among different types of schools. Willmot's study strengthens the view also that qualitative, in addition to quantitative, measures of school life are necessary for a more accurate and more substantial representation of the quality of school life. He concludes that a qualitative examination of schools reveals that schools, in a sense, present a varying quality of school life for each student rather than simply a generalized, certain quality of school life. Also, out of the complex interaction of forces operating in schools there tends to develop a 'school culture' of social and interpersonal environment which is the context of life of the school (p. 268). Such a culture appears to depend on the commitment of the teachers to the school (along with a 'charismatic' principal able to marshal and direct this commitment) and the context of the beliefs that are present.

It is with such conclusions in mind that the present study proceeded. It was intended to provide an understanding of the complex processes of school life particularly where, as a Catholic school, its context of beliefs is assumed so substantially to be present. Despite the limits of this investigation, as a single case study, the gains in terms of the detail of understanding and directions for a wider research in the Catholic school system were to be acknowledged. The data were gathered from all the significant populations of the school community — students, parents and teachers — and the results subjected to discussions with both students and teachers and by interviews with students during the process of the study. Hence there was a relatively sound basis for findings that should be useful to the school system. Beyond this we believed that such investigations as the St Mary's Study could add to, even extend, the research on school effectiveness thereby contributing to information available for assisting the improvement of schools. As suggested by Good and Brophy (1987):

> There is growing evidence that student perceptions of classroom process are valuable sources of information about schools ... Future studies of effective schooling could make better use of student interviews in order to understand how different types of students perceive and act upon the various constraints present in more or less effective schools. (p. 56)

The study at St Mary's College also revealed variations in patterns of the data as indicated in the summary of the student perceptions dimension of the Study. However, we stress that our interest in the quality of school life for St Mary's was partly for its relationship with other aspects of the curriculum. Ainley *et al.* (1984) found that the intention to remain at school to grade 12 was closely linked not only to students' perception of their ability but also to the quality of their school life. They also found that 'curriculum factors, and the extent of a certain co-ordination of the school programme' were similarly related to the quality of school life. This investigation formed part of a total study of the curriculum of St Mary's College and was not merely a separation dimension.

Student perceptions of the quality of school life
As described in the summary of methodology, to investigate the quality of school life at St Mary's College we chose the standardized questionnaire instrument, developed by the Australian Council of Educational Research (ACER) and applied by a number of researchers in Australia.

Analysis of students' responses
A factor analysis of responses to all the questionnaire items resulted in a clustering around six factors which could be identified as General Affect, Negative Affect, Status, Identity, Teachers and Opportunity. This means that General Affect and Positive Affect were re-formed by the analysis into one scale, as have Adventure and Opportunity. Table 21 shows these domains, the clustered items and factor loadings for each item incorporated in the analysis. The factor structure is consistent with that of the ACER analysis.

The results in terms of student responses for each domain are listed at the end of this QSL section (Tables 25 to 32). Note that the model for categorizing the aspects of quality of school life does not envisage the domains as being independent of each other. Rather, together they constitute a view of the elements of school life for students.

Table 22 gives the overall quality of school life scale mean scores and standard deviations for the whole SMC sample together with a quality of school life composite measure (General Affect + Status + Identity + Teachers + Opportunity — Negative Affect). This data provides an initial basis on which to comment on the variability of the individual responses. There is an interesting pattern of variability within individual scales. Also

Table 21   Quality of school life domains, clustered items and factor loadings for analysis

Domain	Clustered Items	Factor Loadings	Domain	Clustered Items	Factor Loadings
General	11	.08	Teachers	4	.60
(and Positive)	40	.60		9	.61
Affect	46	.57		12	.70
	49	.56		15	.60
	52	.45		19	.66
	56	.10		21	.55
	59	.33		26	.51
				37	.51
	7	.07		38	.45
Negative Affect	27	.52		48	.47
	34	.32		51	.60
	43	.60		62	.54
	66	.38		67	.33
				71	.57
Status	2	.36			
	6	.21	Opportunity (and	3	.10
	8	.56	Adventure)	5	.30
	20	.27		10	.30
	22	.57		16	.56
	25	.35		24	.40
	39	.41		28	.23
	41	.18		29	.22
	42	.33		31	.53
	53	.10		33	.29
	64	.18		44	.16
				47	.23
Identity	1	.77		55	.34
	13	.65		60	.62
	14	.27		61	.50
	17	.62		65	.40
	18	.35			
	23	.20			
	32	.63			
	35	.55			
	36	.30			
	45	.50			
	50	.06			
	54	.27			
	57	.11			

clearly some of the dimensions of the quality of school life, measured by the research instrument, exhibit greater variability of responses than others. In this latter case it should be remembered that the range (between maximum and possible scores) varies between scales. Negative Affect in particular is a small scale and it was to be expected that the standard deviation on this scale would be of lower magnitude than on the others. Nevertheless that of Status is also low and itself also reflects the variability in the pattern of responses.

Table 22   *Quality of school life scale and composite measures — whole student sample*
(N = 402)

Scale	Mean	Standard Deviation
General (and Positive) Affect	.38	.22
Negative Affect	.38	.20
Status	.22	.15
Identity	.40	.23
Teachers	.55	.10
Opportunity (and Adventure)	.32	.16
Quality of School Life Composite Total	1.59	.65

Regarding the scales it is clear that some of the dimensions of school life, as measured by the questionnaire instrument, exhibited greater variability than did others. Dispersion was least in relation to Teachers (.10), Status (.15) and Opportunity (.16). There is greater variation of scores on General (.24) and Negative Affect ($-$.10) and the most volatile scale is Identity (.23). In other words, the students are most varied in their reactions to those measures of quality of school life which deal with their sense of self-esteem, their general satisfaction with school as a whole, and the degree of their negative attitudes toward school.

One interpretation of these results is that the most sensitive aspects of quality of school life for St Mary's College students relates to the scales of Identity, General Affect, and Negative Affect (and that the school generates these perceptions in the students with the most varied degrees of success). The least sensitive aspects of quality of school life appear to be in terms of Teachers, Status and Opportunity. It could be that St Mary's, as every school, produces some negative responses in students but few of these students have strong negative attitudes to school life.

Levels of quality of school life
Some of the above points can be pursued further by examining the overall level of responses and scale-to-scale comparisons of the magnitude of the responses. One of the problems of the mean scale scores as they stand is that they tell us little about the absolute levels of response on each scale and the relative strength of responses on different scales. The scale scores cannot be compared directly because the number of items relating to each scale varied and because different factor loadings applied to each item.

In order to assess the relative levels of the Quality of School Life Domains experienced at St Mary's College, and which aspects of school life are most successfully provided for, the data were 'transformed' and some different categories of information created. Table 23 reflects a procedure similar to that of Willmot (1988) and Hunt and Fordham

Table 23 Analysis of level of scale mean scores against scale mid point
(St Mary's College Data)

Scale	Min poss score (1)	Max poss score (2)	Scale mid point (3)	Scale mean (4)	% (+ −) Deviation (3−4)
General Affect	2.69	11.76	7.23	7.61	+5.25
Negative Affect	1.89	7.56	4.73	4.35	−8.03
Status	3.42	13.68	8.55	8.86	+3.82
Identity	5.06	20.04	12.52	12.98	+3.66
Teachers	7.65	30.60	19.13	19.67	+2.82
Opportunity	4.85	19.40	12.13	12.45	+2.53
QSL Composite	21.93	89.92	54.83	57.22	5.76

Note: Students responded on a four-point scale coded as follows: definitely agree 1, mostly agree 2, mostly disagree 3, definitely disagree 4.

A scale mean lower than the mid-point indicates agreement with the scale (Hunt and Fordham, 1983, p. 86) The minimum possible scale score is calculated by summing the factor loadings for each item on the scale. The maximum possible scale score = the sum of the factor loadings × 4.

(1983), which enables us to look at mean scale scores on each dimension in comparing the range of possible scores on each scale. The table shows the scale means against the minimum and maximum possible scores on each scale, and the scale mid point. The percentage deviation of the scale mean (+ or −) from the mid point can then be calculated. This statistic then provides an indication of the absolute level of mean responses for the scale, and can be used in scale to scale comparisons. Table 23 shows that on all the scales (excepting Negative Affect) and on the quality of school life composite measure, there is a positive deviation from the scale mid point, and on one scale and on quality of school life composite this deviation is relatively substantial.

In general St Mary's College students perceive the quality of school life in positive terms (5.76 per cent deviation from the scale). The data suggest that St Mary's College generally appears to be successful at providing experiences and environments which enhance students' general satisfaction with school, the extent to which they are looked up to by significant others, and their sense of self-esteem.

The substantial deviation of Negative Affect (−8.03 per cent) though negative in direction is of course to the enhancement of quality of school life generally. In other words, St Mary's College students tend to disagree with statements such as 'School is a place where I feel depressed'. They are suggesting that they have relatively few negative feelings about school.

Scales which though marginally positive tend to show minor deviations include Teachers and Opportunity. In other words students at St Mary's are slightly more ambivalent in terms of their relationship with

teachers, and the extent to which the school provides opportunities for success.

Placed in overall context, positive attitudes of St Mary's College students towards their school life are mainly carried by their general satisfaction with school ('I get enjoyment from being there'), the extent to which they are looked up to by significant others (School is a place where 'I am thought of as a person who matters'), their sense of self-esteem (School is a place where 'I have become a worthwhile person') and the fact that the school does not appear to generate substantial negative feelings among students.

Quality of School Life: Comparing the Perceptions of Students, Teachers and Parents

In this comparison, percentage totals of the 'agreement' responses for students, teachers and parents have been listed in Table 24 and plotted on a single graph — Figure 10. The item responses have been clustered within the theoretical domains thus enabling us to observe a total pattern as well as that for each domain, which, again are not to be regarded as independent of each other. Note that the teacher and parent responses did not include all the items of the Quality of School Life instrument. However, the domains contain items which are fairly representative.

The overall pattern indicates firstly a fairly high agreement with the item statements by all three groups. That is, with the exception of Negative Affect the responses of all three groups are in a positive direction for all the domains. Of course the low magnitude of agreement for the 'Negative Affect' items indicates that the groups generally feel there is a lack of strong negative attitudes towards school on the part of students. Secondly, the pattern shows a fairly general discordance between the perceptions of teachers and those of students and parents, whose responses plot similarly. However, these generalizations may be qualified as we look at the domains separately. Again we must be cautious in loading too much on to our interpretation of a single item, which does not reflect the variability or sensitivity of the domain as a whole. Keeping the above caveats in mind, we may consider the domains in turn.

General Affect (or general satisfaction with school life)   Students and parents generally are positive in their perceptions as to how the students feel about school. However teachers, though perceiving that the students like to go to school and appear happy there, believe that the students get little enjoyment from their school experience. Overall the teachers see the students' perceptions quite differently from both students themselves and parents. It is also significant that the expectations of teachers, concerning the students' level of satisfaction from school life, is quite high.

Table 24 Results for comparison of students', teachers' and parents' responses — Quality of School Life

Domain	Item statements (Students) school is a place where . . . *	Item No.	Students	Item No.	Teachers	Item No.	Parents
General Affect	I really like to go	11	74	2	100	3	82
	I feel happy	52	88	21	90	22	82
	I get enjoyment from being there	56	81	23	16	24	75
	I feel great	69	73	28	39	29	52
Negative Affect	I feel lonely	27	12	11	47	12	15
	I feel restless	34	24	12	26	13	16
	I feel depressed	43	12	16	47	17	13
	I get upset	66	18	27	72	28	30
Status	I feel important	17	70	5	74	6	54
	People have confidence in me	20	88	9	84	8	84
	People come to me for help	25	72	10	95	11	50
	I know that people think a lot of me	35	70	13	47	14	58
	People look up to me	41	60	15	100	16	49
Identity	Mixing with other people helps me to understand myself	14	90	4	26	5	74
	I learn to get along with other people	18	95	6	58	7	91
	I learn a lot about myself	50	87	19	100	20	71
	I get to know myself better	63	85	25	61	26	85
	I have learnt to accept other people as they are	70	98	29	50	30	76
Teachers	Teachers are fair and just	9	83	1	58	2	79
	Teachers help me to do my best	19	85	7	90	8	84
	Teachers treat me fairly in class	21	89	9	84	10	83
	Teachers listen to what I have to say	51	80	20	84	21	65
Opportunity	I know I can reach a satisfactory standard in my work	44	95	17	37	18	83
	I know the sorts of things I can do well	47	97	18	79	19	93
	I find that learning is a lot of fun	55	74	22	68	23	60
	I get satisfaction from the school work I do	60	87	24	61	25	80
	I know I can do well enough to be successful	65	93	26	72	27	81

* Note Teachers' and parents' are to be read as their perceptions of the students' responses e.g., 'they really like to go'

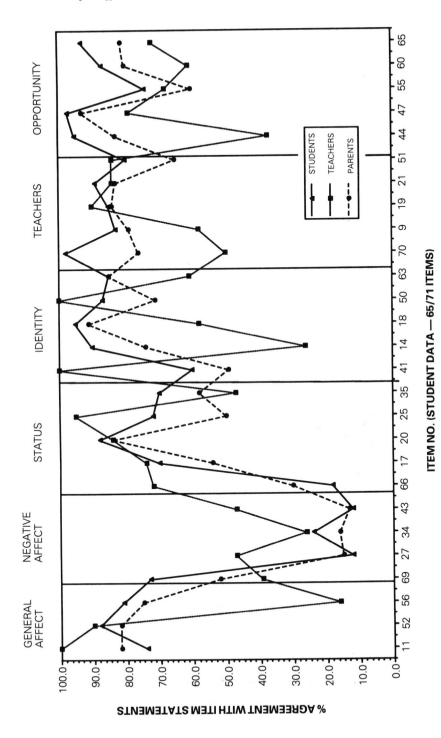

Figure 10 Graphed comparison of students', teachers' and parents' responses for Quality of School Life

Table 25   Results for student responses — General Affect

Item No.	'School is a Place Where ...'	% Agree	% Disagree
11	I really like to go	74	26
46	I feel good about things	89	11
52	I feel happy	88	11
56	I get enjoyment from being there	81	19

Table 26   Results for student responses — Positive Affect

Item No.	'School is a Place Where ...'	% Agree	% Disagree
31	I feel successful	76	24
40	I feel proud of myself	82	18
49	I get excited about things	76	24
61	I feel that things go my way	61	39
69	I feel great	73	27

Negative Affect (or negative feelings toward school life and in general)   As indicated there is generally a low magnitude of agreement with the item statements for this domain. This applies to the students and parents whose responses are in accord. However, the teachers tend to view things much differently. They appear to believe that school is a place where many of the students often feel upset, are lonely or depressed. This variation in perception again appears to reflect in teachers a low expectation that students will have positive feelings about their school life, an expectation not shared by the students or their parents.

Status (or the feeling of being looked up to by significant others at school) Here again the responses by all three groups generally are in a positive direction. In particular students, teachers and parents strongly agree that school is a place where others have confidence in the students. Variation in perceptions here comes mainly from the parents. They appear not nearly as convinced as the students and teachers that school is a place where children are looked up to; feel important; where they know that others think a lot of them, or go to them for help. In this area of the quality of school life there appears to be some discordance in the perceptions of how parents, teachers and students view school as a place where a feeling of status is generated for students.

Identity (the feeling of positive self-esteem)   In this area there is again a general discordance between the perceptions of teachers and those of parents and students, both of whom are generally in accord. In contrast with students and parents, teachers do not readily perceive that students consider school a place where 'mixing with others helps the students

Table 27 Results for student responses — Negative Affect

Item No.	'School is a Place Where ...'	% Agree	% Disagree
7	I feel bored	19	81
27	I feel lonely	12	88
34	I feel restless	24	76
43	I feel depressed	12	88
66	I get upset	18	82

Table 28 Results for student responses — Status

Item No.	'School is a Place Where ...'	% Agree	% Disagree
2	People know they can depend on me	95	5
6	I am thought of as a person who matters	85	15
8	I act in a responsible way	94	6
17	I feel important	70	30
20	People have confidence in me	88	12
22	I try to do what is expected of me	97	3
25	People come to me for help	72	28
35	I know that people think a lot of me	70	30
39	I feel I am a reliable person	94	6
41	People look up to me	60	40
42	I am trusted to work on my own	92	8
53	I try to look after the interests of other students	93	7
59	I feel confident	80	20
64	I am treated with respect	81	19

Table 29 Results for student responses — Identity

Item No.	'School is a Place Where ...'	% Agree	% Disagree
1	I have friends	97	3
10	I know what my strengths and weaknesses are	92	8
13	I feel I belong	85	15
14	Mixing with other people helps me to understand myself	90	10
18	I have learnt to get on with other people	95	5
23	I feel proud to be a student	89	11
32	Other students are very friendly	90	10
36	I feel I have become a worthwhile person	86	14
45	Other students accept me as I am	88	12
50	I learn a lot about myself	87	13
54	I am known by a lot of people	86	14
57	I have learnt to see other people's points of view	97	3
58	Other students listen to what I say	84	16
63	I get to know myself better	85	15
70	I have learnt to accept other people as they are	98	2

Table 30   Results for student responses — Teachers

Item No.	'School is a Place Where ...'	% Agree	% Disagree
4	Teachers are genuinely interested in what I do	78	22
9	Teachers are fair and just	83	19
12	Teachers take a personal interest in helping me with my school work	79	21
15	Teachers recognize any extra effort I make in my work	78	22
19	Teachers help me to do my best	85	15
21	Teachers treat me fairly in class	89	11
26	Teachers encourage me to express my opinions	75	25
37	Teachers take notice of me in class	73	27
38	Teachers give me the marks I deserve	87	13
48	I can talk to teachers about the way they mark my work	58	42
51	Teachers listen to what I say	80	20
62	Teachers are friendly to me in class	86	14
67	I can question the things teachers say about my work	61	39
71	Teachers treat all students equally	46	54

understand themselves'. Though slightly more positive in believing that students regard school as enabling them 'to accept people as they are', 'to get along with others', or 'to get to know themselves better', teachers' opinions are far less positive than the students or parents about these qualities. As the graph pattern shows there is at times a slight variation in the students' and parents' perceptions, but both are relatively high in magnitude of agreement, and therefore very positive, compared with those of the teachers.

Teachers (students' relationships with their teachers)   This domain shows a high positive agreement in the items and reflects the most concordance between the three groups of all the domains. Generally the teachers themselves and parents agree with the students' perceptions of teachers as for the most part treating the students 'fairly' and 'helping them to do their best'. This is a quite positive reflection on the teachers and bears comparison with the low expectations which teachers appear to have of students experience at school. The teachers at St Mary's College were in fact a highly qualified and highly committed group. They might take good comfort from these results and perhaps 'worry' less in this area of students' perceptions and expectations of them. At one point in this domain such 'worry' appears reflected in the feeling of a significant proportion of the teachers group, that the students don't perceive them as 'fair and just'. This contrasts with the high proportion of parents and students themselves, who don't have this perception.

Opportunity (or the relevance to students of their learning and the extent to which they feel they have opportunities for success) The pattern here

Table 31   *Results for student responses — Opportunity*

Item No.	'School is a Place Where ...'	% Agree	% Disagree
3	I know how to cope with the work	91	9
16	I have learnt things that will be useful to me	96	4
28	Learning is easy for me	62	38
30	I can learn whatever I need to know	77	23
44	I know I can reach a satisfactory standard in my work	95	5
47	I know the sorts of things I can do well	97	3
65	I know I can do well enough to be successful	93	7
68	I can learn what I need to get by in life	85	15

Table 32   *Results for student responses — Adventure*

Item No.	'School is a Place Where ...'	% Agree	% Disagree
5	I have learnt to find whatever information I need	90	10
24	I like to do extra work in the subjects that interest me	77	23
29	I am interested in the work we do in class	88	12
33	I like to learn new things	97	3
55	I find that learning is a lot of fun	74	26
60	I get satisfaction from the school work I do	87	13

again shows that teachers in their perceptions of students' reactions, generally differ from the students themselves and the parents. Both parents and students agree in a highly positive direction. Teachers generally do not appear to consider that students feel they can 'reach a satisfactory standard in (their) work', whereas students themselves and parents both are very confident of this. Variations between teachers and the other two groups in other aspects of opportunity perhaps appear not as significant, but are consistent across the pattern.

In terms of a comparison between the perceptions of students, teachers and parents, the representation of quality of school life at St Mary's College appears overall to indicate at least three important factors. First, there is a strong general separation between the views of teachers and the other two groups as to how the students perceive the quality of their experience at school. Relatively the teachers perceptions reflect a less positive view of such experience for students than do the students themselves or the parents. Second, where there is a variation between students and parents perceptions it is the students who appear more positive in general about aspects of the quality of school life represented in these domains. Third, we must remember that for the students their experiences of school in terms of these 'qualities' are presented here in total response scores. The variability of response by various types of students is a complex matter and must be so appreciated. This notwithstanding, the evidence from the quality of school life dimension of the St Mary's College Study shows the need for closer examination of the interactions between the students, parents and teachers, particularly in terms of their

students' and children's perceptions of what they expect of school and the quality of school life provided for them.

The Study generally has revealed some very positive things about the students' perceptions of the quality of their school experiences, and the way the teachers and other students behave, in their interest. But there is variability among groups of students in a number of areas — from academic through to sporting and there is sobering evidence about features of the value and ideological context of the school. These require of the whole of the school community an increase in the frequency, strength and style of much of their communication together and perhaps changes in attitude and approach towards a number of aspects of the school programme. Such response may form a basis for a stronger, more productive educational experience, which is part of an essential foundation for a better quality of life for students.

The Psycho-social Variables

As indicated in the methodology section, the analysis of both the Perception of School study and the Quality of School Life student data incorporated four psycho-social variables: age or grade level; level of academic achievement; year of leaving; and residential locality. This section summarizes findings for each variable mainly where the responses were statistically significant at .01 or .05 levels. Note that in the Quality of School Life dimension of the Study the comparison includes grades 7–12, and not only grades 10–12 as in the Perceptions of School dimension.

Psycho-social Variables Defined
Variable 1. Age or Grade Level   All the present students were located in the natural school settings according to grades. Past students were identified according to their final school grade. In general these also constituted separation of the students into age differences. Each student was given a numeral 'score' according to grade and this was added to her file record.

Variable 2. Level of Achievement   This variable was constructed by use of the School Certificate (grade 10) or Higher School Certificate (grades 11 and/or 12) results. For each student, points were derived from levels 3, 2, and 1 results in four subjects — mathematics and/or science and English and/or another humanities subject together with the two best other subjects. Each student was then given a total point score which was added to her file record. In grades 7–9 inclusive class teachers assigned each student an academic level (numeral 1, 2, or 3).

Variable 3. Year of Leaving   Each student was allocated a grade of exit code numeral, whether grade 10, 11 or 12. For purposes of determining differences in responses of present and past students, the sample was

divided into three groups: 1) students who left school between 1978–80; 2) those who left between 1981 and 1984 and; 3) present students, who included those at school in 1986.

Variable 4. Locality   This was used as a measure of broad socio-economic categorization. It was based on the local government or municipality divisions, the school population being representative of virtually all these divisions. However, this variable proved to be a crude measure and yielded little of significance in the results generally.

Variable 1. Age or Grade Level

Perceptions of School Dimension
Significant differences between the three grades (10–12) were found in both the Perceptions of School and Quality of School Life responses. In the POS study, this was especially so when comparing the grade 10 students with those in grades 11 and 12; and in the QSL when comparing the upper secondary (grades 10–12) with the lower secondary (grades 7–9) students.

The HSC students, in contrast to the grade 10s attached greater importance to independent study skills and traditional subjects; were more likely to approve of their religious education courses and more highly valued being a Catholic. HSC students also tended more to conform to, and approve of, parental and school authority and to see their teachers as good models of leadership. Also, the older the student, the more likely they were to agree that the school had taught them to be a leader and provided opportunities for leadership experience.

The grade 10s, in contrast to grades 11 and 12, were generally more uncertain about themselves and relatively more critical of the school's performance. They tended to value less the school's role in teaching traditional subjects, religious education classes and the importance of being a Catholic. The grade 10s were also comparatively more critical of teachers, the school's success in providing leadership opportunities and in making students aware of social issues. They are more satisfied than the HSCs with the school's work experience and physical education programmes and more likely to agree that cooking and dressmaking skills learnt at school were likely to carry over into other areas.

Expectations of the School   Grades 11 and 12 were more likely than grade 10 to regard it as important that school enables students to understand in depth one or more traditional subjects. Grades 11 and 12 also regarded it as more important than the grade 10s that the school should enable them to organize their own work and time. The grade 12s and grade 11s were also more satisfied than the grade 10s that the school had achieved or

very well achieved the goal of making sure that students are obedient to parents, teachers and all in authority.

Personal and Spiritual Development   The great majority of grade 11 and 12 students agreed with the statement 'Religion helps to answer real questions about the meaning of life'. This compared with agreement of less than half of students in grade 10. Also while most of the senior students considered that 'Being a Catholic is important to me' the percentage of grades 11 and 12 who agreed was significantly higher than that of the grade 10s.

A majority of the grade 12s considered the school's religious education (RE) programme to be important in their religious development. This compared with less than a third of the grades 11 and grades 10.

Concerning personal prayer, the majority of grades 12 and 11, normally prayed several times a week compared with a little over a third of grade 10. A similar pattern existed when students were asked about the importance of some religious, priest or minister to the students' religious development. While half of grade 12 regarded the influence of such a person to be important, only a third of grade 11 and less than 20 per cent of grade 10 agreed.

These results are consistent with Flynn's (1985) findings and support the contention that grade 10 (and sometimes grade 9), is for many students, a time for uncertainty, experimentation and tension as students resolve questions of self-identity, independence from parents, etc. This is also accompanied by a religious 'time-out' which may be part of the overall growth process. By grade 12, it is asserted, most students seem to know who they are and where they are going. Moreover, such students are appreciative of more subtle aspects of the curriculum and see themselves as playing an integral part of the school/parental network. Nevertheless some aspects of such 'natural development' are not endorsed by the data here. Grade 12 and 11 students may have gained a greater appreciation of beauty or of themselves personally than that expressed by grade 10 students, yet no group regarded these as successful outcomes of their schooling.

Leadership and Sport   Grade 12 students were much more satisfied with leadership opportunities provided by the school than were grade 10 or 11 students. Similarly, two thirds of grade 12 compared to just over half of grade 11 and less than half of grade 10 agreed that 'At SMC there were sufficient opportunities to develop leadership in grade 10'. Also grade 12 students (three quarters) were more likely than grade 11 or 10s to perceive teachers as good models of leadership.

When it came to physical education, however, the grade 10s were more positive than the grade 11s and grade 12s. The student interviews

High and middle achievers appear to be more career-minded and suggested more specific work skills to be made part of the school's curriculum. Middle achievers were most satisfied with the school's work experience programme. Lower achievers were more likely to attend Mass and receive Holy Communion. However, they were less positive, than middle or high achievers, that teachers allowed sufficient discussion or tried to make the teaching material relevant to student needs. Lower achievers stated they were less influenced by parents in regard to subject selection.

Objectives of the School   In rating the school's success in making sure that students can organize their own time and work independently, the high achievers were much more likely to regard this goal as not achieved than were low achievers. The high achievers and middle achievers considered the goal of having specific skills needed for chosen work to be much more important than did low achievers. In the science area, the high achievers regarded the goal of understanding science as more important, but much less well achieved than did the middle and low achievers. Finally, the high achievers also regarded the goal of being able to appreciate beauty as more important than did the lower or middle achievers.

Academic Aspects   High and middle achievers more than low achievers agreed that HSC subjects were chosen because they were needed to gain the immediate employment of the student's choice.

Low achievers were less influenced by parents in choosing subjects than high achievers.

In making subjects selections high achievers, more than low and middle groups, were more likely to view the sciences as more important than the humanities. (It should be noted however that overall there was little agreement with this proposition on the part of students.)

Middle achievers and high achievers agreed more than low achievers that appropriate information was readily available regarding specific subjects for specific employment.

Middle level achievers were more likely to agree than high achievers that their choice of HSC subjects will assist in gaining immediate employment. Low achievers were the least likely to agree to this statement.

Low achievers most agreed and high achievers least agreed that one's choice of HSC subjects assists in gaining entrance to a tertiary institution, though it should be noted that overall agreement was very high for all groups.

Vocational   High achievers were much more likely, than middle and low achievers, to agree that craft studies enabled them to do simple repairs at home.

The middle achievers registered greater agreement that work experi-

ence helped them to understand the world of work, though again overall agreement was high.

Personal and Spiritual Development   Regarding the influence of friends in their religious development, half of high achievers regarded friends as important, compared with less than half of middle achievers and one-fifth of low achievers.

Three-quarters of low achievers attended Mass at least on Sundays, compared with approximately half of the high achievers and middle achievers.

Similarly, three-quarters of low achievers received Holy Communion at least on Sundays compared with approximately half of the high achievers and middle achievers.

Leadership and Sport   Differences in response to only one item for this variable were found to be statistically significant. High achievers were more likely than middle and low achievers to agree that they enjoyed activities other than study and sport which they have continued or will continue after leaving school.

Teachers   A majority of low achievers and middle achievers, compared with two-fifths of high achievers, considered that teachers allowed classroom discussion.

Almost half of the low achievers and middle achievers, compared with a little over a third of high achievers, considered that 'many' teachers tried to make their teaching material relevant to students' needs.

Although a high proportion of all students considered that teachers set homework regularly, agreement was highest among middle achievers, followed by high achievers and low achievers.

Quality of School Life Dimension
While the general results show that the majority of students are satisfied with the quality of their school life, it is also clear that low achievers are less satisfied, than middle and high achievers.

General Affect   Though the differences were not statistically significant, the low achievers expressed a much less general satisfaction with school than did the other groups. They were less likely to agree that school was a place where they 'like to go', where they 'feel happy' and 'get enjoyment from being there'.

Status   For the most part, students of differing achievement levels varied little in their perception of the relative personal prestige afforded to them by others at school. The majority of students of all three achievement levels agreed that 'School is a place where I feel important', but about

three-quarters of low achievers, compared with about two-thirds of high and middle achievers, held this view.

A high proportion of all three achivement groups also agreed that 'School is a place where people: have confidence in me; come to me for help; and look up to me'. There were, however, minor variations between groups. With the statement, 'School is a place where I know people look up to me', two-thirds of the high and middle achievers agreed compared with just over half of the low achievers. To the statement, 'School is a place where I am trusted to work on my own', 15 per cent of low achievers expressed disagreed compared with 5 per cent of middle and 9 per cent of achievers. However, to the statement, 'School is a place where I feel confident', more than three-quarters of all three groups responded positively.

Identity   With the statement, 'School is a place where I have learnt to see other peoples' points of view', overall agreement is high for the three groups, but low achievers were less definite in their response. Again, though overall agreement was high, a greater proportion of high achievers and middle achievers agreed with the statement 'School is a place where other students listen to what I say'.

Teachers   With the statement, 'School is a place where teachers are friendly to me in class', almost a quarter of the low achievers disagreed, compared with less than 20 per cent of the middle achievers and less than 10 per cent of the high achievers.

Positive Affect   No statistically significant difference was found between students of different achievement levels, though the responses indicated that low achievers were again less positive than middle or high achievers. They were more likely to disagree that school is a place where they: 'feel proud' of themselves; 'get excited about things'; feel that things are going their way; and that they are 'successful'.

Negative Affect   No statistically significant difference was found. As the general findings show, St Mary's students indicate little sense of alienation in their school life.

Adventure (Sense that learning is self motivating and provides feelings of adequacy and the ability to cope with its demands)   A high proportion of all groups agreed that, 'School is a place where I have learnt to find whatever information I need', with middle achievers recording the greatest agreement followed by low and high achievers.

Opportunity   Although the overall agreement level was high for all groups, the high achievers showed more definite agreement that 'School

is a place where I know how to cope with the work' and 'where I can learn what I need to get by in life'.

Variable 3. Year of Leaving

Perceptions of School Dimension

Summary   The results generally suggest that present students (1986) are more satisfied with their school experience than were either the 1978–80 or 1981–84 groups.

Expectations of School   A higher proportion of the present (1986) and the 1981–84 groups of students regarded as important the school goal of 'appreciation of English literature'. The highest rating came from the 1981–84 group.

Present students are more satisfied than other year groups that the school is successful in 'making sure students understand the world of work', though students in all year groups were generally critical of the school's performance in this area.

Less than half of the present (1986) students considered that the goal of developing in students an appreciation of beauty to be important. This compared with half of the 1978–80 group and more than two-thirds of the 1981–84 group. This goal therefore recedes in importance to students over the period 1978–86.

Only a quarter of present (1986) students agreed that the school was successful in making sure students know of and respond to major social issues (18). However, this is an improvement over past years as the other groups showed even less agreement (less than 20 per cent of the 1981–84 group and only 10 per cent of the 1978–80 group).

Subject Selection   The great majority of students from all three periods agreed that HSC subjects were chosen because of the need for particular subjects to qualify for entrance to a tertiary institution. However, agreement was stronger by the present (1986) group and the 1978–80 group.

Also, the 1978–80 and the present (1986) students, more than the 1981–84 students, agreed that their choice of subjects was because of good results in grade 10.

A very high proportion of students in each period disagreed that their parents had influenced their choice of subjects. The 1978–80 group disagreed slightly more strongly with this statement than did the present (1986) students or those of the 1981–84 group.

Two-thirds of the present (1986) students disagreed that choices were largely determined by organization of subjects into lines. Only about half of the 1978–80 group and about 67 per cent of the 1981–84 group so responded.

A high proportion of 1978–80 students (84 per cent), 1981–84 students (75 per cent) and present (1986) students (82 per cent) disagreed that the sciences appeared to be more important than the humanities.

More than two-thirds of the present (1986) students agreed that appropriate information was readily available regarding the specific subjects required for specific fields of employment. This compared with a little over a third of students in the 1978–80 and 1981–84 periods.

Again, though most students in each period agreed that their choice of subjects assisted or would assist them in gaining entrance to a tertiary institution, the present students registered a stronger agreement (89 per cent) than did the 1978–80 group (81 per cent).

A similar result occurred with responses to the questions as to whether whether students' choice of subjects helped provide a foundation for further study in any discipline and provided a basis for a continuing personal interest. Stronger agreement came from the present students followed by the 1981–84 and 1978–80 groups.

Vocational   Contrary to the general trend, present students were the least satisfied group in this category. For example, three-quarters of the 1978–80 group agreed that craft studies enabled them to do simple repairs at home. This compared with less than half of the 1981–84 group, and 40 per cent of present (1986) students.

In terms of the statement, 'Vocational studies have proven beneficial in my life outside school', the 1978–80 students indicated the greatest agreement, followed by the 1981–84 and present (1986) students. In regard to part B (craft) 84 per cent of the 1978–80 group agreed with the item statement compared with 58 per cent of 1981–84 and 39 per cent of present (1986) students. For part C (dressmaking) 85 per cent of the 1978–80 group agreed with the statement compared with 69 per cent of 1981–84 and 64 per cent of present (1986) students.

In contrast to these trends, 78 per cent of the present (1986) students and 77 per cent of the 1978–80 group considered work experience as helping them to understand the world of work. This compared with 59 per cent for the 1981–84 group.

Personal and Spiritual Development   While a majority of all groups agreed with the statement that 'Religion helps me to answer real questions about the meaning of life', agreement was strongest in the 1981–84 group, followed by the present (1986) and 1978–80 groups.

While there was general disagreement with the statements, 'My education at SMC has helped me in preparing for such things as pregnancy' and 'My education at SMC has helped me in preparing for marriage', that disagreement was least pronounced by present (1986) students. In contrast almost three-quarters of the 1978–80 students and a clear majority of 1981–84 students disagreed with the statement.

All year groups considered that parents were the most important of all the influences upon students' religious development. However, agreement was strongest amongst the 1981–84 group, followed by the 1978–80 and present (1986) groups.

Supporting Flynn's findings of a drop in religious practice once students leave school, a majority of present (1986) students said they normally attended Mass at least on Sundays and received Holy Communion. This compares with just over a third of students in the other two year groups. Also, 30 per cent of the present (1986) group said they rarely or never attended the Sacrament of Confession or Reconciliation. This compared with 56 per cent of the 1981–84 group and 84 per cent of the 1978–80 group.

Leadership and Sport   From 1978 to 1986 there is an increasing number of students who agreed that physical education classes provide a comprehensive and worthwhile programme. Only a third of the 1978–80 group agreed. This compares to a majority of the 1981–84 group and almost three-quarters of present (1986) students. Whether students enjoyed activities at SMC, other than study or sport, which they will continue or have continued after leaving school, a majority of present (1986) students agreed. In contrast less than half of the 1978–80 group and a third of the 1981–84 group agreed.

From 1978 to 1986 there is also an increasing number of students agreeing that at SMC they felt free to make mistakes and learn from those mistakes. A little over a third of the 1978–80 students and less than half of the 1981–84 agreed. This compared with nearly two-thirds of present (1986) students.

From 1978 to 1986 a decreasing number of students agree that there were a sufficient number of PE classes. In the 1978–80, group, about 60 per cent agreed. This compares to less than half of the 1981–84 group and less than a third of present (1986) students.

Teachers   Whilst 20 per cent of the 1978–80 group considered that 'many' teachers make teaching material relevant to students' needs, agreement increased to 45 per cent of the 1981–84 group and just below half of the present (1986) student group.

A high proportion of all year groups considered that 'many' teachers covered a great deal of material in the time allowed. However, agreement was strongest in the 1978–80 group followed by the 1981–84 and present (1986) groups.

While nearly 90 per cent of the 1978–80 students indicated that teachers corrected their work regularly, the agreement level drops to three-quarters in the 1981–84 group and only a majority of present (1986) students.

Student Interviews

Methodology

The authors interviewed twenty-nine present and past students, some in groups of two or three, some individually. The interview questions were based directly upon the Perception of School instrument which focussed on students' perceptions in the areas: 1) academic, 2) vocational, 3) personal and spiritual, and 4) sport and leadership. It was necessary to choose past students residing in the Hobart area. However, these past students were selected from those who had gone to university as well as those who entered the workforce either from grade 10 or grade 12. Similarly, present student selection (based upon consultations with class teachers) was made from those who were likely to go onto university as well as those who were likely to leave school sometime during their upper secondary years (grades 10–12) in order to pursue immediate employment.

Academic

The majority of students defined 'academic' as referring to subjects such as mathematics, English, history. Academic activity was identified as studying, especially through books. The vast majority felt that St Mary's College had benefited them academically. Typical was the following comment:

> I think it [school's academic achievement] was very good actually. I find that it benefited me greatly, especially when I decided to go to uni and go on with my studies. I mean there was no way I would have been able to cope without the education that I had. It involved every facet of the education, and it developed each in me and I found I was quite capable in each subject area, when I went on to further education.

Many students mentioned HSC as a particularly rewarding time in their education because of the freedom, the wide variety of subject choice and the opportunity to specialize. Also frequently and favourably mentioned were the high expectations conveyed to students by staff, peers, administration, etc. Students felt they were expected to do well and consequently developed the confidence that they could and would succeed:

> Well, it [my experience at school] taught me that I could achieve things if I really wanted to, that I wasn't just a mediocre student. It taught me what I was as a student and what I could do. It's encouraged me I think and gave me a bit more confidence than I had before.

> And this year I'd say my teachers have really encouraged me to the fullest and have extended me and have made me work a lot

harder. I don't know, it might be just the teachers I'd struck this year, which I didn't have last year. But they've really pushed me. I really believe now if I want to do, say law or psychology, or something like that, I really believe I could do it.

Most students seemed to appreciate the 'pressure' created by the teachers and academic atmosphere of St Mary's, interpreting it as a sign of concern:

I think they [teachers] were really good, I didn't feel that any teacher was coming down on me; they just tried to push you and make you do your best.

I previously went to a state school before I came here in grade 6 — ____ Primary School which was open plan ... and I would basically say that I could just read and write. My conception of school was 'Do what I want to when I want to' — self expression, which is probably good for me in some ways. But when I came here and we were sitting in rows, it was an absolute shock. But, I needed that — I really need discipline. I'm a really scatty person and need to be told 'You have to do this and you have to do that at such and such a time'. And so, St Mary's has helped a lot. I wouldn't be where I am and have a general knowledge about things if it wasn't for St Mary's.

Another student had a similar experience when transferring to St Mary's after grade 11:

My first year at matric [grade 11] at my other school was a bit disastrous because that school had a terrible, terrible approach to matric. It aims at the mediocre students and not the brighter students. I got two level III's in my first year. Then I came down here and at St Mary's their attitude to matric is just fantastic. I was really pushed and got five really good level III's compared to two the previous year. It's just amazing the difference. Obviously, St Mary's taught me how to work and taught me the importance of trying, whereas at my old school it was sort of half, and the big thing was if you did better than everyone else then they thought you were a bit funny; whereas down here you were encouraged. It was quite good; I really enjoyed myself here.

In fact, two of the students stated that upon attending university they missed the pressure to learn which was present at St Mary's. Other students, who had attended another school prior to St Mary's, stated that at St Mary's academic standards were much higher. Most of those interviewed felt that St Mary's prepared them well for further study and that they fared well against students from other schools. The following comments from students were typical:

Student 1:   I went to Tech after leaving St Mary's and I found it different because they don't make you work. If you don't work it's up to you, but St Mary's made you work, which I found was good.

Student 2:   When I was studying for my apprenticeship I found it a lot easier than the other girls study-wise, so I am sure they [SMC teachers] helped me by showing me how to study. So I seemed to find it quite easy whereas at school [St Mary's] I didn't find my work easy and had to work to get through it. But, when I left school, I found it a lot easier.

These comments, as well as other evidence from the St Mary's Study, would seem to cast doubt on the apparent 'evidence' that more 'private' school students are represented in the university drop-out statistics than those of the more liberal state schools.

One student stated that St Mary's generated a love of learning which she felt would be lifelong:

I think it started me off to be interested to learn more and I realized while at St Mary's that there were particular subjects which would interest me long term. So I've gone on studying particular subjects and I think that when I finish university I'll still be involved in academic activities for the rest of my life probably. I think that's fairly well associated with St Mary's. I found that the subject was interesting for itself, as well as for passing exams.

Two students also referred to the fact that St Mary's was an all girls school as a positive factor in their academic development.

When asked about the broad range of subjects most students favoured them, although a few thought there were too many subject offerings:

In High School we were doing 14 subjects or something like that, and sometimes I think it's just too much. I do five subjects at Art School and I find it hard to swap to another subject and [type of] thinking. Eight different subjects in a day, 45 minutes each, it's just not long enough. It's nice to have a broad knowledge of things, but sometimes I wonder in trying to do it all, if we really get a lot from it.

Several students expressed a concern about the large class sizes, especially in the lower secondary level and the large number of subjects which students are required to do, especially in grades 9 and 10. Also, cited was the 'hidden curriculum,' which stated mathematics/science subjects are for boys, arts subjects for the girls, as noted by the fact that most of the sciences courses at HSC level are offered at St Virgil's, while most of the arts courses are taught at St Mary's.

Finally, one student suggested the need for a student tutorial programme in which students could help tutor each other:

> I'm not a particularly intelligent person and I have to work harder than everybody else to get where I want, but I think there should be some sort of tutorial — maybe between student and student — set up some time to help people in that way. Sometimes you can learn more through talking to a fellow student than you could through talking to a teacher, and maybe that could be set up.

Vocational
A few students at first thought of 'vocational' only in terms of a religious calling. Most students defined vocation in more general terms:

> Q: What do you mean by vocational?
> A: Choosing a career, choosing what you're going to do with your life.

Two students, however, saw an integration of vocation as both a worldly and a spiritual direction:

> Q: What do you mean by vocational?
> A: What direction you're heading in — your physical career, how you're going to earn your bread. But, also what you're going to do in terms of what you think you owe society, or not necessarily that, but what you think you should give back.
> Q: That's interesting, you're suggesting there's a religious dimension to vocational. Is that part of the whole, or is it different or separate, I mean.
> A: I mean it depends how you live your life, but I mean your spiritual life. Like you don't have to be religious or anything, but you know married or single, or research scientist or whatever, there's still a spiritual dimension to your vocation.

As noted in the three responses below, some students attributed their choice of vocation to influential teachers, to subjects and activities they most enjoyed, and to the school's work experience programme:

> Q: What is it about the school that maybe helped you figure out what you want too? Was it through your courses, or work experience?
> Student 1: St Mary's has given me a taste of different subjects, quite a wide range, and it makes it easier to choose what you want to be.
> Student 2: Well, it [St Mary's] helped me to decide what I want to do in life. I've decided what I want to do and it's helped me with all the choices of things I can do. Like yesterday, I went up on the bus to Launceston to look at the college up there.

That was arranged by the school — and the subjects you can choose for matric — that's helped me.

Student 3: It was through some of the subjects, and then again in work experience, that was good, and also, some of the teachers and discussing it with them and getting their views.

Other students, however, knew their vocation even before coming to school.

Q: What led you to decide you were going to go into nursing? Did St Mary's give you any guidance as to say nursing versus other things?

A: No. I was going to be a nurse since I was about five years old. That was what I was always going to do, and I sort of did my subjects and worked my things here around what I was aiming to do.

Almost every student spoke highly of their work experience obtained through the school. Indeed, several spoke of the need for more work experience opportunities.

Student 1: I didn't think there was enough work experience and things like that, but I must admit that in the field that I ended up in and wanted to go into, it was very hard to get work experience — so that probably had nothing to do with the school anyway.

Student 2: As far as I was concerned, I think I was so unsure of what I was going to do, I just didn't have a clue. If you could be told more about different jobs and a bit more work experience, it would have helped.

Students were also asked about their cooking and sewing classes and many responded that these subjects were very useful in later life, regardless of one's vocation [the survey results, however, showed significant differences among students. Past students were more positive than present students, and cooking and sewing received higher approval ratings than craft].

Finally, students were asked if they had any ideas about how the school might better fulfil its vocational role. Among the suggestions were:

1 More emphasis on job seeking skills — interviewing techniques, letter writing, resumes, etc;
2 More work experience;
3 More assistance in subject selection taking into account student abilities and future employment prospects as well as the need for a well-rounded education.

Student 1: I think there needs to be somebody to help you make the choices when you go to matric (matriculation) because I chose completely the wrong subjects. I thought I could handle them at the time, but then I wasn't able to so I took on too much. If somebody had been there to say, 'just do a couple', it would have been better.

Student 2: ... encourage students to not choose subjects that will simply get them their matric or that their friends are doing, but subjects that maybe they haven't ever done before. Here's an opportunity to study something at a greater depth not just for the sake of getting qualifications for enrolling at a university, but for your own knowledge. I'd love to go back and do some matric subjects because I know that I've got gaps, things that I know nothing about, like history. I didn't do any history and that would have been really interesting.

4   More testing to help students discover the kinds of jobs and careers in which they might be interested.

5   More help in grade 11 and 12 in regard to university requirements, application deadlines, etc.

I think it's a good idea to take students down to the university and look around at all the different departments to see if that's what students want to do, because I didn't have a clue what courses were available down there. And all the application dates for things, like medicine — I never heard about that. I think if you're interested you have to go and find out for yourself, but at the beginning of second year matric we weren't told 'if you want to do this, the closing date is such and such, and if you want to go up north, this is what you have to do'.

6   Need to have more people coming to the school to talk about careers.

7   Need more counselling, especially to encourage girls to think about careers in science, engineering, computers, etc.

Personal and Spiritual Development

Personal development was typically defined by the students as:

total development, including your academic or intellectual development, your social development, ability to interact and things like that. Spiritual development is one part of personal development.

Another student put it this way:

Personal development is understanding more about yourself and realizing your capabilities and limitations and how to cope with

them both. Realizing where you are in relation to everyone else and understanding what you can do and develop aims and things like that.

Most students saw personal and spiritual development as 'intertwined': 'I think the spiritual helps the personal development and also personal helps with spiritual'. Several students also mentioned that we learn much about ourselves by the way in which others see us. The school was generally seen to play a major role in personal development, especially in the upper secondary level where students were given opportunities for leadership and responsibility.

> In fourth year [grade 10], especially, we organized a lot of class socials and things like that, and we think that was really great in developing personal ability. A lot of responsibility was given to you as well in those years. I remember I was class captain and that did wonders for me and my self-confidence. Having to get up and make speeches in front of people, and then also getting into matric when we were getting into debating and that sort of thing. Those sort of things were important, especially once you finish school. I mean, if you haven't got confidence in yourself first, you're going to struggle once you get out there. I think a lot more could be done in the first three years [grades 7–9] — encouraging more debating, class captains and that sort of thing, even changing captains every term just to give everyone a bit of responsibility. As a teacher now, or as a student teacher, I'm out in schools and I see that some children obviously at home don't get, 'Oh you're a good boy, keep going, keep trying'. They don't get encouragement from home. So of course when they get to school, they feel a bit down, and they can't look you in the eye and can't stand up for themselves. I think that if you give them, I've noticed this myself with this one boy, if you gave him a responsibility, it made him feel really something. If you can do that to everyone, if you continue it on all through the years of schooling, once he finishes he's just going to be that much better a person. I really notice it now when I'm out [on student teaching], so many things you can pick up, that maybe ones you lacked in, you can help others.

Class teachers, parents, special friends, significant others were seen as important to both personal and spiritual development:

> Q: What do you mean by the words personal development and spiritual development?
> A: How I mature through the school. Spiritually a lot of the nuns helped me along the way. Sr _____ was one that was very helpful to me. Any problems — I could always go to her and

turn to her. Personally a lot of the students were very good to me. I just felt with the groups that I was in I could see myself developing and maturing which was very good. In terms of personal development I'd say it [the school] has done a lot. I'm very happy. I'll send all my children to St Mary's and St Virgil's.

Q: Yes, well that's a good test isn't it?

A: Yes I think it's been terrific. I really think the teachers and the students and everybody have helped me a lot, and I really appreciate that.

Because spiritual development is so inextricably linked with personal development, many of the comments above and below apply to both.

Many students acknowledged the difficulty of a school, or any institution, fostering spiritual development, especially in a society so dominated by materialistic concerns:

Well it's kind of an uphill battle, like Mrs _____ [religion teacher] said to try to tell people at matric level, you can't do this or you can't do that. When everything around, like in magazines and on the screen, says you do your own thing, get what you want, go for it, don't worry about other people, it's cool to be sleeping around, or whatever. It's hard to have somebody say, 'Oh that's wrong'.

It was further recognized that the family plays the key role in personal and spiritual growth; that if the seeds of spirituality are not planted there, the school is likely to have little impact. This conclusion is indicated very powerfully by the survey results in which students considered their parents as the single greatest influence on their religious development:

I think if you're ready to accept your faith and go to church and learn about it well then you develop spiritually. But some people don't want to accept it and they won't listen. I remember some people in my religion class said 'Oh no, religion again' and they just didn't listen. It's up to the individual, and if you've got the family background at home, I think that helps a lot. Spiritually, I come from a very Catholic family. That's really good, and the support at home has always been really good, and I don't know whether St Mary's developed me and further or whether ... because I was just, well not the sort of person that gives up on God just because something goes wrong or anything — because I've got a good home. I think St Mary's just continued it further.

Many students also pointed out that spiritual development and religious instruction did not just occur in religion classes, but pervaded the entire

school. As one student put it when referring to the impact of the school on her religious development: 'It's more than the actual religions; it's the whole environment of St Mary's College'.

Many students credited the school for giving them a deep and meaningful faith:

Student 1:   St Mary's has given me a really deep faith. It has also given me a fairly good knowledge of the faith and it has given me the ability to communicate with people.

Student 2:   Religion lessons have taught me a lot I didn't know about religion. I did learn a bit about the church last year that I didn't know, and it was quite interesting.

The Catholic tradition and rituals, especially school retreats and Graduation Masses were viewed as particularly important in fostering spirituality. Also emphasized was the opportunity for daily prayer and availability of the sacraments:

One of the other things that St Mary's gave me for my spiritual development would be an appreciation of tradition. That by being part of a tradition we can have particular ways of developing spiritually, like the retreat even — that yearly excursion off to spend time with God or thinking about God, and that helps me in a religious context. And I think prayer was fostered in the school, particularly at matric level we were encouraged to be prayerful and my position of head prefect was very much a position of praying for a group of people that I was leading. That was the way I was in charge that meant I wasn't in charge. They were prayerfully my responsibility to pray for and think of, whether it's my family, my special group of friends, the people that I work with, but that is a responsibility I have, and I think that aspect of spiritual development I learnt at St Mary's ... I especially enjoyed our last retreat. I got a lot out of that and also about myself as well because we had a group gathering, all the lights out and with candles and you could really feel the friendliness about you and you could even feel God there present, and I always feel the same when I get in that situation.

Speaking specifically about the retreats, another student said:

Retreats were good. They gave you a group identity perhaps, that there was a particular thing that was important to that group at that time. That used to come across in retreats. It could be friendship or love or peace or sharing which would be what that group wanted discussed at that particular time. So we learnt something about our spiritual development in that way. I felt that everyone was closer at the retreats too.

Q: Because of that, were you able to find out things about
yourself that you weren't aware of before or about yourself in
relationship with others that you didn't know before?

A: You learnt about hearing I think — how we can by sharing
with other people receive some kind of support and overcome
problems and have a positive approach to life.

Q: Was that in it for you too?

A: Yes we all got closer together and closer to God I felt. I
think too you learn about the idea of a retreat so that you can
go off sometime by yourself and have time to just be alone or
with a group to pray or something. It is difficult to have a
retreat once you leave school, and it takes a lot of time and
effort to look up and find out about things. The prayer aspect
is important too, I guess. The daily prayer idea is good and it is
good that it was continued and that it still goes on. Availability
of the sacraments I thought was great.

Another student commented about the 'all girls' nature of the retreat.

St Mary's really helped. Our retreats were absolutely wonderful.
I can still remember them. It was just so nice and we all got so
close — that's why I think it's really lovely going to an all girls
school, too, because I really think girls need each other when they
are going through high school because boys are pretty horrible at
school. Being all girls we could be affectionate to each other and
the nuns really encouraged that. I can remember one occasion we
were having Mass ... and we all started crying. We got really
hyped up and we just all burst into tears.

When asked about suggestions for improvement, the following comments were made regarding religion classes.

1 Many students expressed the desire to learn more about the
   Church and Christian doctrine, especially as articulated by Vatican II.

2 More discussion about religious vocations.

3 More emphasis on learning about other religions. Also, those
   students who did Religious Studies Level 3, an externally examined subject featuring a unit on comparative religion, commented favourably on this aspect: 'I liked learning about other
   religions because that was more interesting. . . . I liked to learn
   about the other religions and how they differed'.

4 Several students were concerned that religion classes in the lower
   secondary school did not foster enough discussion — that there
   was too much art work and picture drawing, and not enough
   doctrine.

5 One student perceived a low priority given to the religion classes

in comparison to other subjects. 'If class teachers had to plan things, or there needed to be a meeting the RE Class was always sacrificed.'

6   While acknowledging the importance of morality, it was felt that there was too much emphasis on sexual issues over and above other moral issues — justice, poverty, war, etc.

I think you can discuss justice issues and I think I came out of St Mary's with a very low general knowledge about things happening in the world and how to act towards conservationism and countries at war, civil war, politicians, and advertising. I think that should be part of our spiritual and personal development, which the school has to pick up. I guess we see it under a religious lesson time because that's the only time when there can be that freedom of what is covered.

7   A few students stressed the need for more apologetics in religion classes so students can profess and defend their faith.

Well, I have strongly developed ideas about this because I'm considering teaching religion, but I'm really biased about what I think should be taught in a school and I think students need, before they leave, apologetics, some way to be able to stand up for and profess their faith in terms that make sense to everybody. I think we need to be ethical ... we have to be able to answer questions in a way in which people can understand without our Catholic background... I find that there are intelligent and clever people, and remarkable people, who through the ages have been Catholic and have considered that that's been the truth for their lives. Now people think you're a bit silly if you don't realize that there's no God. That's already been dealt with in history.

8   Other students stressed the need for more knowledge of the scriptures.

Well, in grade 7, 8 and 9, I didn't really see the relevance of much of religion towards what our religion was actually trying to teach us. I think, I don't know, it happens a lot in a schools I suppose — religion tended to take on the form of drawing pretty pictures, drawing the host and drawing the chalis and things like that, and then, especially around Easter time where there were all types of things like Lent happening. But, we didn't really look at scripture and I know I'm very ignorant of what is actually in the Bible, and I think that's maybe a fault of the school. However, in grade 10, our teacher really extended it and he wasn't the sort of person who would put up with just drawing pictures and religion as just a symbolic thing, he really went into it. That really started to

develop because we had really meaningful class Masses and those type of things. I think that was a great benefit to me. And then going on to religion in matric, studying all the different religions and everything, I think that was also important in order to appreciate the other religions. Because you often don't become aware of them because without knowing them you just kind of take their religions as 'Oh I'm Catholic, I don't really care what you are'. I think it is important to have an awareness of what they believe in and why they believe it. Once you get to uni, there are a lot of people who are against religious people. They call Catholics 'micks' and all that sort of thing and get on your back. That's another thing; if you don't know what you are talking about, you've obviously will look a bit dumb and you think they have every right to question why you are a Catholic if you do not know these sort of things. I think that's another reason why in first, second and third year they should develop that — why Catholics, and looking at what we are actually — the history of the Catholic religion.

9 Finally, a couple of students mentioned the need for the school to better help students maintain contact with friends once they leave St Mary's.

Leadership
Student discussion about leadership was especially perceptive, as shown by different definitions which students gave of leadership and the qualities of a good leader.

Attributes of a Leader

The following qualities of leadership were listed by students:

— ability to communicate
— flexibility
— open mindedness
— capacity to lead a group
— ability to organize things
— ability to express an opinion
— courage to do what is right
— ability to set an example
— ability to listen to people's ideas
— able to exercise authority without 'bossing' people around
— cooperation
— able to bring out the best in others
— ability to take responsibility for things

— ability to work with different people
— confidence
— able to help others to lead

Important Statements about Leadership

While the above characteristics stress the 'obvious' leaders, students also recognized that there are quiet leaders who lead primarily by example. Other students pointed out that we are all leaders in a way; we all have potential to be leaders and will lead in some circumstances.

> I think it's nice for us all to be encouraged to be leaders. It doesn't mean you have to stand up and lecture to the people or something like that, but I think we should all realize that leadership is in everyone.

Several students highlighted leadership in a Christian context.

> To be a good Christian leader is also to be able to get people to believe in themselves and to get people to be able to show their own qualities because you can't expect to do everything yourself. If you can get other people to have a go as well then you're succeeding.

And another student:

> Q: What has St Mary's done for you in the area of leadership?
> A: It's given me an idea of how to lead students in music as well as in faith.
> Q: Can you enlarge on that at all, the music would be fairly obvious, but in terms of the faith area?
> A: By giving me such a love of Christ, that the younger students can see that and it will probably give something to them.

Most of those interviewed felt that St Mary's had helped them develop their leadership skills.

> Q: What about leadership skills?
> A: Well, since I've been at St Mary's I'm more likely now to say what I think and to do what I think for me is right, rather than sit back and wait for somebody else to say what they think is right and then follow them. I'm more likely to go out and do what I think is right first.

The school leadership camp (held for Higher School Certificate or Matriculation classes at the start of the year) was mentioned by several students as providing valuable training for leadership.

It [leadership camp] helped me afterwards because we did it at the beginning of the year before I went into second year matric, and that year I was deputy head. I think I learnt a lot of things just from seeing other people who were going to be leaders as well, sort of comparing what qualities they had and what you had and I don't think I really thought about the weekend until a long time afterwards. We had little games that we played, leadership bits and pieces, and you could see how other people did things. And later that year I would say to myself, 'Oh yes — that week', that was a good way to do it, and you could exhibit those traits yourself when you came to being a leader.

Those interviewed who had been or were school prefects commented on the honour of holding such a position of responsibility: 'It was lovely being a prefect. A real honour. I felt very proud'. Another student observed:

I think it [prefect system] is a great idea. I've seen other schools where they don't have that and their attitude is, 'Oh well, if kids don't want to look neat and tidy, if kids don't want to conform, well who cares? It's none of our business'. [At St Mary's] You're given the role and given some chance to show leadership. It really benefits you later on in life because you really know what is expected of you, what's expected of others.

Student Suggestions about Leadership

Among the suggestions about how leadership might be improved were:

1   Many students suggested the need to provide more leadership opportunities for grade 10 students, especially since for some of those students grade 10 will be their last year of formal education.

Leadership opportunities have been really great this year [grade 12] and pretty good last year. I think that grade 10s get a hard deal really. They don't get much of a chance. They're sort of in the middle. If they were at a public school they'd be prefects at the top of their schooling. So therefore they'd get to do a lot. And a lot of students leave school in fourth year, and they're going to miss out on all that opportunity. I mean they have never had the opportunities that the grade 11 and grade 12s have.

2   A few students also felt that grade 11s didn't get enough leadership opportunities; and a few felt even the prefects were not given enough to do.

> I don't think the prefects are given much to do. It was really only the head and the two deputies. [For example], we often represented the school at functions, and I think a few more of the prefects should have gone.

3   The formation of a School Council was also suggested as a way to get more students involved in leadership roles.

4   Another suggestion was to develop new ways to get students from different years to know and work with one another.

Teachers

Many comments above have already spoken of the influence of teachers on the academic, personal and spiritual development of students. Suffice it to say here that comments about teachers were generally favourable, especially of those teachers who were perceived as 'getting down on the students' level':

> I think as a teacher in today's society you've got to change, to be flexible. That is one of the main problems the teachers — the teachers just aren't on the children's level and they've got to be. They've got to get down there and mix in with them, get on their level. I know it's hard these days, but there are ways and means. You can do a lot more things as a class together — you [the teacher] being one of them. I know with _____ [teacher's name], he/she fostered that a lot in fourth year [grade 10]. _____ was probably the best teacher I ever had, and that continued on in matric as well. But also _____, she was also great.

Students were also perceptive in noting a change in student/teacher relationships as students matured.

> In grade 8, I don't think you thought you could consider a teacher as a friend or someone that you could confide in. The teacher was just the figure in front of the class who came and presented you with knowledge. You had to present stuff for that person, whereas in matric, some of them, not all of them, I suppose because of our maturity, were able to speak on more adult terms with students.

Another characteristic of outstanding teachers was a demonstrated love for their subject and a caring attitude towards their students:

> There again, it [teacher's enthusiasm for her subject] decided my vocation, the direction I'm going to take in my life artistically. So if it wasn't for _____ in matric taking me for art, I honestly don't know what I would be doing now. I've always had a flair, I've always enjoyed it but _____ has such a passion for it. She really enjoyed it and she builds that into all of us, all her students, because she's such a Christian loving person. She makes you

really enjoy her subject and she puts her love for it into you in a strange sort of way. You have to have a feel for it first too. But if it wasn't for me doing matric art here, I don't know what I would be doing. Because, too, you need encouragement and you need someone to say 'That's good', 'That's working', or 'Throw that out the window'. Some places you just don't get it. Lots of people say about private schools that they 'mollycoddle' you, which they do in a way. When you have things which they do in a way, when you have things in on a certain day and they chase you up. Well when you go to university, then no one is going to chase you up if you haven't got it, then that's it. But it's nice and I think it does help you in the long run to know someone cares. It's not very nice being one in hundreds of kids in matric.

Teachers were also mentioned in reference to developing the leadership talents of their students.

I'd go into the art room after school and we'd talk for ages about everything and that made me feel good because I felt I was a bit of a friend of the teacher. It means that a person is getting a sense of how valuable she is and that enables a student to react more favourably because you feel that there is a sense of responsibility, and it's not all about, 'The teacher makes me do this. If the teacher doesn't make me do this then I don't do it'. There were a number of cases when I was here that I felt I didn't get very good examples from my teachers. I thought, 'Oh yuk, what awful people'. And you think about it even more when you get older. As we were saying before, my life is still affected by this place. I still think about it; I think about something we did or something happens and I think — such and such would have done this like that.

These comments help qualify the survey result which showed that 41 per cent of students disagreed with the item statement that 'the teachers were good models of leadership'. Although a student might have a general perception that teachers as a group were not effective leadership models, almost every student interviewed spoke of the special and powerful influence of at least one particular teacher. Finally, a few students observed that actions speak louder than words: 'It's the personality of the teachers and their own standards that really come across in religion'.

Sport
Opinions about sport and physical education were more divided than any other category, especially regarding the compulsory aspect of physical education (PE) classes, attitudes toward competition and duration of classes.

School study questionnaire. Moreover, the qualitative data from the interviews helped to further illuminate and refine the exact nature of student perceptions about their quality of school life. Finally, the perceptions of students, recorded in their own words, constitutes valuable qualitative evidence of the nature and quality of education provided by St Mary's College.

Responding to the Results: Reactions of Teachers and Students

Students' Reactions: Perceptions of School

As noted in the Interim Report, the focus of the St Mary's College Study was two fold. It firstly aimed to gather information from students both past and present regarding their perceptions of the total programme of the senior school. The attendant purpose was to gain information from all the senior students of the school regarding their experience of the quality of their school life. However, the researchers realized that the validity of such information would be enhanced if we sought the students' comment and opinion apart from the 'pen and paper' means. Hence we interviewed a representative sample of students concurrently with the collection of data via the questionnaire instruments. In addition we presented the analyzed results to meetings of all the current (1986) students of grades 10, 11 and 12. These meetings were informal, lasted an hour each, and were conducted without the presence of members of staff. There were two meetings for each grade; one for the 'Perceptions of School' results, and the second for the 'Quality of School Life' results.

The following method was employed. The results were presented on the screen in terms of each category and domain. Students were given time to read then react generally. The researcher subsequently probed the items (of the questionnaires) in order to gain more depth. Finally the students were asked to make general and summary comments. All the student responses were recorded and periodically 'read back' to the students for accuracy.

The following summary records the main responses of the students in terms of the importance they placed upon them. For convenience and order, the summary is presented under the categories and domains of the two questionnaire instruments (Perception of School and Quality of School Life).

Expectations of School Here the major response related to the finding that students regarded the 'affective' areas of schooling as more important objectives, but ones less well achieved by the school. The students considered this a 'logical' result. They wondered why the school did not realize more that they as young people were unsure of themselves and, surrounded by 'pressures' to perform and to 'keep up', were more likely

to focus continually on themselves rather than 'intellectual' tasks. This 'logic' was particularly applicable to grade 10 students, they said, who were younger. Also, students argued, the abrupt change from grade 9 to the 'senior ranks' was conducive to such introspection. That students of the earlier years (1978–81 especially) were not as convinced of the significance of the 'affective' areas of school objectives was due to the 'fact', the students asserted, that in the earlier years students 'weren't subjected to as great a set of pressures'.

The next item of main concern to students was the result in which 'an appreciation of beauty' was of little importance and of little achievement by the school, according to the students. This was confirmed in the discussion. It was explained, the students said, by the overwhelming competitive atmosphere, the quest for jobs and such associated pressures. Nevertheless they asserted that an appreciation of beauty was 'essential to education' and they considered this to be lacking in their experience at school.

The third point of focus in discussion of 'Expectations of School' concerned the question of their response to social issues. In the results the students answered that whilst they regarded the objective of the school in helping them to respond to major social issues as very important this was not well achieved by the school on their behalf. Students reacted to this result by stating that the reason was obvious to them but not, evidently, to the school. For students, there was a natural link between a focus on self-esteem and concern with social issues, and this was especially so at grade 10. As their 'personal aims' were achieved so would they be able to respond to social issues, they argued.

Academic Aspects Two points considered important by students were raised in this category. First was the extent to which the ready availability of information affected their choice of subjects for their higher school certificate (or matriculation). The students argued that the availability of time was integral to the availability of information. That the grade 10 group (as the results showed) were much more likely to agree that appropriate information was readily available regarding subjects chosen for future academic purposes, the grade 12 group (final year students) asserted, was due to the greater availability of time and therefore a greater willingness to search on the part of the grade 10s. This did not deny the importance, the students asserted, of the urgency of the possibility of gathering specific detail as a measure of what subjects could or should be chosen for matriculation. The students' discussion of this point did not include their defining of 'availability of time'. They assumed that time available meant time they were able (rather than willing) to give. Nevertheless the interesting point from the researcher's point of view was that this matter of 'ready availability of information and of time' was so significant to the students.

The second issue for the students was the relative importance of influences upon them in their choice of subjects to study for matriculation. The results indicated that 'parents' and 'friends' choices' were the least influential factors and the most influential was their own intrinsic interest in the subject. The students firstly confirmed the negligible influence of parents. But regarding their friends' influence, they asserted that 'friends' and 'intrinsic interest' are admixed which could have affected the results where 'friends' influence was concerned. Nevertheless they confirmed the result that it was not because of friends that subject choices would be made. Again, to confirm the importance to the students of this area the students unanimously declared that an added support to them would be to invite past students to talk to present students about subject choices — the influences in their choices, the problems afterwards, etc. Even the grade 12s, they said, could help the grade 10s in this.

Vocational Aspects   In this area the students simply confirmed the results and felt that no further discussion was needed.

Personal and Spiritual Development   There were four main areas which students chose to discuss. The first concerned the result that more than half the students had agreed with the statement, 'At times I'm afraid of losing my faith'. Two perceptions emerged from discussion with the students. The first was their distinction between faith education which meant education in the sacraments, doctrine etc, and that relating religion to life. That a greater proportion of grade 10 than grade 12s at times feared of losing their faith was due, they said, to a greater concentration by grade 10s upon the sacraments and doctrine, whereas for grade 12 there was a greater concentration of 'relating religion to life'. (Some students ascribed the differentiation of the response of the grade 10 students to the fairly characteristic 'aggressiveness' and critical nature of the grade 10s.) However, this pointed to the second perception; students perceived the necessity for education in the sacraments and doctrine, etc, but at the same time time declared, 'make the sacraments and doctrine more related to life'. For these students their religious education at school exhibited a dilemma; it was either 'doctrine' or 'religion related to life'. They felt the need for a deeper education in the faith, one which combined the attainment of both these objectives, instruction in church doctrine and relevance of religion for life.

The second issue concerned their religious practice. Some students at first asserted that the questions on their practice of prayer implied a narrow definition of prayer. The proportion of those students who practised prayer was low, they argued, because prayer was assumed to be 'only the kneeling down in church kind'. However, after debate on this point, the students as a whole agreed that no matter how widely prayer

had been defined the result would have been the same. Thus they confirmed the result — that less than half the students prayed up to several times a week and more than a quarter of the total prayed 'occasionally during the year' or never.

The third issue came from the questions students had responded to concerning moral and religious issues. In particular they raised the apparent contradiction in the results which showed that whilst 79 per cent of the total student sample considered that 'being a Catholic is very important to me' on the other hand, 50 per cent of them had agreed that it was 'alright' for those not married to 'live together'. The present researcher indicated to the students that some of the staff, who also had sighted the results, wondered whether the students saw the question as implying that it was alright (for others) not married to live together, but not a practice they would indulge in personally. The students' response to this was interesting. They understood the question as a general moral proposition. But, more significantly perhaps, they considered there was no real conflict between the two results above. Rather they considered the state of 'being a Catholic' to be of greater importance than a single moral practice such as non-married people 'living together'. The importance of being a Catholic they said was that it allowed for 'personal interpretation' of their Catholic belief and practice.

Finally in this category, questions of influence upon the students' religious development gained focus. The result which showed that nearly three-quarters of the total student sample considered the 'instruction and example of parents/guardians to be the greatest influence' was confirmed in discussion with the students. 'Yes', they stated, other influences are of some importance, but their relationship with their parents/guardians is continuous. There was no question by the students that this parental influence was ever inappropriate.

Aspects of Leadership and Sport In 'reading' the students views in this category it is important to be aware that St Mary's College students are given a practical and thorough grounding in leadership in their senior years at school. This training takes many forms, including a weekend in leadership 'training' at the beginning of their matriculation years. Four points emerged for discussion.

First, the results showed that three quarters of the students thought that school had helped them understand what leadership is. On the other hand, less than half the students considered their teachers to be 'good models of leadership'. The students saw no conflict in these results and regarded them as factual.

Second, the results showed that there were quite insufficient opportunities for them to develop leadership as a whole, particularly in comparison with grades 11 and 12. This result was confirmed in the students' discussion among all three grade levels. The students also confirmed the

result which showed the great majority of them considered there to be an insufficient number of classes in physical education. Yet they insisted and agreed that this again applied mainly to the grade 10 group. The students thus raised what they considered a significant matter for the school's attention — the leadership training and physical education needs of grade 10 students. The reader will better realize this significance when they know that grade 10 Tasmanian schools constitute the end of the secondary phase of schooling. Students may then leave school or proceed to the two final years for matriculation examinations. Hence grade 10 students are in a delicate position in a 'matriculation' school as St Mary's College is. Especially, those students who leave school after grade 10 may miss out on these processes of personal development — as these results appear to indicate. Without special attention, the grade 10s in a school such as St Mary's may enjoy fewer leadership opportunities than their counterparts in schools where the grade 10 class is oldest age group.

The Q-Line This special subject line for higher school certificate students which offers increased alternatives to the more 'academic' subjects has proven popular among students. This was reflected in the results which the students felt no need further to discuss, except simply to confirm them.

Teachers The students' discussion centred on two features which perhaps encapsulate the definition of 'good teaching' from their point of view. The first was the result that less than half of all the students considered that teachers extended students to the limits of their abilities. It is to be noted that the students did not consider this an exaggerated possibility. They understood the contextual nature of the question — ie 'limits of their abilities'. They recognized it as referring to what was possible for them in the classroom on a daily basis. However the students made suggestions as to why the result was so. They considered that the question of a teacher 'extending' students was a matter of individual autonomy. They were unanimous in their statement that a teacher will 'extend' a student to the 'limits of (her) abilities', if she wants to be so extended, or more particularly if she wants to do her part in the process. On the other hand, the students considered that high achievers are often 'held back' in the classroom, especially in grade 10, and that this is sometimes due to 'peer pressure'. That is, an important inhibition to a teacher's 'extending' students 'to the limits' is the peer pressure placed on high achievers.

The second issue concerned the result that only 22 per cent of all the students considered that teachers 'succeed in making their classes interesting'. The students opened discussion with a tribute to the mythology of 'school'. It is a 'fact of life', they asserted, 'and it will always be like this'. On the other hand, they concluded that the matter of 'interest' was often

subject specific, though they insisted that the general result still held true. The students also agreed that some phases of class experience differed from and were less interesting than others. They agreed for instance that classes in grade 10 were less 'interesting' and less 'exciting' than in grade 11, just as grade 6 was compared with grade 7. The students acknowledged between them the 'big change' that occurred when moving up from primary (grade 6) to secondary (grade 7), or from junior to senior school. The students appeared thoughtful but made no comment when told that there was no statistical difference between age or grade levels for any of the results in this 'teachers' category. (Statistical difference had been explained to them at the beginning of the discussion sessions.) Finally the students were aware of the contrast in presentation between 'television' and 'teaching', but as a group made no comment upon the influence of television upon their experience of teaching.

Students Reactions: Quality of School Life
Results for this second dimension of the study were also presented to the students for comment and discussion. However, the more personal nature of much of the questions precluded the breadth of discussion which ensued in the more programmatic detail of the 'Perceptions of School' dimension. Also the fact that the data for this dimension were collected from present (1986 and 1987) students and didn't include opinion from outside years, may have been slightly inhibiting. Nevertheless some interesting points emerged which were representative of student reaction to the results.

General Satisfaction with School   This section comprised results for two domains, viz General and Positive Affects. The discussion focussed mainly on the result for the item 'School is a place where I get enjoyment from being there', which the students considered was a fairly representative item, their response to which indicated their attitude generally to school. They confirmed the analyzed result that in general students get satisfaction from being at school. When considering the contrasting result for grade 9 compared with all the other grades, the senior students explained that grade 9 presents a number of demands, not experienced in other grades, which influence their general response to school. The students considered grade 9 to be somewhat 'a peak working year', in which they have little room for simple enjoyment of school and in which they often have mixed emotions about being there. Also they are able to look forward, they said, with 'more knowledge' to the senior years and contrast their own academic experience in which they, unlike the senior grades, appear to have to work harder without their results appearing to count. Grade 9 students may experience the first disappointments at the academic levels in which they are placed. For them school was more

difficult to be satisfied with, they stated, and in grade 9 friends 'meant a lot'.

Relationship with Teachers Here the results expressed an ambivalence in the students' perceptions of teachers and the ways in which they relate to students. The students stated simply that this was bound to be so. When they considered the fact in the results that the lower the grades the less critical of teachers the students appeared to be, again they saw this as inevitable. The demands on them in the senior years are much greater. They have many subjects but relate to fewer teachers and they have to 'cope with higher levels of academic work in the matric (matriculation) years which is often not recognized by teachers'. The students seemed to consider that because the matriculation years were 'voluntary' their efforts were less likely to be recognized. On the other hand, the students considered that there were certain realities in the senior years which were 'a fact of life' — for example, that teachers didn't encourage senior students to express (their opinion) was a fact of life, they said, and in any case 'there's no time for opinions'. This latter question led to fairly intense discussion about the predominance of the examinations at matriculation, a 'system' they said which 'needs examining'.

Status and Identity The students' discussion of this area indicated the importance to them of the factors of being able to 'feel important' and to have feelings of self-worth. Furthermore this importance does not diminish over time and remains as strong in grade 12 as it appears to be in grade 7. Indeed one result indicated that grade 12 students felt less important in school than did students in all other grades. On the other hand the results showed that low achievers felt less important in school than did others, but generally considered school a place 'where other students listen to what I say'. The point here is that the area of feeling important and self-worthy, as well as being significant to students, was an area that held a great deal of ambiguity for students, which factors they confirmed in their discussion, but which they appeared to accept as part of the reality of school life.

Conclusion
Student discussion of this dimension — Quality of School Life — was interesting in its affirmation of the results. Students in their discussions focussed upon the very features which the results clearly showed were those which carried the positive attitudes towards school. In fact the effect was similar in their discussion of the results for the 'Perceptions of School' dimension of the Study. The sessions were significant for the fact that in virtually all the questions discussed there was no contradiction of the results, though there was often a broadening and deepening of the insights they had presented through the more empirical means of questionnaires. And, of course, the students expressed much satisfaction at

being given the chance to comment on the results and to discuss them with their fellow students. For our part as researchers, the reaction sessions proved to be thoroughly enjoyable and heartening occasions.

Teacher's Reactions: Perceptions of School
It is to be remembered than an interim report of results for the two dimensions of the Study was presented to principal and staff in a plenary meeting where teachers were free to discuss and comment on the results.

These reactions were more formally arranged because it was felt necessary to have teachers provide specific comment on areas most direct-ly related to their own teaching. Hence seven groups of teachers were formed to deal with the categories they felt most akin to. These discussed the relevant results and then presented written reports to the present researchers. In addition teachers were asked to comment, if they wished in writing, upon any or all of the other categories.

The teachers' reaction took the form of analytical comment upon the student responses in some detail and also included a number of recom-mendations as to ways in which the programme, and the school environ-ment (the quality of school life) might be improved for the students. The reactions are presented here in summary (though little has been omitted) and deal firstly with categories in the 'Perception of School' dimension then with the 'Quality of School Life'.

Expectations of School   The teaching staff were firstly concerned with the students' perception of an apparent gap between the importance placed upon education about jobs and careers and the low degree to which this was achieved. Whilst suggesting that students often do not take sufficient advantage of the school resources available in this area, the teachers made two other useful suggestions. One was to include career education earlier in the senior years (grades 7 and 8). The second was the possibility of testing students for aptitudes in grade 9 for those students expecting to leave in grade 10 and (again) at grade 11, the results of which testing should be available to students.

In view of the importance placed by students on their ability to organize their work and to work independently, the staff thought that a 'degree of negotiation' could well proceed between older and younger students in order to help them in becoming more responsible, more able to take 'initiative'. The teachers concluded that 'greater attention' needs to be paid to concepts of 'self-motivation and initiative' in the school.

Academic Aspects   There were two main concerns for discussion in this category. The first was the relationship of students' academic work to their possible careers. Teachers felt that a more structured career path was warranted for students in the matriculation years (grades 11 and 12). Specifically they considered that more precise follow-up of the work-

experience programme was needed. The second point related to data which indicated in this category a difference in perceptions between students from the Kingborough locality and students from all other areas. The teachers felt that such data should be remembered when the 'final picture' of this Study was drawn. (In fact as the evaluation proceeded the socio-economic variable did not present differences for most of the categories studied.)

Vocational Aspects Teachers firstly wondered whether students had understood some questions in this category. For instance they wondered what the statement, 'more vocational studies are required at higher school certificate (level) if students are to be prepared for life after school', 'meant' to the students (which presumably might cast some doubt on the high agreement of students with the statement). Also the staff felt that students did not value leisure education as a useful means of opening up a career. The teachers felt disenchanted by the fact that leisure education was not regarded as a 'vocational option' for students.

Other staff responses, not from within the discussion group, felt the results generally to be 'fairly straightforward' and 'what would be expected', (which was the view of the students when they responded to these results). However, there was general agreement by staff on two further points: firstly, that greater participation by grades 11 and 12 (the matriculation group) in the work-experience programme would be a worthwhile improvement. (This group also agreed, as had the first staff group, for more planned 'follow-up' of the work experience.) Secondly the area of the crafts could well include, they said, more activities of 'home-repairs' for all students and particularly for the low and middle achievers, who would be perhaps 'capable of (such) smaller tasks'. In fact the organization of weekend 'workshops' on particular areas of interest such as 'home maintenance' might, the staff suggested, be worth consideration.

Personal and Spiritual Development The results for this category reflected a diminishing of faith and practice in students. The teachers noted this and registered some concerns. In other words, the teachers did not merely accept the generally negative results as a temporary phase which maturity would rectify. Summarily, the teachers raised two main issues. First, they confirmed the crucial role played by the parents and considered that they as teachers might increasingly assist parents in 'playing their role'. Specifically this could be in areas such as 'biological education' (for informing students about pregnancy, etc). Gaining cooperation of parents in religious education should include their attendance at Mass and Reconciliation and clearly defined 'support' in matters of sexual morality and guidance within the teachings of the Church. Suggestions from

outside the discussion group included raising the level of religious education to that of other subjects such that it 'be examined and given an award'. Also it was suggested that the teachers themselves be given group lectures on 'the teachings of the church' and 'controversial topics', at least annually since 'there are differences of opinion among staff on Church teachings'.

The second main area which concerned the teachers related to the results which indicated the conflict being experienced by students between 'social acceptance' and 'religious moral standards', and also the apparent lesser significance of 'active (humanistic) service' and 'active worship'. The staff concluded that the school must aim for and assist children in maintaining a balance in such service. Taking all the input — from within and beyond this discussion group — there was general agreement among staff for a greater effort in assisting the students to be educated in all areas of their religious faith. Teachers often employed terms such as 'concern', 'saddening', 'worrying', hence the recommendations were based on conviction as much as rational assessment.

Aspects of Leadership and Sport   There were two main points of discussion under the term leadership. The teachers of this group firstly wondered what the students understood by leadership, given the 'discrepancy' in the results, which showed that three-quarters of the students agreed the school had helped them understand what leadership is, whilst just over half the students felt that the teachers were good models of leadership. They noted the evidence from the age/grade variable which showed that the older students were more positive about the teachers as leadership models, hence indicating, they said, that students' attitudes in this area show a 'marked difference as they mature'. The students themselves saw no conflict in the above results. On the other hand the teachers' comments reflected a very thoughtful and insightful discussion on the notion of leadership. They insisted, for instance, that understandings of leadership should be integral to religion and that verbally erudite dominant lessons which are 'purely anecdotal cliche-ridden discussions' do not 'allow room for new, more thoughtful leaders to emerge' nor do such discussion provide time for (necessary) personal reflection. There was little doubt that questions of leadership — what it is and how it should be encouraged — were high on the agenda of teachers concern.

In terms of sport and physical education, the teachers noted that there had ben an improved student response in the area of physical education over recent years, most students now stating that there were sufficient PE lessons. In this respect the staff noted that it would be 'interesting to assess' the timetabling of PE 'alongside' the subject of leisure. On the negative side the staff appeared sympathetic to the students perception that physical education was 'sport oriented' and that there was a 'strong emphasis on competitiveness'.

The Q-line The teachers in this discussion group made some useful comments. Firstly they thought it necessary to discount the perceptions of grade 10 who lacked experience of the 'Q-line' and whose observations could be based only on 'anecdote' or 'hearsay'. This is a fair point, though the researcher felt the questions needed to be addressed to students who were about to enter the 'Q-line' arrangement. Also perhaps it is not unusual for students of a next lower year to have some idea of a subject area, particularly one which is a popular alternative. The staff also questioned the reliability of the question which asked whether Q-line subjects were 'sufficiently practical'. The staff argued (correctly in the researchers' view) that a more precise definition of 'practical' was warranted. This is a case which illustrates part of the main purpose of the evaluation where the data and results may lead to further probing for more answers. This question could be asked again.

Teachers Predictably this group's statement of comment was one of the lengthiest and most detailed. In fact the teachers' comments were characterized by a lack of defensiveness and reflected a quite professional approach to analyzing the student perceptions of them and their teaching. In some instances their comments were almost exactly the same as the students. For instance, to the result that only 22 per cent of students regarded teachers as succeeding in 'making their classes interesting', the students and teachers agreed that this was among other things often a question of method rather than content, that 'what works for one class may not work for another', and that probably a real obstacle to 'interesting' classes was the priority of examinations.

In regard to the result that less than one third of the students considered that teachers were 'understanding of students' study problems', the teachers recognized this as a 'problem that needs to be addressed'. They proposed the establishment of a staff committee to 'outline avenues for improvement', and included such suggestions as a 'formal instruction session' for the HSC students at or near the beginning of the year in order to raise the consciousness of teacher and student expectations, possible areas of problems and study techniques. Also a senior student tutor scheme was suggested in which grade 12 students 'passed on information' to grade 11s and grade 11s to grade 10s, one period a week. In place of the class period all the staff could be involved for accommodating small groups to advise on general and specific study techniques, and one period a week could be timetabled for this. Also formal instruction in 'library and research' skills could be provided with an ongoing communication about this area provided for with a 'designated teacher'. Attention should be given, the staff stated, to a 'structured homework timetable', with 'restricted subjects for nightly homework'. Staff could complete a 'strategy' for each year group to 'aid student study skills'. These constituted a set of cogent suggestions which

in the researchers' opinion could prove of great general value to the outcomes of student work.

In another sense the student responses appeared to alert the teachers to their continuing need to be kept 'abreast of progressing educational theory and methodology'. This was applicable, for example, to the extremely low agreement of students to the statement that 'teachers try to make their classes entertaining rather than useful'. They related this to the indication in the results that only few of the teachers (22 per cent) in the students' minds 'succeeded' in making their classes 'interesting'. The teachers themselves appeared to perceive the significance of the entertainment industry which presents to the young the vision of instant gratification, instant knowledge, packaged in an instantly accessible form. The teachers' expression of a desire for updating, we perhaps may infer, reflects the understanding that teaching is fraught with obstacles raised within the society which teachers are trying to serve.

Teachers Reactions: The Quality of School Life
General Satisfaction with School (this category combines the two listed formally in the research as General Affect and Positive Affect). The teachers felt that the opposing responses of satisfaction and complaint about school was an 'inconsistency typical of the age group and not a fault of the school'. However, it would be fair to say that the results don't actually reflect inconsistency but rather that students are generally satisfied with school. Although some students have 'complaints', very few of these students have strong negative attitudes towards their school life. The result for the category of Negative Affect, discussed next, supports this view.

Negative Attitudes Towards School   The teachers firstly considered that the term 'alienation' was inappropriate for the descriptor. (The researchers are inclined to agree, but it is the term employed in the standardized instrument of the research and we were bound to use it.) Nevertheless the teachers did confirm the results as a 'true indication of the school'. The very little sense of 'alienation' felt by the students towards the school would be due to the fact, the teachers said, that St Marys College 'generates a feeling of care and concern for all' and there were bound to be students who were, as people in any group, 'lonely' or 'depressed'.

Status and Identity (two categories)   The teachers expressed concern at the high percentage of students who did not find school 'a place where they feel confident' or '(are) treated with respect'. They found this result 'disturbing' in fact and felt that ways should be found to change the situation. The staff also considered that the evident lack in feelings of a sense of status and self-worth (described in these categories) points to 'a need to cater more for low achievers'. Certainly the results overall for

these categories indicate that low achievers appear less secure in terms of the 'quality' of their school experience.

Teachers   Given the result that more than a third of the students felt unable to talk to teachers, or question the things teachers say, about their work, the teachers conceded that more 'needs to be done to explain to (students) what is being done with their work'. This is an important recognition by the teachers of the need for a communicative clarity and openness, and if 'more' were to be done in this area the outcomes would surely prove of long-term benefit. The staff saw a contradiction in the results which on the one hand showed that more than 80 per cent of students considered teachers 'fair and just' whereas less than half (46 per cent) of the students felt teachers 'treat(ed) all students equally'. The teachers in the discussion group thought that the word 'equally' may have been variously interpreted by students. The discussion group concluded that it was not the teachers' aim to treat students equally due to the fact of differing abilities which require different responses. Nevertheless the staff generally agreed that students of lower achievement need to be well identified so that 'careful' even 'special' attention may be given to them. The same principle ought, they said, to apply to students in all achievement groupings, but in this as in the categories of Status and Identity the needs of low achievers were raised as of specific concern to the staff. Finally there was a general note that although students appeared generally to regard students favourably more time needs to be gained in order to 'free' teachers for 'interviews with students regarding their work'.

Adventure and Opportunity   In both these categories staff appeared generally satisfied that the results reflected what teachers ought to be achieving. Yet the fact that 12 per cent of students were not 'interested in the work (they) do in class', suggested that teachers might still 'aim higher'.

   This teacher group also looked closely at the summary of interviews under 'personal and spiritual development' and 'leadership and sport' and found 'agreement on all points'. Their conclusions here were perhaps symbolic or representative of a critically rational reflection of the results generally, when they stated:

> Religious education should not, indeed, cannot be piecemeal, anecdotal and ill-informed. No worthwhile discussion on moral issues or religious beliefs and practices can take place unless on a firm foundation of education and knowledge. Without this knowledge all that occurs is self-opinionated, and often self-serving chit chat during which those persons with self-confidence, loud voices and momentarily strong opinions make themselves heard to the exclusion of people whose opinions, often better based and formulated, are therefore never heard.

Also the teacher group echoed the conclusion of the group dealing with the leadership category as they concluded: 'A willingness to make oneself the dominant member of a group is a deceptive sign of leadership, confusing as it does, true leadership with dominating character'.

Concluding Comment

The teachers' reactions raised quite specific concerns recognized by them, but also considered these concerns in ways that enabled them to produce strategies and ideas which provided a basis for substantive action. This was a characteristic of the teacher discussion and suggested that their meetings had been productive for themselves and their work, in addition to a form of useful validation for the researchers.

Chapter 5

The Concept of Vision

Introduction

Chapter 3 discussed the role of evaluation within the broader context of school improvement and Chapter 4 described and presented the results of a 'real' evaluation conducted at St Mary's College. The process of evaluation forces a school community to focus on essentials. Indeed, the essence of evaluation assumes some scale by which one can measure, weigh or judge these priorities. Evaluation, in this broad sense, requires a school community to consider its concept of the educational good — its vision of the ideal. A school's vision encapsulates its course for the future; and an evaluation measures and monitors the extent to which the school remains true to its educational course. As schools today battle the turbulent seas of societal change, it is crucial that their educational course be frequently and accurately monitored. This chapter explores the latest theoretical developments in such educational chart making — the role of vision in education. A compelling educational vision is the vital, driving force of school improvement. Here we define and illustrate the ways in which educational vision provides the guiding light which gives sense, purpose and direction to all aspects of the school's informal and formal curriculum. Presented in this chapter is the special vision of St Mary's College which provides the backdrop to an educational drama in which the authors were fortunate to play a part. It is an example which also provides the background for discussions, in later chapters, of social capital, school management and the effective implementation of change. The St Mary's vision was also the focal point which led the authors to spend three years investigating, in one Catholic school, the ways by which we are able to measure the extent to which an educational vision has become a school reality and, having measured the present, how a school community can work towards making its educational dream come true for the future.

The Nature of Educational Vision

'A vision is a blueprint of a desired state. It is an image of a preferred condition that we work to achieve in the future' (Sheive and Schoenheit, 1987, p. 94). It is a quality of leadership, for to lead is to communicate a vision. Building on the seminal work of Starratt (1986), Burns (1978) and others, Bennis and Nanus (1985) interviewed ninety people whom their colleagues identified as exceptional leaders. From their interviews emerged four key themes relating to vision and leadership. First, outstanding leaders direct their attention to and focus others' attention on a vision. Second, they communicate that vision through symbols, myths, legends and actions. Third, outstanding leaders position themselves in their field to maximize their organization's strengths and communicate the vision. And fourth, outstanding leaders reflect in their own person the underlying values and beliefs of the vision.

Writing about vision in educational leadership, Starratt (1986) declares that a vision will remain unfulfilled if it goes no further than the leader. Rather the vision must be 'owned' by teachers, parents and students. A vision must be communicated — shared in such a way that the people within the organization adopt the vision for themselves and make it their own. But, communicating a vision does not happen by circulating a dry, boring 'strategic' planning or policy statement. People do not become enthusiastic about statistics and projections. They do respond to the values underlying a particular vision. They do respond to leaders who are articulate, enthusiastic, sincere and feel strongly about what they are doing. In many respects a vision is caught, rather than taught. A vision which is not shared will not be fulfilled.

Starratt also makes the point that vision is not something to be put into a speech and brought out for special occasions. Indeed, the vision of the school must be reflected in the day-to-day activities of the organization. Vision must pervade the standard operational procedures, general policies and all aspects of the school. The vision must be such an integral part of things that it continues even if certain people leave the school. It is important to realize that vision is not some abstract philosophy which is drafted by a few people at the top. An effective vision reflects a collaborative consensus, a unification of values which forms the foundation of day-to-day decisions which must be taken in light of an over-arching and shared expectation of where the school is going.

In order to lead with vision, leaders must be active and forward thinking, rather than reactive and absorbed in the past. They must be passionately committed and feel deeply about, love, what they are doing. Leaders must also think more about leadership and make the time to contemplate and envision their future. Unfortunately, school leaders have tended to be so absorbed in the management of the here and now as to

have given comparatively little thought to a vision for the future. Accordingly, British educator, David Hargreaves (1988) has spoken of the pressing need for school leaders to be more holistic, to look to the future and engage in forward planning. Educational vision then is about the need to reflect on, and plan for, the future, rather than merely reacting to, and fretting about, the past. It is about the power of dreams, the might of metaphor and the almost super-human potential unleashed by a unification of values and purpose.

How Does an Educational Vision Come About?

Excellent schools, companies and other organizations are characterized by leaders with vision, see e.g., Lightfoot, 1983; Rutter *et al.*, 1979. Yet, despite the fact that there have been several studies depicting leaders of vision, we know very little about the sources of vision, just as we know little about the source of dreams. Indeed, the answer to the question posed here is as fundamental as the nature of man himself. Another reason why so little is known about the origins of vision undoubtedly lies in the fact that, like the Nile, there are thousands, maybe millions, of tributaries which feed into the current of one's life. One's vision often evolves from a rich variety of sources — influential people in early childhood, special moments and events, both planned and accidental, literature, music, the qualities of a particular culture or sub-culture, and a thousand other causal factors. For world-renowned scientist, humanist and Pulitzer-prizewinning author, Rene Dubos, for example, his mother and school teacher were the two persons who influenced him most during his early years. Of his mother, he writes:

> In the village where I grew up I remember distinctly a conversation with my mother one evening while I was helping her to wash the dishes in the kitchen when I was approximately ten years of age. As she frequently did, she expressed her desire that I move into a broader life than what she had known, not only more prosperous but also more intellectually rewarding. My mother had received little formal education, having left school to work as a seamstress at the age of twelve, but this was a time when primary education was excellent all over France ... Late in that particular evening, she opened the *Petit Dictionnaire Larousse*, the only learned book in our home, at the special section devoted to the 'Grandes Ecoles'. This provided both of us with material for daydreaming as to what my future should be. I do not know whether she had a clear notion of what the Grandes Ecoles stood for but it is certain that my attempts at a life of scholarship have

their origin in her attitude, not only on that particular evening, but throughout my teenage years. Whenever I have been successful as a scholar or otherwise, there comes to my mind the pink pages at the end of the Larousse dictionary where, for the first time, I read the brief descriptions of the Grandes Ecoles and thus obtained a somewhat concrete image of a world larger in scope and more sophisticated than the one in which I had lived. (1981, p. 76)

The biographies of great visionary leaders like Martin Luther King Jr, Mother Teresa and Mahatma Gandhi, also suggest that the origins of vision are both variable and numerous, sometimes focussing on painful experiences; at other times special people in one's life; at other times still, evolving gradually over a course of years. However, a common thread running through every great and powerful vision is that it:

> has its roots in those deep, core meanings about human life, its dignity, grandeur, beauty, value, etc. It tends to be expressed in myth, poetry, metaphor. It is concerned with values such as freedom, honour, selflessness, altruism, loyalty, devotion to fatherland (or to some community) integrity and dignity of the person, equality, peace and harmony among peoples, the rule of law, the elevation of reason and civility, wisdom, self governance, courage, character, a perfect performance, creative expression, harmony with nature, etc. (Starratt, 1988, p. 3)

Categories or Levels of Vision

In their study of 'Vision and the Work Life of Educational Leaders', Sheive and Schoenheit (1987) identify distinct categories of vision. One category is that of 'organizational vision' — desired future states of the excellent school. The outstanding principals they studied possessed personalized, highly detailed visions of excellent schools and effective schooling. However, a second category of vision, expressed by some principals, went beyond organizational vision to a wider category which Sheive and Schoenheit (1987, pp. 97–8) labelled 'universal vision'. These leaders, in addition to their personalized vision of excellence, devoted considerable effort to the attainment of a larger, more universal vision, for example, in terms of the concept of equity of educational opportunity.

Other categories of vision involve an individual's career path, the future of a particular department or subject, the future of the school's extra curricular programme, a vision of the football programme, the building development plan, and so on. Unfortunately, these other visions have not always been viewed in relation to the larger vision of the school

as a whole. For example, Hargreaves (1988) has noted that staff development plans have usually focussed on the needs, goals and vision of the individual staff member. He argues that staff development should be primarily focussed around the needs of the school so that individual and school visions become one.

While Sheive and Schoenheit's analysis suggests that educational vision operates at different levels, it is important to stress that a school, in order to be effective, needs a fusion of these visions; a philosophical coherence, an agreement on fundamental values. Such a fusion will establish the connection between the values, needs and motives of teachers, students and staff, on the one hand, and the desired vision of school on the other (W Greenfield, 1987).

The St Mary's College Vision

As a result of such studies as Coleman and Hoffer's *Public and Private Schools: The Impact of Communities* (1987) and Lesko's *Symbolizing Society* (1988), the unique vision of Catholic schools have recently been the focus of much attention. For this reason, the authors present here a detailed statement of the exceptional educational vision of St Mary's College. We do not maintain that other schools, even other Catholic schools, should necessarily be influenced by the specifics of the St Mary's vision. Indeed, each school community (principal, staff, parents and students) must work out, develop and forge their own unique vision of education which reflects their particular circumstances. At the same time, however, a current example of a vision statement which is articulate, value-laden, celebratory and future-looking might prove useful to a school community considering or reconsidering its vision. Thus the point is not simply the Christian ideology with which many readers might not sympathize. It is to emphasize the manner in which the clarity of a school's consensus values can be the basis for a vision statement which has persuasiveness, integrity and rigour.

St Mary's College Vision Statement

As an educational community sponsored by the Catholic church and the Presentation Sisters of Tasmania, St Mary's College contributes to the schooling of young Australians, particularly, though not entirely, those of the Catholic faith. St Mary's aims to provide an excellent education which meets the requirements of the appropriate governmental authorities but also takes into account the significance that Christian values and the Christian faith tradition may have within education (*The Catholic School*, paragraph 3). Therefore, the vision of St Mary's is to ensure that

as a Catholic school it is in all aspects firmly established upon Christian principles. Furthermore, the College aims to help each student become all that it is possible for her to become — spiritually, intellectually, socially and physically.

Given that the personal development of the students is based on the Christian Gospel way of life — faith and the fullness of human living — the particular aims of the College are:

a) to assist in the introduction of the students to the knowledge and appreciation of the gift of faith;
b) to assist students' development as prayerful persons within the Christian community, especially by their participation in the Mass and the Sacraments; and
c) to assist students in their total development as persons.

Like other Catholic schools, St Mary's aims to create for the school community an atmosphere enlivened by the Gospel spirit of freedom, compassion and charity.

St Mary's College determines to help the young person in such a way that the development of her own personality will be matched by the growth of the new creation which she became by Christian Baptism. The College further strives to relate all human culture eventually to the Christian news of salvation, so that the light of faith will illumine the knowledge which the students gradually gain of themselves, the world, of life and of mankind.

St Mary's strives to be a place where young people may exercise their sacred right to be; to weigh moral values with an upright conscience, to embrace them by personal choice and to know and love God more adequately (St Mary's College Prospectus).

Values and Beliefs Inherent in the School's Vision

The vision of St Mary's College is shared by the students, teachers, families and wider parish group whom together comprise the school community. It is a view of a desired future state towards which the St Mary's community is aiming. The extensive curriculum evaluation was partly designed to determine how well the school's vision has been actualized and what future steps might be necessary in order for the school to move closer to that vision's fulfilment. Starratt (1988), proposed a theory of leadership which is described as 'communal institutionalizing of a vision'. 'Vision', he says,

includes beliefs about how children develop into full human beings, about the variety and depth of learning which human

beings are capable of, about the future the young will face in their adult years. Much more is the leader's vision rooted in meanings and experiences of human life that are very basic, very cultural, that touch upon the essence of what it means to be a human person, upon the fundamental building blocks of human community. (pp. 16–17)

It is in this sense that beliefs are inherent in the St Mary's vision. Such beliefs would include the following:

a) There is no such thing as a value-free or value-neutral education. Education and leadership in education are equally 'value charged' (Greenfield, 1986). The school is a 'moral institution' (Greenfield, 1987) and schools must address such moral (and in this case religious) questions as: Is there a God? What is the good life? Is there freedom? Is there punishment of evil deeds? Is there certain knowledge? What is a good society? (Bloom, 1987). The Catholic Church has a rich philosophical, social, historical and literary tradition which provides a wealth of insight to these questions. Moreover, it is a tradition which is still evolving as each generation interprets the faith in the light of its particular cultural and contemporary problems.

b) Education is a product of partnership and participation, the outcome of concerted efforts by school, home and parish. A strong sense of purpose unites the endeavours of these three entities. Education is not a duty nor a developmental task that rests on or is secured by teachers alone (Simmons, 1985).

c) Inherent in a Christian or Catholic philosophy is a sense of optimism and hope, a celebration of life. Neither a nation nor a person can achieve a good life with a disposition towards cynicism, fatalism and despair. The Resurrection of Christ and its message of joy to the world is the central doctrine of faith. Moreover, the long history of the Church is eloquent testimony to an eternal optimism even in the face of the severest persecution (Dubos, 1981, pp. 134–5).

d) An attendant corollary of optimism is the perspective that there is no such thing as a problem without a gift for you in its hands. A problem is an opportunity to grow. As the early martyrs showed, adversity can be the greatest teacher and the seed from which a deeper faith will grow.

e) Developing one's talents to the full and using them in the service of others is an important tenet underlying the school's philosophy. 'Teach us to number our days and recognize how few they are; help us to spend them as we should' (Psalm 90:12). The school begins from the principle that its educational programme is intentionally directed to the growth of the whole person.

f) St Mary's College is part of the Catholic Church, but is also an instrument of society. It must help develop persons who are both re-

sponsible and inner-directed, capable of choosing freely in conformity with their conscience. It must be a community whose values are communicated through the genuine interpersonal relationships of its members, and through both individual and corporate adherence to its vision.

g) The St Mary's College motto, 'God is the fountain of all knowledge. Mary is our Mother', implies that teaching and education constitute a sacred trust. These are 'saturated with significance' (Starratt, p. 18). Also, the examples of Mary, after whom the school is named, and of Nano Nagle, the foundress of the Presentation Order of Nuns who founded and administered the College, serves as a special inspiration to the community in leading their lives, in obedience to God's will, and in striving always to bring dignity to all that is done; doing the most ordinary things in extraordinary ways.

h) The fundamental aim of teaching is towards the individual students' assimilation of Christian values. It does not stop at an integration of faith and culture, but aims to lead the student to a personal integration of faith and life.

i) St Mary's aims to teach its pupils to discern their Creator in the voice of the universe. He is revealed for their sakes, and so that they may better serve both God and their fellow man. In the daily life of the school, each student learns that she is called to be a living witness of God's love for people by the way she acts. Each person must know that she is part of the salvation history which has Christ, the Saviour of the World, as its ultimate goal.

j) In order to maintain and enhance its Catholic ethos, St Mary's College requires the best qualified teachers possible for religion. Moreover, religion must not be reduced to a mere subject to be taught in the curriculum. ('Faith is caught, not taught.') Religious concerns must of necessity pervade all aspects of the school.

k) St Mary's is a community, promoting a faith relationship with Christ in whom all values find fulfilment. Faith, however, is principally assimilated through contact with people whose daily lives bear witness to it. Faith is born and grows inside community. It must also be continually fed and stimulated by its source of life, the saving Word of Christ who is God Incarnate. This Word is expressed in the Sacred Scripture, in tradition, especially liturgical and sacramental tradition, and in the lives of people, past and present, who bear witness to that Word.

It is beyond the scope or intention of this book to present a full statement of Catholic doctrine, but these key beliefs should at least portray a small fragment of the rich and intricate tapestry of faith which provides the backdrop for the St Mary's College vision of education. Again the point here is the ideological unity which gives meaning to the school's statement of vision.

Other Examples of Vision Statements

St Virgil's College Mission Statement:
A Vision by any other Name

Another form of vision statement is expressed in terms of management literature, *viz*, a 'mission' statement (Brown, 1984). Below is an example of a school mission statement from another Catholic school, St Virgil's College, which is an all-boys school run by the Christian Brothers. Guided by a team of outside facilitators the community of St Virgil's, after many meetings and much discussion, formulated a seventeen–page mission statement, part of which follows.

GIVING MEANING TO OUR MISSION

Preamble
'Like other schools ... Catholic schools are called to a renewal of purpose, and some to re-organization' (*To Teach as Jesus Did*).

This Mission Statement acknowledges traditions and values of our past, the perceptions and interests of our present situation, and within that framework, attempts to articulate a vision of the future in terms of these issues:

* Christian identity
* Community
* Development
* Curriculum

It is the culmination of valuable contributions of time, effort and interest by members of the College community over the past fifteen months....

The document's importance is enhanced considerably because of the involvement of the total school community — parents, students, teachers and administrators.

'Giving Meaning to our Mission' is welcomed as a significant contribution to the future development of St Virgil's College.

The Church's best hope for its schools in the 80s and 90s is that they be educative communities which are respectful of personal dignity and in which all members can learn and be evangelized.

Evangelization is the bringing of the Good News of the Kingdom to the people of God on their journey towards salvation. This is what we ask for in the Lord's Prayer when we pray 'Thy Kingdom come': the need we acknowledge for God's power to be experienced as a strength both in our personal lives, and in the life we share with others. Where this need is consciously acknowledged in a group, such as the school

community, there is an openness to build the values of the Gospel into the fabric of that group, that is, into the life of the school.

The process devised to assist school communities develop a mission statement aimed to help achieve three objectives:

1 To explore the values and understandings that hold the group together — the strengths of the group.
2 To become consciously and critically aware of the Gospel values alive in the group.
3 To initiate some long-range plans for the development of the school as a 'gospel'-oriented educative community.

There are many values in the Gospel and each age and culture takes to heart that set of values which seems most important to conditions of time and place. The Christian Brothers as part of the Church highlight the need to be an evangelizing presence to the poor and the disadvantaged; as well, their 200 year old service to young people has been built on the principle that religious development is the foundation of all human dignity.

Edmund Rice was a wealthy business man of Waterford, Ireland, at the turn of the eighteenth century. At the age of twenty five his young wife died leaving him a daughter to care for in a special way. Though grief-stricken he continued his business, attended to his need for prayer, was a loving father to his child and with generosity went out to the poor of his city. Touched by the ignorance and the state of hopelessness of the youth of Waterford he began a new life dedicated to their service. To further that mission he founded the Christian Brothers in 1802.

The Church today missions us to explore the values of justice, reconciliation, peace, solidarity with the needy, community and participation as vital to the 'coming of the kingdom'.

The basic question in School Development is 'How can the school most effectively respond to the movement of the Spirit in our times?' The question can only be answered after a process of reflection. The shape of a school's mission statement will provide some response to this pressing query.

Mission understanding
St Virgil's College, founded in 1911, is an evolving Christian community committed to the ministry of Catholic education. The generous support, often in hardship, of parents, students and staff in the formative years of the College, has given rise to a strong sense of ongoing tradition. The community witnessed the spirit of Edmund Rice through the hard work, sacrifices and total commitment to the Church of the Christian Brothers.

We acknowledge that we live in times of dynamic changes in society,

in education and in the Church. New and different needs and expectations are emerging. The College community is being challenged to respond in a positive and visible manner to the changes being thrust upon us. In these years of transition, we value the increasing importance of lay teachers and the greater responsibility they are being called to accept in the mission of the Church. We value more highly a discipline based on the Gospel value of justice. We seek to promote student participation in all aspects of school life that contribute to the development of each person to his/her full potential. The need to widen our curriculum making it more relevant to the changing needs of students is becoming more evident. We see the need to offer more opportunities in life skills. We affirm the need to instil in our College community of students, staff and parents, the courage to bear witness through example, integrity, openness and faithfulness and by challenging values contrary to those of the Gospel of Jesus Christ. Given our Catholic heritage, we realize the importance, and the inherent value, of celebrating life and faith events in community. We see the need to provide for times of reflection and evaluation to help us remain true to our Catholic tradition based on the Gospel values of compassion, justice, trust, forgiveness and peace.

Moving into the future, we recognize that St Virgil's College has an obligation to serve especially, but not exclusively, the Catholic community. We believe in reaching out to the students of all socio-economic levels, but with Christ as our model and being inspired by the example of Edmund Rice, the founder of the Christian Brothers, we hold a special concern for the socially and materially disadvantaged.

We acknowledge the decisive role of parents as partners in education, and students as the focus of our educational endeavours. Hence, we seek to embrace a collegial and collaborative model of decision making involving parents, students and teachers.

Again, we may or may not empathize with the religious or ideological expression in this example. Nevertheless, we may note the consistency of significance given to a consensus and unity of values by the whole school community which form the basis of a rich educational vision.

An Example of a Vision of a Tertiary Institution:
The Gold Coast College of Advanced Education, Queensland, Australia

The Gold Coast College of Advanced Education established in 1986 is one of Queensland's newest colleges. It will increase participation in higher education by serving the needs of a unique and internationally acclaimed centre of tourism and business enterprise in the south-eastern part of the State ... As a college of advanced education, it is committed to providing a diverse range

of high-quality educational programmes with a strong vocational emphasis. Given the Gold Coast's national and international role as a major Pacific rim centre of tourism, the College's courses and continuing education programmes will have a particular orientation to a tourist and international setting. It will also serve industrial, technological and information-based developments in the region and State.

The Gold Coast College of Advanced Education seeks to develop an intellectually stimulating, enterprising and caring environment. Accordingly, it aims to extend educational opportunities by adopting innovative approaches to staffing, to the design of courses, to teaching strategies, scheduling of programmes, and the generation and utilization of resources. It will prepare graduates who are competent, educated people, able to grasp opportunity and capable of assuming leadership in commercial, cultural and community endeavours, consistent with the entrepreneurial spirit of the region. The enterprising approach of the College will also be reflected through the establishment of consultancy centres providing opportunities for its staff and students to make contributions through research and development projects. (Gold Coast College of Advanced Education, Student Handbook, 1988)

The Gold Coast College's educational vision is thus encapsulated in its well defined sense of the nature of its task as a unique educational institution. Its vision also incorporates the nature of the people and region it serves and its values of shared endeavour with the surrounding community.

Other Expressions of Vision

These three ideological statements incorporated the visions of those educational institutions. They are formally articulated yet thoroughly value based, as are all educational institutions. However, it is important to realize that a vision can be expressed in many ways, a formal vision statement, being but one of the many. It might also take the form of a scenario of the perfect school, the ideal classroom, the great coach, the best English lesson and so on. Visions can also be expressed in traditions, myths, rituals, stories, legends, song, symbol and, of course, one of the most powerful statements of vision, action or conduct. The most effective leaders use a combination of these to ensure that the vision permeates the whole school and is shared by the entire school community (Starratt, 1986; 1988; Peters and Austin, 1985). As these vision statements show, however, no matter how it is expressed, vision is about a future sense of direction and purpose. It is also founded upon a bedrock of fundamental

values and beliefs about the nature of man and what is important in life. Therein lies both its mystery and its power. Let us now probe deeper into the mystery and power of vision and examine its role in the overall context of school improvement.

From Educational Vision to School Reality: The Role of Leadership

Earlier, in discussing the nature of vision, we indicated that an educational vision may not be realized if it does not go beyond the leader. We also intimated what is implied in a leader's possession and sharing of this vision. Now we must answer the question: How does a vision become reality? We begin by discussing the leader's role in this crucial transformation.

An educational vision becomes reality when it illuminates the ordinary events of school life with dramatic significance; is articulated in compelling ways by school leaders, and is shared with colleagues; when it becomes implanted in the structures and processes of the organization; when day-to-day decisions are made in light of it; and when all members of the organization celebrate the vision in ritual, ceremonies and art forms (Starratt, 1988, p. 15). Similarly, employing Sergiovanni's (1984) theoretical framework, such vision becomes reality when all the forces of leadership merge to ensure that the culture, symbols, educational concerns, human relationships and organizational structures all stem from and reflect that vision.

Sheive and Schoenheit (1987, pp. 99–103) provide a useful outline of the steps which leaders take to actualize their visions, a topic treated more elaborately in Chapter 8. First, leaders see the vision, a fusion of strongly held values reflecting a desired future state. Second, leaders, through a process of conscious reflection, commit themselves to the vision; they own it. Third, the leader articulates the vision and shares it with others. The private vision becomes a public one. Fourth, they develop strategies to work toward the fulfilment of vision. And fifth, they mobilize people. They search for and reward those who most strongly share their vision and who themselves become visionary leaders. They fire others up and invest time, money and energy in developing skills, creating and taking every opportunity to move the school toward the realization of its vision. Although these steps are stated separately, in the reality of the school, the exercise of visionary leadership involves both complex and over-lapping activities (W. Greenfield, 1987, p. 12). As will be explained in the chapter on change, there are many interrelated causal factors which are involved in bringing about school improvements which work towards the fulfilment of a particular educational vision.

Finally, visionary leadership is not a one-way process which eman-

ates from the principal down to subordinates. As W. Greenfield (1987, p. 16) states:

> Operationally, leadership is a reciprocal process that depends for its success on the capacity of the principal to 'tap' latent levels of motivation and morality among teachers, to *engage* teachers in the pursuit of increasingly higher levels of motivation and morality such that both the principal and the teacher are transformed in the pursuit of higher ends.

The Reflection of Vision in School Life: The Role of Organizational Culture

In order to understand how a school's vision can be reflected in the day-to-day running of the school, we must further understand the concept of organizational culture. Over the last few years there has been a distinct move away from quantitative rational models of school management and towards more qualitative and dynamic models of school leadership. Peters and Austin (1985), Deal (1985 and 1987), Kelley and Bredeson (1987), and others, stress the importance of understanding the school's symbols and culture as a prerequisite to making a more effective school. Deal (1985) explains that:

> Culture is an expression that tries to capture the informal, implicit — often unconscious — side of business or any human organization. Although there are many definitions of the term, culture in everyday usage is typically described as 'the way we do things around here.' It consists of patterns of thought, behaviour, and artifacts that symbolize and give meaning to the workplace. Meaning derives from the elements of culture: shared values and beliefs, heroes and heroines, ritual and ceremony, stories, and an informal network of cultural players. (p. 605)

An effective vision permeates the culture, the very bones of the organization. Let us explore how this happens. In the process perhaps we shall see why culture is so important to the transformation of vision into reality, and thus to school improvement. To do so we next discuss some of the individual components of school culture. While the analytical framework is derived from Deal, the examples emanate from the authors' experience of St Mary's College.

Shared Values and Beliefs

The heart and soul of any effective organization is a system of shared beliefs and values. Such shared beliefs and values provide the fuel for an

effective vision, focus the organization's goals and energize a community to action. In the case of St Mary's College, whose vision statement was presented earlier, the central place of Catholic values and religious beliefs is evident everywhere. The majority of staff members are practising Catholics. Religious studies is a compulsory subject for every student and every grade. Each morning every class begins with a prayer. Mass is offered to students each week. Holy Days of the Church are carefully planned and celebrated by the whole school community. Graduations, student government structure, school rules for student conduct, assemblies — all aspects of student life are given a religious focus. Religious art work, literature and messages are in abundance on school walls, in mottos and in school literature. Academic subjects, music, student groups, drama and other formal and informal curriculum offerings frequently have a religious theme. Indeed, so strong is the commitment to Catholic values that these are not confined to school hours. These expressions of a particular set of values are expected to be practised in the lives of staff and students outside, as well as inside, the school. A similar dominance of religious values was found by Kelley and Bredeson (1987) in their study of St Mary's Catholic High School in the United States.

Heroes and Heroines and Stories

Deal found that 'effective businesses anoint and celebrate heroes and heroines ... whose thoughts, deeds, and personal qualities represent core company values' (1985, p. 606). Accordingly, a vision requires heroes and heroines, human beings who exemplify the vision in action. Organizational members need someone to look up to, to emulate, to model. The Catholic Church, of which St Mary's College (Australia) and St Mary's Catholic High School (USA) are a part, is rich in heroes and heroines — the life of Jesus, and those of the Apostles and Saints — whose feast days are celebrated in the Mass and on special occasions. The vision of St Mary's is especially reflected in Mary, the mother of Jesus, and after whom the school is named. Statutes and portrayals of Mary abound and her life example is held out as an ideal model for all to follow. Finally, St Mary's College (Australia) is a Presentation Order school. The Presentation sisters were founded by Ireland's Nano Nagel and her story of dedication, prayer and concern for the less fortunate is often repeated and symbolized. Thus two of the sporting houses into which the school is divided are Nagel and Presentation.

A vision is also spread by stories. These will include stories about the lives of Jesus and the Saints, as mentioned above, but it will also involve other stories about past and present principals, parents, students and teachers. These stories relate positive episodes about the philosophy, values and past successes of the school community.

Ritual

Studies by Deal and Kennedy (1982), Peters and Waterman (1982) and others have also found that successful companies have distinctive rituals of work, management and personal exchange, (Deal 1985, p. 606). For Catholic schools, like St Mary's College, the nature of these rituals is greatly influenced by the wider Catholic Church to which the school belongs. This explains, for example, the great similarity between the St Mary's High School of the Kelley and Bredesen study in the United States and St Mary's College in Australia. Other aspects of ritual, how-ever, will be influenced by the fact that a school is a particular order school which will have a special character distinct from other schools. In the case of St Mary's College in Australia, for example, the fact that Nano Nagel originally established Presentation schools to provide educa-tion for the poor and disadvantaged, means that Presentation schools have a policy that no Catholic child will be turned away because of an inability to pay. Also the school places special emphasis on raising money for the missions and other worthy causes — again a reflection of its founder and church community influence. Finally, still other aspects of ritual will be impressed by the nature of the school leader. Sr Barbara Amott, the Principal of St Mary's College, believes in and values, among other things, a tightly-run, well disciplined school which emphasizes high achievement standards, especially in academic work. The result is a tidy, orderly and comparatively competitive school environment which would be contrasted with less competitive, more informal and less orderly Catholic schools in the same region. The point is that the school's vision is reflected in its rituals.

Ceremony

'Effective companies have regular ceremonies that dramatize and re-inforce core values and beliefs' (Deal, 1985, p. 607). The ceremonies (graduation, assemblies, retreats, feast days, etc) of St Mary's College have already been referred to above. The St Mary's College graduation, however, is particularly worthy of mention, because state schools seem to observe nothing like it. Briefly, the graduation ceremony culminates, for most of the students, thirteen years of Catholic education. As with other major celebrations, the occasion is celebrated with a Mass, but with the difference that more work, planning, care, pain and love go into this occasion than almost any other. The students plan all the readings and songs. The whole school practises the music (sometimes taking ordinary class time to do so) to make sure that the whole community know their roles and can play their parts with understanding and feeling. The Mass is usually celebrated by the Archbishop and attended by numerous priests,

past students, parents and grandparents (the latter of whom are often past graduates of St Mary's). The Mass (affectionately called the 'tissue' Mass because of all the emotion) is followed by a reception where the graduating students are presented with special mementos from the school. Also the Principal and head prefect make speeches which summarize the year, the vision of that particular graduating class and its contribution to the 120 plus year history of the College. It is a beautiful ceremony and one which aptly reflects the school's vision and the commitment of the people who comprise the school community.

Informal Network of Cultural Players

'In most strongly performing companies there is an informal collection of people whose chief function is to keep watch over the culture, to carry and reinforce the values' (Deal, 1985, p. 607). Two aspects of St Mary's College make this feature of its culture especially powerful: 1) the fact that the College is situated in Hobart, Tasmania, the capital of an island state of Australia; and 2) the fact that the school is one of the oldest in Australia, and has been attended by many of the parents, grandparents and even great grandparents of present students. Thus, if a St Mary's student (who is easily identified by the school uniform) misbehaves on the bus or while in town, or even out of uniform and after school hours, the behaviour is likely to be noticed by someone connected with the College. Those 'someones' (the cultural gatekeepers) inform the Principal and she takes the appropriate action. Parents, too, are a major factor in this cultural network through their membership in the wider Catholic community. Indeed, so powerful is this feature of Catholic schools that Coleman and Hoffer (1987) argue it is the main reason such schools are so successful in maintaining a high standard of education. This 'social capital' feature of Catholic schools is accordingly the focus of discussion in Chapter 6.

An educational vision, to be effective, must therefore be inextricably bound up with the school's culture, some of the elements of which are stories, heroes and heroines, rituals, and ceremonies. Indeed, the culture of the Catholic Church 'may well be one of the best organizational models extant' (Beare, 1987). As Deal and Kennedy conclude:

> ... The Catholic Church has something in common with IBM, Mary Kay, McDonald's, the Polaris Service, the US Forest Service, and countless other successful organizations — all of them capture some of the religious tone. These corporations are human institutions and capture many of the expressive aspects of living ... (like) soul, spirit, magic heart, ethos, mission, saga.... (Deal and Kennedy, 1982, p. 195)

Educational Vision and Dramatic Consciousness

In order for vision to permeate the culture of a school it must be reflected in its daily life and routines. This aspect of vision, recently articulated by Starratt (1988), derives from Irving Goffman's (1959) symbolic-interactionist research which seeks to understand how persons perceive and define reality in specific, day-to-day social situations. Goffman perceived the social situation as a 'drama'. How we as individuals play our roles in the drama depends greatly upon the context and such factors as time, place and mood. Goffman also suggests that we all engage in 'impression management' whereby we attempt to control the shared definition of the situation, 'managing' for our own ends the impressions other participants get from the social interaction (Goodman and Marx, 1978).

Applying Goffman's theory to vision in leadership, Starratt contends that leaders must be conscious of the 'roles' they play in the social drama of their school community. Sometimes the roles which leaders play are dictated by precise social constructs which amount to a virtual script which the leader must follow. Thus the principal, acting in the roles of policy maker, leader, chief person in charge, etc, participates in what Starratt terms 'bureaucratic drama'. However, sometimes the principal must carry out a role and perform in a situation where he or she is not sure how to act. There is the need to improvise. '[I]t is in improvisation that the human drama expresses individuality, freedom and creativity' (1988, p. 9).

Starratt suggests that while principals and teachers are players in the social drama, they are also coaches and critics. They can step back from the drama and reflect on its meaning and significance. 'Dramatic consciousness flows from one's vision of what a school should be, could be' (Starratt, 1988, p. 10). As a result of leadership vision, one is able, in poet William Blake's words, to 'see the world in a grain of sand and eternity in a flower'. One is able to sense the long term significance of even the smallest of day-to-day events:

> Everyday in school, children are moving towards the choice of life or death, of belief in the ultimate goodness of life, or belief in the ultimate cruelty of life. They may not frame those beliefs in such stark existential terminology, but that is what is happening ... So what possibilities teachers hold out for children that day in school is enormously important. That children find some success in the arduous, yet marvellous task of thinking about and making sense out of the world is enormously important. The task of teaching is saturated with signficance. (Starratt, 1985, p. 18)

Thus a powerful vision instils in community's leaders a heightened sense of awareness, a dramatic consciousness of the possibilities of each

moment. Vision helps principals, teachers and parents to see that they can and do make a difference in the lives of their students and in the lives of one another. As noted by Schein (1985) leaders are able to embed their own assumptions in the ongoing daily life of their organizations:

> (1) through what they pay attention to and reward, (2) through the role modeling they do, (3) through the manner in which they deal with critical incidents, (4) through the criteria they use for recruitment, selection, promotion and excommunication they communicate both explicitly and implicitly the assumptions they really hold, and (5) through the conflicts and inconsistencies which get communicated and become part of the culture. (p. 242)

Educational Vision and the Reflective Practitioner

As with Goffman's dramaturgical approach to symbolic interaction, Donald Schon's (1983 and 1987) theory of the 'reflective practitioner' also contributes to our understanding of vision. Schon argues that most professional schools only teach standard scientific theories and how to apply them to straightforward cases. They thus fail to equip future doctors, lawyers, engineers and other professionals adequately to deal with the difficult problems which they will encounter in actual practice. Schon suggests that professional education should be centred on enhancing the practitioner's ability for 'reflection-in-action'. This implies learning by doing, problem solving and developing the ability for continued learning and problem solving throughout one's professional career.

Schon's ideas, however, also provide a useful blueprint for considering the school leader, the professional educator, who: through reflection formulates a vision; articulates that vision through the formation of an 'educational platform'; and uses what Argyris (1982) originally termed 'double loop learning' to continually monitor the extent to which current practice reflects the vision in action. Let us delve more deeply into each of these three aspects.

Naming or Labelling

Numerous writers from such fields as linguistics, philosophy and social psychology have referred to the power of naming or labelling. The point is that once we name something we are then disposed to perceive and judge it in certain ways and according to particular criteria. Our language thus is a map which, like all maps, includes certain details of reality and ignores others (Whorf, 1956). The formulation of a vision is, in many respects, an act of naming particular values and beliefs (a concept of the

'good') which are proffered as a map for the future. The power to name is the power to decide what we look at, and to determine what we see and therefore where we go. This is the positive side of naming. However, just as naming can be a positive affirmation of the values inherent in a vision, it can also lead us astray if our reality is misnamed, just as an incorrect map will lead us to the wrong destination. Starratt (1988) gives the example of a student sent to the office with a homework problem. If we name the problem as 'laziness' we will take one approach. If it is named as a 'learning disability' problem, the principal will take another approach. If it is labelled as a 'broken home' problem, the approach is different still. The point is that the act of naming has a great influence over the whole process of vision formulation, problem solving and other thought processes.

A final aspect of naming which is relevant to vision is that of group reflective practice. Starratt (1988) points out that we are more likely to correctly name a problem if we engage others in the process, if we ask others, 'Do you see what I see?'. This collective reflective practice can have a profound effect both on the collective formation of a shared vision and on the development of group problem solving and other skills necessary to make a vision work. Holt (1987) makes a similar point when he notes that all school improvement, in reality, involves a determination of the nature of the educational good for that particular school community; and that educational change will not be effective unless the whole school community is involved in making that determination. In short, he is stressing the value of, and need for, collective reflective practice.

Educational Platform

A second important element of reflective practice is what Sergiovanni and Starratt (1983) term 'educational platform'. An educational platform is comprised of particular values and beliefs. It can support and help justify what is; or it can articulate, through words or deeds, the values and beliefs which support a vision of what is to be. Studies by Argyris and Schon (1974) found that administrators frequently had two platforms: one which they verbalized when asked about their values and beliefs; and another one which they demonstrated in action. And, just as schools can have both a stated curriculum and a hidden curriculum which runs counter to it, so too leaders can express one set of values and beliefs, yet contradict, by their actions, those same beliefs and values. Thus, Argyris and Schon suggest there is a need to encourage leaders to write out their platform, to refer to it often, especially in solving difficult problems, and to reflect on it so that it becomes a real guide to their actions and decisions. While there is no set formula which must be followed in the construction of an educational platform, Sergiovanni and Starratt offer

the following practical guidelines of the kinds of things which might be included.

1   *Aims of Education.* Among other things, a vision statement articulates values and beliefs about the aims of education. These aims need to be stated in specific terms, not abstract concepts. They should relate specifically to the education of the young people in your specific school.

2   *Image of the Learner.* This aspect of the vision focusses on the attitudes and assumptions about how one best teaches and learns. Are all students taught in the same way? Are students viewed as active or passive participants in the learning process? Is the focus more on a group of students or on individualized learning?

3   *Image of the Teacher.* What is the vision of a teacher? Helper? Friend? Social engineer? Stimulator? Commander? How does the administration view teachers? Are they mere employees? A team of professionals? Isolated and independent professionals with sole control over their classrooms?

4   *Value of the Curriculum.* What kind of learning is valued in the school? Is all learning viewed as intrinsically valuable? Do mathematics and science reign supreme over the humanities? What about the informal curriculum? What about the relative importance of practical versus theoretical subjects?

5   *Preferred Pedagogy.* Are inductive teaching methods considered best? What about student-initiated learning? Are teachers encouraged to be eclectic in their approach?

6   *Teacher-Student Relationships.* Is the emphasis on caring relationships or subject matter content? To what extent are the needs of the whole child catered for? Is the emphasis on group or individual development? Do teachers and administrative staff reflect, in their relationships with students, the values which are espoused in their stated aims of education?

7   *School Climate.* Is the school climate relaxed, open and informal? Or, does it tend to be more strict, closed and formal? Is the organization of the school flexible and spontaneous or more orderly, structured and predictable?

8   *Major Achievements of Students This Year.* The more detailed the vision, the more real it is likely to be in the lives of the school community. Does the school, as a whole, have goals to which it is committed for this year? Do individuals have related goals which are part of and related to the broader school vision?

9   *Social Significance of the Students' Learning.* What is the main emphasis? Students learning skills which are immediately useful

for work? Learning for the sake of learning? Good citizenship? Learning about the cultural heritage of one's civilization?

10 *The Language of Discourse in Learning Situations.* In most learning situations, is knowledge viewed as impartial, neutral? Is the emphasis on quantitative measurement and precise definitions, or on creativity and imagination? To what extent are the moral uses of knowledge and artistic sensibility catered for? Art, music, history, literature, and even mathematics and science are not value free. How do these subjects reflect and expound upon the values inherent in the school's vision?

11 *Relationship of Parents and Community to the School.* What is the perceived role of parents in the education of children? What about the culture, values and mores of the community in which the school is embedded?

Obviously, not all of these eleven areas will be part of every educational platform. They are merely intended as guidelines to help educational leaders become more reflective practitioners and better able to judge the extent to which their vision is becoming reality.

Double Loop Learning

A third aspect of reflective practice, as developed by Schon (1983) and Argyris (1982) and recently addressed by Starratt (1988), is termed 'double loop learning'. Argyris contrasts double loop learning with single loop learning. In single loop learning a person decides on a course of action in solving a problem and then evaluates whether that action has met with success. Double loop learning goes further to ask why certain actions were successful and others were not. Double loop learning is multi-faceted and incorporates the wider context of which a particular action is but a part. Starratt provides the following concrete example of double loop learning by a school principal:

> ... a principal who is a double loop learner will not simply be talking to a ninth grade maths teacher, but to a second year, ninth grade maths teacher, whose evaluation reports at the end of her first year were unfavourable, who is aware that her tenure approval hinges on showing improving this year, who needs to work more closely with her maths supervisor who doesn't know anything about coaching inexperienced teachers, whose case the local teacher union leadership is watching carefully due to past failures of the school to assist inexperienced teachers. That administrator is much more conscious that he not only wants to help this teacher, but that the future level of cooperation of the union

may hinge on his careful handling of this teacher. The administrator is aware of his own feelings, that he needs to win this one. Those feelings also caution him to balance his need to be fair and helpful to this teacher with his responsibility to the school children to weed out hopelessly incompetent teachers. (1988, pp. 13–14)

The effective implementation of vision incorporates the best of reflective practice. And, the concepts of naming, educational platform and double loop learning provide valuable insights into how the reflective school leader, in concert with a reflective school community, can bridge the gap between vision and reality.

The Need for More Research on Vision

Thanks to the seminal work of Blumberg and Greenfield (1980) on school principals, Peters and Waterman (1982) and Bennis and Nanus (1985) on the role of vision in successful business organizations, and the educational research and writings of Starratt (1986), Sheive and Schoenheit (1987), W. Greenfield (1987), Beare, Caldwell and Millikan (1988) and others, the concept of vision is now receiving considerable attention. At the same time, there is an urgent need for much more research, quantitative and qualitative, on the concept of vision. We need, for example, to learn much more about research-in-action linkages. How can the different aspects of the concept of vision be put into action? How and why do symbols, rituals, stories and metaphors work so powerfully to communicate vision? How does an educational leader, who has yet to articulate a vision, go about it? How is a vision best articulated to others? What are the best strategies to empower others who share the vision? What can be done about competing visions within the same school? How does the school leader capture the interest and gain the invaluable contribution of parents towards the school's vision? How can schools and educational bureaucracies best be structured to promote visions of excellence? How do we engage students in the process of formulating and promoting the school's vision? These are just a few of the micro areas of vision which await further development. There are also larger questions to be answered (Alvesson, 1987). What is the relationship between one group with a particular vision and other groups led by different visions? How is vision affected by the dependence of organizations on the general culture in which they exist? What differences exist between organizations bound together by vision and those bonded by something less strong, for example a shared common perception of reality as opposed to common values? How do the political character of organizations and the political behaviour of organizational members, make an impact upon vision? To

the extent that a vision is based upon a particular ideology, what is the role of that ideology in relation to vision and other aspects of organizational behaviour? While the discussion of vision in this chapter hopefully has contributed at least partial answers to some of these questions, there is still much work to be done.

Conclusion

This chapter has explored the concept of educational vision and its relationship to evaluation, school management and other aspects of school improvement. For many educators struggling to cope with the here and now, thinking about education in the next century occupies but a fleeting moment of their time. But, whether we like it or not, the twenty-first century is, in many real ways, already here since the choices we make today will govern the course of future events. Indeed, the kindergarten class of 1989 will be the grade 12 class of the year 2000. The youth now in classrooms all over the world will spend most of their lives in the twenty-first century. While many things about the future of education are unclear, one thing is certain. The world of tomorrow will be dramatically different from that of today. Thus, more than ever before, we need educational leaders, men and women, who are visionaries. We need people who can escape the chains of the present and dream of the future; who can forge and articulate a vision of a desired educational state. We need leaders to provide a brightly burning torch which can inflame the hearts and minds of others, thus lighting the way for society, a school, to shape its own course rather than stumbling in the dark or passively accepting destiny. Rapidly accelerating change, increased complexity, and growing interdependence are among the features of the modern world which demand leaders who know who they are, where they are going and how they are going to get there. Schein concludes, 'Leaders do not have a choice about whether to communicate. They have a choice only about how much to manage what they communicate' (1985, p. 243). In managing what they communicate educational leaders must be versatile, holistic, outward looking; above all, people with vision.

On a wider scale, the insights gained regarding the importance of vision, and the ways in which a vision can come to permeate the life of a school community, may be of benefit to other schools. In an age of rapid change and great challenges, all schools must, more than ever before, give careful thought and attention to their unique vision of education. As we have seen, a school evaluation — incorporating students, staff and parents — has a central role to play in enabling a school to remain focussed upon, and work towards the fulfilment of, its vision of education.

In the special case of St Mary's College, if it can keep the above

'transforming' factors in mind as it proceeds to bring about school improvement, its vision will be well on the way to becoming reality — a reality rich in the social capital which Coleman and Hoffer (1987) found to be so vital in producing excellent schools. It is to this concept of 'social capital' we now turn as the next chapter explores further the context of school improvement.

Chapter 6

The Idea of Social Capital

Introduction

As we saw in the previous chapter, an educational vision is a picture of a desired future state, a collective sharing of values, norms, beliefs and expectations about schooling and the form it should take. This chapter builds on the concept of vision by further considering the social structure of parents, teachers and students which comprises the school community. It is our contention that the strength of a school's social structure — its network of shared beliefs, norms, values and expectations — is one of the most powerful influences for effective school improvement.

In their book, *Public and Private High Schools: The Impact of Communities* (1987) Coleman and Hoffer depict an American society and a state secondary school system which are severely constrained because of the declining 'social capital' in society. This chapter discusses the findings of the Coleman and Hoffer study regarding the phenomenon of social capital and considers their implications for Catholic schools in particular and for schools generally in Western societies. The last part of the chapter suggests possible future directions that might be taken by government, schools, parents and industry to preserve and nurture the social capital which is so important for successful schooling.

The Relationship Between Family and School

Education, viewed in its widest sense means the transmission of knowledge, values, norms, beliefs and expectations to people of all ages. In its narrower sense, education refers to the experience of formal schooling. It is in the wider sense, especially, that the family plays a primary and fundamental role in a child's education (Musgrave, 1988; Foster, 1980). Foster points out that:

the process of socialization involves the *transmission of the culture* into which an individual is born and, as well, *the acquisition of the uniquely human attributes* which can come only from interaction with other human beings ... This encompasses language, beliefs and ideas about the nature of the social world, values and attitudes denoting desired social relations in this world, and a sense of place, a sense of where one as an individual fits into the scheme of things. (1981, p. 152)

The influence of the family on a child is also aptly described by Conway:

Compared to the influence of a zealous and pervasive mother, a resolute father, a concerned sibling, mentor or close childhood friend, the most clever of political spellbinders is a crude amateur hammering upon invisible doors. (1978, pp. 34–5)

A vast body of literature has explored the links between the family and school. Even a summary of the literature on family/school/society relationships would require a separate book. The focus here, however, is on the more recent concept of cultural capital as developed by such writers as Bourdieu and Passeron in France during the 1970s, Halsey (1978) and Harker (1984) in the UK, Coleman *et al.* (1966) and Bowles and Gintis (1976) in America, and Connell *et al.* (1982, 1985) in Australia.

In America, Coleman *et al.* (1966) found that differing educational achievements among different students were often due more to family background and related cultural factors than to school influences. Also taking a structural view of schools in the wider setting of society, Bowles and Gintis in *Schooling in Capitalist America* (1976) emphasized the links between school, family and the economy.

Bourdieu and Passeron (1977) posited a cultural reproduction theory. This suggests that schools, by focussing on a particular and dominant culture (with its attendant values, beliefs, expectations, assumptions) thereby discriminate against students who come to the school without the requisite cultural capital to cope with, understand and take advantage of the education which the school offers. Consequently, those students fail who come from families lacking the cultural capital upon which the school curriculum is premised. Similarly, Halsey (1978) and Harker (1984) have analyzed the ways in which the family determines one's status and culture by providing the child with a language environment for early learning, self-perception, level of confidence, set of values and expectations which may or may not be appropriate to the language environment, values and assumptions which the child will encounter later on in school.

Connell (1983, pp. 152–3) has argued that Bourdieu's theory is essentially a cognitive one which focusses solely on the 'pedagogic work' and the more formal aspects of the curriculum. He suggests that a

psychological and developmental, as well as a cognitive, account is necessary to explain both the conscious and unconscious processes, and the means by which certain cultural groups become disadvantaged (Musgrave, 1988, pp. 64–71).

In light of this background to the developing concept of cultural capital, let us turn to Coleman and Hoffer's recent work (mentioned at the beginning) on the related concept of social capital. In contrast to the cultural capital of the family, Coleman and Hoffer take a broader view to explore the educational significance, not of a single family, but of the whole network of adult human relationships in which the child and his or her family are embedded. The authors submit that the insights gained from such a holistic view hold much relevance for school leaders, school communities and society at large. Their findings especially highlight the positive influence on children's schooling of a family and wider social network which are united by a shared vision — a unification of shared expectations, values and beliefs.

The 1987 Coleman and Hoffer Study

The 1987 study by Coleman and Hoffer had its genesis in an earlier study by Coleman, Hoffer and Kilgore (1981) which showed that students in Catholic and other private schools (in 1980) scored higher on achievement tests in mathematics and verbal skills (but not in science) than did students of similar backgrounds in public schools. After considerable controversy about the limits of the first study, a follow-up study was conducted of grade 12 students during 1982 who were in grade 10 in 1980. This made it possible to measure the growth of achievement over the two-year period. Regarding academic achievement during high school, Coleman and Hoffer found that Catholic and other religious schools:

> bring about greater growth for the average student in both verbal
> and mathematical skills than do public schools, but not in science
> knowledge nor in civics ... (p. 212)

The superior performance of Catholic schools in educating disadvantaged students was even more striking. In the US public schools, 14.3 per cent of the grade 10s in the 1980 study had dropped out of school by grade 12. This compares with 11.9 per cent drop-out rate for non-Catholic private schools and 3.4 per cent for the Catholic schools. Indeed, the Catholic school success in this area was so much greater than their state school counterparts that the US Secretary for Education, William Bennett, on 7 April 1988 called on Catholic schools to enrol the 'worst 5 or 10 percent' of public school students and ask state or local governments to help pay for teaching them.

Hoffer contend that the extent to which the individual will avail himself or herself of those opportunities will be greatly influenced by the social capital which exists in the family and surrounding adult enclave.

Private Non-Religious School Orientation

Private schools which are not part of a wider religious community see the school as an agent of the family, but in a very individualistic sense. There does not exist this community of families which makes up the network of religious-based schools. The religiously-based school, in contrast, sees school as an agent of the religious community of which the family is a part.

Catholic School Orientation

In contrast to the state school emphasis on individualism, opportunities and rewards, Catholic schools, especially since the Second Vatican Council, have stressed the importance of an education founded upon Christian values and a sense of community. Vernacular services, greater participation by the laity in school and parish life and ecumenical harmony with Protestant, Jewish and Greek Orthodox Churches are just a few examples of such community emphasis (Hunt and Kunkel, 1984, p. 11). Moreover, as stated by the US National Conference of Catholic Bishops:

> Since the Christian vocation is a call to transform oneself and society with God's help, the educational efforts of the Church must encompass the twin purposes of personal sanctification and social reform in light of Christian values ... The educational efforts of the Church must therefore be directed to forming persons-in-community, for the education of the individual Christian is important not only to his solitary destiny but also to the destinies of the many communities in which he lives (National Conference of Catholic Bishops, 1972, pp. 3–4).

Not only are Catholic schools an integral part of the parish life which surrounds them, but they are also bonded to a world-wide Church which has a rich tradition of beliefs and underlying values which are reflected, expounded upon and celebrated in symbols, rituals, myths and ceremonies. This intricate network of relationships — reflecting common traditions, beliefs, values, and expectations — is responsible for the rich social capital of Catholic schools, and in turn, has a very supportive, positive and powerful effect on the children who attend those schools.

Why Social Capital is so Important

Human development involves much more than the biological processes we all must go through to become adults. As Dubos puts it:

> Becoming human implies the passage of *Homo sapiens* out of nature into culture. For each person, this process results from an evolution which is guided, and indeed to a large extent imposed, by the set of assumptions of the social group to which that particular person belongs — assumptions which influence practically every aspect of individual life. (1981, p. 61)

Traditionally children were socialized, given their set of assumptions, by the family and wider community of adults of which that family was an integral part. However, as the family has become denuded of adults and the neighbourhood has lost its character as an interdependent community, the institutions which formerly socialized our children are crumbling. Children are increasingly growing up in a social context dominated by mass media and populated primarily by other children.

A wealth of research has shown that a child's success in education depends, not only on the characteristics of the school (in providing opportunities, demands, rewards), but on the qualities the child brings from the home. These qualities from home are characterized by Coleman as 'attitudes, effort, and conception of self' (Coleman, 1987, p. 38). As these resources — the social capital — decrease at home, they will not be replaced by economic capital — pouring money into school resources, for example, which take the form of more opportunity, rewards and demands. The dangers of not replenishing our social capital, says Coleman, are two fold:

> One danger lies in the possibility that nothing will replace these informal institutions, and children will grow up in an environment consisting primarily of commercial recreation (music, clothes, thrill-generating activities) and populated primarily by other children. A second danger lies in the possibility that the old institutions will be replaced by consciously designed new ones, but institutions inferior to the ones they replaced. (1987, p. 37)

Reasons for the Decline of Social Capital in Modern Societies

There are many complex and interrelated reasons for the decline of social capital in modern society. Just a few of the major reasons will be discussed here. Changes in the family, the primary agency of socialization have

certainly been a major factor in the decline of social capital. The extended and supportive kin network provided by the extended family was lost with the advent of the nuclear family. Also, as industry moved from the home to the factory, fathers not only were absent from their children, but also absent from the wider community of families — the neighbourhood. More recently, a majority of mothers, too, have left the home with the result that the adults in the family devote most of their time and energy to one world and the children are left in another. This 'other' world of children among children is also more and more influenced by mass media and other technologies, including forms of transport and artefacts of leisure, which have further broken down family and neighbourhood or community ties. Indeed, since the advent of electricity and better heating family homes often find each individual member in their own room rather than sharing and socializing around a communal hearth. The potential of the modern 'family' room so called has been seriously inhibited by the television set, stereo and video games. The 'family' room has thus lost much of its socializing influence and has ceased to be the spiritual and social centre of community life. Also, in a society where industry and technology require greater mobility there is less incentive for families to lay down permanent 'roots'. There is also greater affluence in Western societies thus making people less dependent upon one another and in turn further breaking down the social fabric. Since the 1960s there has existed also a value crisis in society. Consequently, youths and adults are often pulled between conflicting messages. Finally, politically and philosophically many people have disengaged themselves from the public domain and opted instead to spend their time and energies in developing individual human resources.

Popkewitz (1983, p. 11) reminds us that 'the patterns of school conduct are always rooted in assumptions about the nature of society, of individuality and the relation of the individual to that society'. This philosophical emphasis on individualism as opposed to community (relationships) is reflected and promoted in most secondary schools. As explained earlier, classrooms in non-religious schools thus often assume that learning occurs for and by individuals. Declining employment prospects, teacher specialization and the encouragement of children to learn technical skills and develop expertise in limited areas further enhances the individualism and competiveness of school life, (Lesko, 1988, Chapter 1). Thus most government and non-religious private schools reflect an emphasis on individualism and revolve around a system of rewards and opportunities by which the individual is encouraged to develop. This described emphasis on individualism, however, fails to take into account the fact that the extent to which the individual will advantage himself or herself of school opportunities will be greatly affected by the social capital which the child brings to the school.

Rebuilding Social Capital: What Can Parents Do?

If a loss of social capital is caused by the denuding of adults from the home and surrounding community, the obvious place to start rebuilding social capital is in the home and by the parents. Simply put, parents must make it a higher priority in their lives to play a stronger and more involved role in their children's lives. Indeed, one US study given wide media coverage in Australia indicated that fathers spent an average of only 17 seconds a day in which undivided attention was given to their children. Similarly, the Times Educational Supplement recently reported on a Carnegie Foundation study in which half of the students in grade 8 indicated that at the end of the school day they returned to an empty home. Forty per cent of those surveyed said they wish they could spend more time with their mothers and fathers. Many students said they often felt lonely and lacked contact with adults.

Parents would also do well to emulate many of the Asian families in Australia, the United States and elsewhere. Coleman found it was common for Asian parents to order two copies of textbooks — one for the child and one for the parent. Interestingly, several studies have commented on the strength and support of Asian families and communities, but have failed to emphasize what those results say about the corresponding depletion of social capital in other families. Similarly, comparative studies between the United States and Japan show that Japanese parents are actively involved with their children's school work while American parents are encouraging, but not actively supervising their children's homework. Deciding to become more involved with children will, of necessity for most, entail the making of a number of crucial choices. If spending time is important for our children's development we may have to forego other activities or alter them in order to pay more attention to our children. An even more difficult series of choices involves choosing between building our own human capital and the family's social capital. The 1970s and 1980s (the me-decades) have seen an increasing emphasis on individualism — jogging, night classes, fitness groups, etc. Building human capital is important, but one must be careful that human capital is not being developed at the expense of social capital. We should therefore attempt wherever possible to have the 'me' become 'WE'. Similarly, when looking at job promotions and moving the family, we should consider all the costs — social as well as economic.

Some parents fail to become active in their children's education because they suffer a crises of confidence, especially when confronted with 'new maths' and other curriculum developments. Although primary schools have been exemplary in their efforts to involve parents in schools, it is still rare to see a parent in the secondary school, especially upper secondary. Thus, schools must assist parents in becoming more involved

by offering guidance, support and training in the new skills required for understanding and assisting their children with new knowledge. And, while schools need to do more to welcome parents and involve them in the life of the school, parents, too, should be confident that their help can and will make a difference. Indeed, educators and parents sometimes forget that they are the child's first and most influential teacher. As such they impart to their children the gift of language, basic values, ideals and expectations which will shape the course of the child's life. Thus the famous lines from Wordsworth that 'the child is father of the man', should serve as a powerful message to parents of just how significant their own role as teachers of their children.

In choosing schools and communities parents should seek out communities where there are strong relationships among the parents. We should ask about the involvement of the parents and friends association and the role of parents in the school, as much as we ask about the school's academic record. Similarly, if the parent involvement in our children's school is lacking, we should try to take steps to improve things by becoming active ourselves.

Parents should also make an active effort to get in touch with the world of children. For example, across the United States there are groups of adults who have formed discussion groups to read and discuss children's literature in an effort to better understand their children and their perceptions and experiences.

Finally, a family's social capital can be improved by increasing human capital which is supportive of the family. Thus, the Asian parent's ordering of an extra copy of textbooks increases their human capital, but does so in a way which is supportive of the family's social capital. So, take piano lessons, tennis lessons, university classes — whatever — but do it and share it with the family, is one obvious response.

The Role of the School in Building Social Capital

The Message for Catholic and Religiously-Based Schools

Coleman and Hoffers' results contain at least three important and timely messages for Catholic and other religiously-based schools. First, it is crucial that Catholic and other religious schools recognize, cherish and build upon the strength of their social capital; and that they be wary of forces which threaten to undermine it. The authors contend that a clearly articulated and compelling vision, regular evaluation and a collaborative approach to school management are all vital for ensuring that a school's social capital is maintained, and even enhanced. Just how easily social capital, and therefore educational effectiveness, can be subtlely and almost

imperceptibly undermined is illustrated by Nancy Lesko (1988) who suggests that a growing tension exists in many Catholic schools between two competing visions. The traditional vision sees the school founded upon relationships which are in turn based upon norms, values, beliefs and traditions of a wider religious community. However, a second and competing vision of individualism is often found in Catholic and religious schools today. This second vision sees individuals within the school as in conflict and competition with one another. Evidence of these conflicting visions was also found in the St Mary's College Study and are fully discussed in a later chapter. As Catholic schools and religiously-based schools strive to show that they are academically equal or superior to state and non-religious private schools, they must ensure that short-term academic gains are not achieved at the expense of a breakdown in the school community. Indeed, there is increasing concern, especially among Catholic educators, that religious issues are no longer central to the policies of many Catholic schools. Administrators, board members, parents, students and teachers are becoming increasingly preoccupied about individual skill levels and academic achievement, with the result that there is a de-emphasis on moral and religious issues (Morrison, 1978). These and other aspects of social capital are further addressed in our discussion of findings from the St Mary's College Project.

Second, as Catholic and other religious schools continue to battle for public dollars, they must be sure that those dollars do not come at the expense of a decline in social capital. Otherwise, there is the risk that religious schools will lose their unique religious ethos and will become inseparable from their state school counterparts. Thus religious school leaders should be wary lest governmental bureaucratic dictates lead to a school which is less religious and more secular.

A third concern emanating from the Coleman and Hoffer concept of social capital involves the impact on Catholic schools caused by the decline in the number of religious nuns, brothers and priests who have traditionally taught in these schools. Ciriello's (1988, pp. 10–15) research on the commitment of Catholic school teachers found at least three types of motivation or commitment patterns amongst lay Catholic teachers. One group of lay teachers (about 54 per cent) chose to work in Catholic schools because of the importance of religion in their lives and the emphasis of the school on religious concerns. A second group (about 20 per cent) taught at a Catholic school primarily because they were interested in the general teaching opportunities afforded, and not because of any religious commitment. A third group (about 5 per cent) chose to teach in a Catholic school because of its convenience to home and the match between teaching job and outside responsibilities. The remainder (about 21 per cent) appeared to be low in all three motivations listed above, and it was unclear why they were teaching in a Catholic school. Ciriello and other researchers have found that there is a connection

between a teacher's commitment and the instructional goals that teacher has for his or her students. Ciriello concludes that there is:

> a need for concrete actions to insure that those who are hired into Catholic schools hold in esteem the religious purpose of the schools and that those who are currently employed in the schools are encouraged to take responsibility for the implementation of the specific school goals. This calls for attention to be given to initial selection criteria, socialization activities, and staff development processes that support the mission and culture of the Catholic school. (1988, p. 12)

The Coleman and Hoffer study therefore suggests that religious schools must not take their social capital for granted. Rather, it is vital that they remain vigilant and guarded lest they run the risk of losing the very thing which makes them special, different and educationally effective. Social capital does not remain static. In a world where the family and a sense of community are in general decline, religious schools must work harder than ever before to protect and preserve that which is the source of so much of their educational success — their social capital.

Implications for Schools in General

It would require a separate book to adequately address this question. All that is attempted here is to present a few key ideas.

Despite the alleged value neutrality maintained by some educators, the authors submit that schools are moral institutions and principals and teachers are moral agents who have a vision for their school — a picture of a desired future state (Beare, Caldwell and Millikan, 1988; Caldwell and Spinks, 1986 and 1988; Greenfield, 1987; Starratt, 1986). Moreover the vision of education for a particular school includes:

> beliefs about how children develop into full human beings, about the variety and depth of learning which human beings are capable of, about the future the young will face in their adult years... Much more is the leader's vision rooted in meaning and experiences of human life that are very basic, very cultural, that touch upon the essence of what it means to be a human person, upon the fundamental building blocks of human community. (Starratt, 1986, pp. 16–17)

It is important that the educational vision and underlying beliefs of the school community reflect the importance of social capital and be grounded upon a philosophy which sees individuals and society as inextricably related. This entails the belief that there is no such thing as a value-free or value neutral education and that individuals must be con-

cerned with the public realm and the good of society (Lesko, 1988, pp. 9–10). To have real significance the importance of social capital must be reflected in the ordinary events of school life, articulated by school leaders, shared with colleagues and be evidenced in the day-to-day decisions of the school (Starratt, 1986, p. 15). Similarly, employing Sergiovanni's (1984) theoretical framework, such vision becomes reality when all the forces of leadership merge to ensure that the culture, symbols, educational concerns, human relationships and organizational structures all stem from and reflect that vision.

Guided by a vision which values social capital, the principal and other school leaders must consciously develop a sense of community and cohesion within the school. There should be less emphasis on individualism and competition within the school and more on cooperation and working together to pursue common goals. In this respect interschool competitions (in debating, music and academic subjects as well as sport) can help unify a whole school and give students a sense of dedication, pride and commitment to a community cause. At the same time, the principal should strive to empower others (students, parents, staff and wider community) and give them a stake in making the school community work. For example, Coleman and Hoffer cite school superintendent, Alonzo Crim in Atlanta, Georgia who acquired business sponsorship for each of his pupils who were in the bottom 10 per cent of the school. These community leaders took a special role in sponsoring a student through the completion of school and effective integration into the work force (Coleman and Hoffer, 1987, pp. 240–1). And in Hobart, Tasmania, a Catholic school principal (grades K-12), Sr Barbara Amott, requires all of the secondary students to involve primary students in their activities, to get to know and spend time with each other, thus developing a real sense of school community. Isolated examples of these kinds of activities are to be found in most schools. However, the important point is that building community and relationships are not one-time, one shot efforts. A network of relationships must pervade the very bones of the school and be celebrated in the ritual, ceremonies and art forms of the school.

It is also important for the principal to develop an active parents and friends group and to involve parents in the school. As indicated earlier, while there has been some notable progress made by primary schools in getting parents involved, secondary schools have a long way to go and much to gain in this area. A number of principals have had significant success in getting parents involved by informing and showing parents exactly how they can help their child with reading, homework, sex education, and other areas. Some school leaders have initiated home visits and thus won the support of parents. Schools should also go out of their way to make parents feel welcome. This is especially true for parents who themselves were not successful in school and perhaps carry with them a number of negative fears and expectations from their past experience of

education. Also, there is no doubt that part of the success of collaborative approaches to school management, such as the model developed by Caldwell and Spinks (1986), lies in the fact that parents are made active partners in the schooling of their children. These are just a few of the many strategies which are possible to forge new and powerful links between parents and school. In many schools, gaining greater participation of parents in school community affairs, will require that parents, as well as their children, be provided with appropriate skills, how to: organize; chair a meeting; engage in fund raising; work successfully in small groups; establish active parental networks and so on.

The wider community, too, can be involved as in work-experience programmes in Australia and the RSA Education for Capability campaign in the UK which fosters closer links between school and community in finding ways in which the capabilities of young people can be released and enhanced (Burgess, 1986). Another example is the school-business compact in which local industry gives preference to students from a particular area provided they meet specified standards relating to attendance, academic achievement, etc. These have proven immensely successful in the UK and the USA. One of the most ambitious school-community partnership ventures is the Annie E. Casey Foundation's New Futures Initiative (Wehlage and Lipman, 1988; Wehlage *et al.*, 1989) in which five US cities have received financial assistance from the Casey Foundation to establish a partnership between school and community which tackles the problems of youth, pregnancy, poor retention rates, unemployment, etc.

The principal should also encourage activities which bring adults and children and families together. For example, one of the authors initiated a school chess club which involved almost 100 students from kindergarten through grade 12. Twenty of the players accompanied the author on Friday nights to play in the local chess club which included university professors, computer analysts, teachers, research scientists, the unemployed, retired pensioners — people from all walks of life. One of the writer's most poignant memories is that of a 7-year-old Vietnamese boy (and a very good chess player) engaged in a match with an 86-year-old retired opthamologist. Both were concentrating their fullest and enjoying their chess, but sharing far more than a chess game. For that student, whose parents were still in Vietnam, the chess club — the enclave of adults of which he was an important part — added greatly to his social capital and played a significant role in his excellent school performance. Thus chess clubs, an active 'old scholars' group, parent-student sporting matches, family days, and so on are just a few of the many ways in which schools can help children become intricately linked to a community of adults, thereby enhancing social capital.

With the 'greying' of Australia, America, the UK, Japan and other countries it is also important to utilize a virtually untapped and tragically wasted natural resource — our elderly. A few schools are beginning to

realize the tremendous contribution these people can make to enhancing the social capital of the school. Hopefully schools and governments will make available the structures to bridge the gap between these generations so that we can begin to rebuild our lost social capital.

Finally, it is important that principals and school leaders routinely evaluate their school communities and involve teachers, staff, students and parents in measuring the extent to which the school's vision and social capital are in fact being maintained, as well as seeking new ways in which social capital and general school improvement may be further enhanced.

The Role of Industry and Government in Preserving and Enhancing Social Capital

We have already mentioned the success of school-business compacts in helping those students who are most likely to lack significant social capital. Coleman and Hoffer (p. 211) suggest a few ways in which industry can also help rebuild the social capital which has been diminished by fact that first the father, and now a majority of mothers, have left the home to join the workforce. They suggest that we seriously examine the ways in which the family can become part of the workplace — the single institution (outside the home and sometimes the neighbourhood) which constitutes the central locus of activities for most adults of both sexes. Already an increasing number of businesses, especially in the United States, offer day-care services, as part of their employees' benefits. Perhaps, too, schools can be set up either solely or principally for employees.

Even if these structures are not feasible or are too radical, other possibilities can surely be found to enhance social capital. For example, industry could re-examine its policy of moving executives from one location to another every few years. Such moves often harm the community which has lost a valuable family and discourage the family moved from establishing 'roots' elsewhere because they know they will be moving again. Promotion structures should be designed which maintain rather than diminish the social capital.

Governments, too, need to establish programmes and policies which help maintain and enhance social capital. Through tax incentives, industry should be encouraged to adopt programmes such as those suggested above. In its urban planning governments should build social capital by designing integrated communities which create the equivalent of a small diversified village where children can observe work and trades close at hand and even play a role in them. The psychological, social and emotional gains for the children of those communities will enhance social capital and

avoid the decay of the inner city and blight of suburbia so prevalent today (Dubos, 1981).

For those parents choosing to remain at home, tax structures and governmental support should make it possible to do so thereby recognizing the valuable contribution made to our social capital. Through its education policies, government can also encourage schools to establish policies which build and enhance social capital. One very encouraging sign in Australia and the UK is the encouragement of greater local autonomy and a collaborative approach (Caldwell and Spinks, 1986 and 1988) to school management which involves parents, teachers, students and community members in the decision-making process. These policies recognize that significant educational reform will only come from the bottom up and must be initiated by the schools themselves and with teachers, parents, students and community given a greater stake in the outcome. Governments should continue to promote greater links between the school and wider community. They should also foster experimental schools which attempt new structures, like the school in the workplace mentioned above, which seek to provide greater parental involvement in the schooling of their children.

Conclusion

This chapter has reviewed the findings of the Coleman and Hoffer study (1987) which stress the importance of social capital in the education of children. The decline of social capital in modern society has also been chronicled with an emphasis on how that decline impacts the education and development of children. Finally, the writers highlight some ways in which parents, schools, government and industry can help stop the erosion of, and work to re-build, the social capital of youth and society. At a time when many are concerned about our environment, natural resources and quality of life, let us not neglect the fundamental social capital which will be the basis for a happy and successful future life for our children.

The Role of Management in School Improvement

Introduction

We have seen in earlier chapters that an effective paradigm of school improvement is one which takes into account the different contexts — historical, epistemological, philosophical, sociological, political and psychological — in which such education proceeds. We have also discussed the significance of the part played by social capital in one of those important contexts, that is the network of community values, beliefs, expectations, norms, etc in which the school and the child are embedded. Where the social capital is strong and the community unified around a consensus of clear and compelling values and beliefs, the school is likely to possess a powerful vision which is a major force in bringing about an excellent school. We have also noted the role played by evaluation in rediscovering and measuring the extent to which a school's vision has become a reality. We have shown too that the process of school improvement includes the vital element of management. This chapter considers that very practical dimension. It attempts to provide a useful model and some helpful suggestions regarding the ways in which a school can best be managed to take account of and accommodate the emerging concepts of educational evaluation, vision, social capital and leadership.

For reasons outlined below, the authors highly recommend a collaborative school management model, especially along the lines of that advocated by Caldwell and Spinks (1988) in *The Self-Managing School*. This is not to say, however, that any one model is best for all schools. Indeed, as indicated in the initial chapter, the local context of each school community is unique, and that a model which works well for one school in one setting may be inappropriate for another school in a different setting. We agree with Lovegrove *et al.* (1982, p. 71) that '[E]ach school is an enormously complicated social organism — there can be no crisp set of conclusions, no unequivocal answers — the school does not readily lend itself to improvement on the basis of generalisations'. The Caldwell and

Spinks Model of Collaborative School Management, however, is not a set of school improvement generalizations. Rather, it provides a very practical strategy focussing on the process of collaboration and providing a workable management framework, which takes into account the particular circumstances of each school.

Why Collaborative Management?

The process of management is concerned primarily with the stability of the organization by the establishment of efficient and effective routines, processes of control, coordination between different factets of the organization, policy formation, evaluation, communication and effective decision making (Sergiovanni, 1984; Greenfield, 1987). It is beyond the scope of this work exhaustively to evaluate a range of different management models. Instead, we have elected to focus our attention on a collaborative approach to management. Several factors led to this decision. First, as Caldwell and Spinks (1988, p. 6) show, there are a number of important arguments in support of self-management by schools. Political-economic theorists suggest that the goals of equality, efficiency and liberty are enhanced by school-site management, which is by its very nature more democratic. In contrast to a central budgeting method, self-managing schools promote efficiency, adjustment to local needs and greater innovation. They do this by involving those who arguably have the greatest interest in making sure that scarce resources are utilized wisely and fairly. These are the school leaders, staff, students, parents and other adults who form the local school community.

The latest organizational theory, too, supports the value and desirability of school 'self' management. Peters and Waterman (1982) in their study of America's best-run companies found that big companies like IBM were successful because they remained highly decentralized. At the same time the successful companies were highly centralized when it came to basic and fundamental values like the importance of customer service. Extending the work of Peters and Waterman to schools, the school effectiveness movement has shown that the school, the decentralized educational unit, is also the primary unit of educational change (Purkey and Smith, 1985; Finn, 1984; Hopkins and Wideen, 1984). As Oldroyd and Tiller (1987) point out, the acceptance of such evidence — that has almost become axiomatic — 'follows many attempts to effect change from the outside, which appear to have had little impact' (p. 14). They argue further that the reasons for this failure are complex but, they state, 'the immunity of schools to change from outside stems from their cultural uniqueness which is rarely recognized by, or accessible to, external agents ...' (p. 14).

Holt (1987) and Caldwell and Spinks (1988) suggest that school-

based management is consistent with the movement toward greater pro-fessionalism amongst teachers who seek more autonomy and a greater stake in educational leadership. The emphasis on school-based manage-ment is also reflected in an international trend toward collaborative man-agement models in many countries, especially in the UK, the USA, Canada, Australia and New Zealand. As an outstanding example, on October 1st, 1989 the entire system of government schools in New Zealand came under the complete jurisdiction of local Boards of Trustees. Each school community had elected the members of its board, to whom were added the principal of the school, teachers and a student represen-tative. According to educators, this constitutes a system of such radical change as to be virtually without parallel in the Western world. It is a system of education that had remained intact for more than a hundred years and has changed dramatically in a relatively short time span. It represents a changed power relationship between state authorities and local control, a different form of financing the educational institutions, and, most significantly, a new division of responsibility between profes-sionals (principals and teachers), parents and the local community. There have been criticisms, and claims, that the change will have the effect of reducing services, increasing existing inequities in educational provision, and that the changes are 'not a very subtle way of reducing expenditure'. Nevertheless a number of schools (visited by one of the authors) see it as an opportunity of great potential for participatory and collaborative education.

This trend, we believe, is symptomatic of world-wide mega trends (discussed in the Chapter 2), especially the trend from representative toward greater participitory democracy, a move away from centralized government and towards decentralized government and social services, and the increasing emphasis on self-help as opposed to government help. Collaborative management is also compatible with the trend toward greater student and parent involvement within schools.

Finally, the emphasis on collaborative management should be of special interest to Catholic schools as religious orders decline in number and lay people assume an increasingly larger role in educational leader-ship. Collaborative management is also consistent with the recent signi-ficant movement within the Catholic Church from an authoritative hierarchical structure to a more traditional collegial model which depends upon collaboration amongst the community of believers.

The Degree of Collaboration

Caldwell and Spinks (1988) point out that there are different degrees of collaboration which are possible within a particular school. For example, some school leaders do consult others, but exercise for themselves the

actual decision-making power. At the other end of the spectrum, a headteacher, staff and school community make decisions through a formal structure such as a school council or board of governors. Caldwell and Spinks favour full collaboration. Supported by the systems analysis of Russell Ackoff (1981) they present a compelling case for a 'corporate' or collegial approach to planning which, in the terminology of Ackoff, is *interactive*-focussing on the past, present and future of the organization simultaneously. Ackoff maintains that:

> It is through participation in interactive planning that members of an organisation can develop. In addition, participation enables them to acquire an understanding of the organisation and makes it possible for them to serve organisational ends more effectively. This, in turn, facilitates organisation development.
>
> It is better to plan for oneself, no matter how badly, than to be planned for by others, no matter how well.
>
> In interactive planning, plans are not prepared by internal or external planning units and then submitted to executives for approval. Rather, executives engage directly in the planning process. Doing so is one of their major responsibilities. Furthermore, all those who are normally planned for are also given an opportunity to engage in the process.
>
> ... the proper role of professional planners and planning units inside or outside the organisation ... [is to] provide whatever motivation, information, knowledge, understanding, wisdom and imagination are required by others to plan effectively for themselves. (Ackoff, 1981, pp. 53–74; Caldwell and Spinks, 1988, pp. 63–64)

Based upon these and other Ackoff principles, Caldwell and Spinks (1988) list the following characteristics of 'Collaborative School Management':

1 Policy-making and planning should be considered a continuous process, linking the often unsystematic, fragmented processes which have been the subject of frustration and ineffectiveness in the past ('the principle of continuity').
2 Policy-making and planning at the unit level — 'the programme' — should be considered a component of a comprehensive process for the organization as a whole — 'the school' (the holistic principle).
3 Policy-making and planning should be 'all-over-at-once' rather than 'top-down' or 'bottom-up', with appropriate involvement of people at all levels: communication should be multi-

directional, flowing up, down and across lines of authority ('the participative principle').

4   Policy-making and planning should take account of past, present and future, recognizing the achievements of the past and present by basing many policies and plans on existing practice but anticipating the desired future by setting other new policies and planning accordingly ('interactive planning'). (pp. 64–5)

The Caldwell and Spinks Model of Collaborative Management

The Caldwell and Spinks Collaborative Management Model evolved over a seven year period. In the case of St Mary's College, a fully collaborative model is still evolving. By its process the St Mary's Project, however, exemplified a major collaborative step in seeking the views of students (past and present), staff and parents regarding the quality of education provided by the school. This illustrates the point that schools should not seek to become fully collaborative overnight. Caldwell and Spinks indicate that a minimum of three to five years should be allowed to implement a collaborative model of school management.

The Caldwell and Spinks Collaborative School Management Cycle has six phases: 1) Goal-setting and need identification; 2) Policy-making, with policies consisting of purposes and broad guidelines; 3) Planning programmes; 4) Preparation and approval of programme budgets; 5) implementation; and 6) Evaluation. This cycle is similar to other models proposed in various management and administrative texts. The special contribution made by the Caldwell-Spinks model, however, emanates from the clear delineation of those phases which are the concern of the group responsible for policy. It also organizes planning activities around programmes which reflect the normal patterns of work in the school.

School Improvement Through Collaborative Management

Collaborative school management provides the broad 'managerial' guidelines to bring about school improvement. However, it is important to realize that the management cycle described above is not put into place all at once. In fact, a school could start the collaborative management process at various stages in the cycle. For example, St Mary's College began the process with a comprehensive evaluation. Other schools begin with a vision or mission statement which focusses on broad goals and needs. Caldwell and Spinks suggest it takes three to five years to get all the stages of collaborative management into operation.

Finally, while the collaborative management cycle provides the general school improvement strategy, it is also important to be mindful that management is inextricably linked with school vision, leadership, evaluation, school culture and the historical and political context in which the management operates.

The Need for Institutional Support

Since the majority of schools tend to be part of an educational system, it is also important to indicate how the system may bring about a process of school-based management for the purpose of improvement. Caldwell and Spinks recommend the 'stepping stone' strategy proffered by Havelock (1973). They suggest: 1) introductory meetings to all schools in a region; 2) a call for volunteer schools which will be provided with technical support to help them become skilled in collaborative management; 3) working with individuals who show promise and the protection of innovators from 'resisters' who seek to discredit them; 4) bringing the programme to the attention of those who may be considered 'early adopters'. They should be encouraged to talk with 'resisters' or would be 'resisters'; and 5) finally, encourage opinion leaders to implement collaborative school management and enlist their support to introduce it to the remaining schools (Caldwell and Spinks, 1988, p. 169).

Timar and Kirp (1988) stress that significant school improvement will not eventuate simply by giving schools more autonomy. Encouragement and support must come from the larger state organization. State policy planners are important in setting broad educational guidelines. However, they also must realize that individual school communities need time to develop the skills necessary to make collaborative management work. State and national bodies must therefore avoid the popular tendency to seek instant results. Rather:

> A theory of institutional support is anchored in the conviction that everyone in schools is responsible for planning, budgeting and programme evaluation. Budgets are tied to assessment and diagnosis: targeting money where it is most needed. Responsibility is not segmented and parcelled out among a host of players in the educational process. For schools to take responsibility for their efficacy means that schools must behave like organizations rather than a conglomeration of related activity centres or a shopping mall. In order to rebuild their institutional coherence, schools must also exercise authority by affirming the fundamental worth of education in everything they do ... The authority of schools must also be predicated on the belief that there is a body of knowledge that is worth teaching. That belief must form the

organizational and intellectual base on which schools are structured. (pp. 135–6)

Finally, institutional support should come from schools of education and professional organizations as well as school systems. As Timar and Kirp conclude:

Presently, teachers think of themselves as responsible for a certain number of students in a classroom. Teachers are not expected to assume responsibility for the entire school, especially not for long range planning. Organizational cultures are built on participatory decision-making, planning, goal setting and problem solving. Professional norms and teacher attitudes are shaped by the workplace, professional organizations and teacher training programmes. Before teachers can be expected to take on broader responsibilities, they must be socialized to assume those responsibilities and must be taught the skills to carry them out. Schools of education and professional organizations are the obvious agents to promote this element of educational reform. (p. 136)

The Enhancement of Teachers as Professionals

Assuming the proper institutional support, one of the major benefits of a collaborative approach to school management is the resultant empowerment of teachers. In traditional hierarchical management models, teachers have often lived an isolated and lonely existence confined to the domain of their own classroom. Thus Lortie (1975, p. 232) found that teacher development is 'impeded by mutual isolation, vague yet demanding goals, dilemmas of outcome assessment, restricted in-service training, rigidities in assignment, and working conditions which produce a "more-of-the-same" syndrome among classroom teachers'. Similarly, Lightfoot (1983, pp. 9–10) observed that teachers 'use pet frameworks for viewing the world', react to change issues 'autobiographically' and emphasize 'what is wrong rather than the search for what is right'.

However, Jones and Maloy (1988), after studying numerous efforts in adopting collaborative approaches to school improvement, concluded that:

When given opportunities, however, those same teachers have enthusiastically acted to improve their instruction and their school's climate. They entered the profession because they wanted to help others to learn; and despite their frustrations with bureaucratic rules, institutional barriers to change, and uninterested colleagues, they continue to find deep personal rewards in their teaching. When partnerships between educators and out-

side organizations work, they stimulate crucial dialogues about curriculum, climate and educational purposes that foster an evolving awareness by teachers of their complex professional roles. (pp. 27–8)

Through collaborative management teachers are enhanced as professionals who have a vital stake in determining the nature of the educational good in their school community. Teachers are not isolated in their classrooms, but share in a vibrant and rich educational community which is conducive to achievement and personal growth, not only on the part of students, but of all involved in the educational process (Jones and Maloy, 1988).

The Special Role of Parents and Students

The special role of parents and other adults in the educational success of children was highlighted in the discussion of social capital in Chapter 6. Despite the importance of parental involvement in the education of their children, Lightfoot (1978) observed that parents, schools and community members are often 'worlds apart'. 'Families and schools are engaged in a complementary sociocultural task and yet they find themselves in great conflict with one another' (p. 20). One of the great values of the process of collaborative school management is that parents become partners in the education of their children. By being more involved in the school, participating parents are more likely to understand the complexities of the formal learning processes in schools (Marsh, 1988). Indeed, learning more about the learning processes within the school is an important way in which parents may increase their participation. With that understanding parents will do a better job in helping their children intellectually, socially and emotionally (Long, 1986). They will also be more willing to support educators in their efforts and give a high political priority to education (Bastiani, 1987).

Catholic schools, especially, should be interested in a collaborative model of school management because it facilitates a closer family and school partnership. As stated by the Catholic Education Council for England and Wales (1965):

The need for close contact between the two main influences on the child, home and school, is great. Parents and teachers can pool their resources in the cases of individual children, the teacher gaining the advantage of the parent's unique knowledge and of information about home circumstances, the parents benefiting from the greater objectivity of the teacher who can draw on

experience of a wider range of children and encourage or reassure parents ... (p. 11)

The Catholic Church regards the family as the basic social unit in society. More than this 'the Christian family is at the heart of the Church's mission to exemplify God's love for His children — most especially in the impersonal and neutral life which is currently fostered by an isolationist, individualistic civil society' (Buetow, 1988, p. 153). As Coleman and Hoffer (1987) have shown, the network of close relationships among family, school and church found in Catholic communities provides a rich source of social capital for the young people embedded in that community. Accordingly, a collaborative framework of school management which taps into and reflects that rich network can only work to further enhance the quality of education.

Another significant benefit of collaborative school management is a greater participation of students in the life of the school. Writers like Boud (1988) tell us that schools should place greater emphasis on teaching students to be autonomous learners. This means, among other things, giving more attention to the process of their learning. Through the process of collaborative school management students can be given the opportunity to be active, responsible and engaged with their learning tasks (Marsh, 1988). Moreover, the feedback and involvement of students is invaluable in accurately gauging the extent to which the school's goals are being met. Finally, although little research has been conducted in this area, it seems that the participation of students in school improvement activities often leads to positive collegiate relationships with their teachers (Dunn, 1986, p. 3).

Conclusion

In such areas as law, medicine, politics and the environment, people are beginning to realize that the issues at stake are too important to be left to the experts. Thus new structures are emerging which call for and enable experts, administrators, governments and community members to participate and share in policy-making. The school is undoubtedly one of the major agencies of socialization for all human beings. Indeed, the quality and nature of a person's education is a major factor in the shaping of individual, group and national destinies. Thus education is likewise too important to be left to the experts. It is vital for our common future that parents, governments, administrators, teachers, students — all who hold membership in a school community — be involved, in collaborating for a common purpose. That purpose is making the school effective and responsive to the educational needs of those whom it serves. This more

democratic view of education leads us to conclude with Gutmann: 'The policies that result from our democratic deliberations will not always be the right ones, but they will be more enlightened — by the values and concerns of the many communities that constitute a democracy — than those that would be made by unaccountable educational experts' (1987, p. 11).

Chapter 8

Making School Improvement Work: The Effective Management of Change

Introduction

From an exploration of the context of school improvement emerged a focus upon its central feature — evaluation. We then described a 'live' and practical instance of school evaluation, through the reporting of findings from the St Mary's School Project. The process of this 'real' evaluation also illuminated for us two other contextual ideas — vision and social capital. However, two vital questions still remain. How in fact may the vision, recaptured through the evaluative experience, be realized? How may the strengths of social capital — the cherished norms, the best loved values, the supportive interrelational network — be nourished and preserved?

This chapter attempts an answer to these questions and does this via the notion of managing change. Since school improvement implies change we must determine which are the most effective means by which it may be managed.

Assumptions Underlying the Process of Effective School Improvement

Any model for school improvement or change necessarily reflects a number of underlying assumptions. To illuminate the change process, we return to the St Mary's College Study and identify the major assumptions underlying that specific case of school evaluation for improvement. The following nine assumptions did not merely attend this evaluation: they provided both a basis and an impetus for continual, creative assessment of the school's life and work. In addition, these assumptions, we consider, may also provide a theoretical structure upon which change for school improvement can be established. Finally, although the assumptions are

discussed separately, it is important for readers to realize that they are interrelated and logically connected.

The Possibility of Change: The Case Against Determinism

The most fundamental value or belief underlying educational change is that change is possible. We would not support arguments that men are fated to accept relationships which are 'necessary, determined and outside their control' (Godet, 1987, p. 9, citing Karl Marx). It is true that an earlier technological optimism, in which the rise of technology was coincident with a belief in the control of our destiny, in recent times has given way to technological pessimism. However, such cyclical actions and reactions have frequently occurred in history (Dubos, 1981). In contrast to groups like the Club of Rome and others we do not believe that man can do little else than sit by helplessly as the hand of fate moves unalterably toward the midnight hour of planned or accidental destruction. Trend is not destiny. We have the power to take control, to shape new visions, to build new relationships, to work towards a desired future state, a brave new educational world that is creative, not destructive. St Mary's College undertook the challenge of self-evaluation because the members of that community implicitly believed that change and improvement were possible.

The School as the Essential Unit of Change

The second assumption is, as Hopkins and Wideen (1984, p. 1) put it, that 'the school is the essential unit of change in the education system'. The last decade of research into effective schools supports the view that attempts at educational change when imposed from outside the school has little impact (Oldroyd and Tiller, 1987, p. 14). The reasons for this resistance to super-imposed change are multi-faceted and complex, but stem primarily from the cultural uniqueness of schools (Dalin and Rust, 1983; Bolam, 1982; Joyce and Showers, 1980). This cultural uniqueness 'is rarely recognised by, or accessible to, external agents or trainers' (Oldroyd and Tiller, p. 14). At the same time, however, the role of the school within the wider society remains an important consideration (Wissler and Oritiz, 1987). While stressing the importance of initiating change at the school level, we should be careful not to regard schools as closed systems, separate either from a wider school system or from society (Alvesson, 1987, p. 6). This point has been dramatically made in the recent work of Coleman and Hoffer (1987) in their much publicized *Public and Private High Schools: The Impact of Communities* which emphasizes the educational role played by social capital — 'the norms, the

social networks, and the relationships between adults and children that are of value for the child's growing up' (p. 36). In addition there is a new political reality for many schools. St Mary's found that evaluation became inevitable as the Federal government increasingly intruded into the affairs of schools, including the non-government, so-called private schools. The school believed it vital that their own 'evidence' would be the valid evidence for external as well as internal purposes of accountability.

Schools Can and Do Make a Difference

The third assumption underlying our approach to educational change is that schools can and do make a difference in the lives of students. The modern school effectiveness debate began in response to James Coleman's research on American schools, *Report on Equality of Educational Opportunity* (1966), which concluded that schools have little impact on the academic performance of students independent of the home background of those students. (See also Flynn, 1985, pp. 266–75.) However, the last two decades of the school effectiveness movement have demonstrated that schools may make a difference to all students and that the processes at work within schools have an important bearing on students' achievements. (See for example: Beare, Caldwell and Millikan, 1988; Caldwell and Spinks, 1988, 1986; Duignan, 1986; Flynn, 1985; Murphy, Well, Hallinger and Mitman, 1985: Tymko, 1984; Cuban, 1984; Purkey and Smith, 1985; Pursell and Cookson, 1982; Rutter *et al.*, 1979.)

The Importance of Evaluation-based Change

The fourth assumption is that enlightened decision-making leading to effective educational change is founded upon an accurate base of data. This means that evaluation should be an inherent part of the school's management structure. It is evaluation, however, that is not one-off, occasional, but is frequent and cyclical. Indeed, responding again to the political reality for schools, in a contracting educational system where educational needs must compete against defence, public welfare and other areas, it becomes increasingly important that schools and school leaders be able to command as well as account for their share of public funds (Glassman, 1986). It is also important that evaluation methodologies be employed which do not merely report but which genuinely and strongly reflect the rich complexities inherent in a school culture. This constitutes further reason why an evaluation (as was explained in Chapter 3) should be viewed as a regular activity and not a one-time event. Moreover, evaluation will need to include both quantitative and qualitative measures of the school's formal and informal curriculum (Murphy and Torrance,

1987). Most importantly, we argue in this book that the key to this evaluative data is that firstly derived from the students themselves.

The Difficult Path from Research to Action, from Theory to Practice

A fifth assumption in our approach to educational improvement refers to the specifically evaluative process in which change for improvement originates. It implies a more specific orientation for educational research and researchers. Although the most effective change is that which evolves from within the school, this is not to deny the role of educational research. On the contrary, it is vital both in validating existing educational practices and pointing the way toward new directions of change (Hoy and Miskel, 1982, p. 62). Regrettably, however, as Miles and Ekholm (1986) demonstrate, in the past, researchers have 'leapt too quickly from the descriptive to the prescriptive, and nurtured the Promethean illusion that by following our conceptual tracks, policy planners and administrators could get there operationally as well'. This does not mean, they conclude, that we abandon the quest for school improvement. However, it does mean that we must abandon the 'master plan' and reorganize the task, accepting a more modest scenario to take into account specific school contexts and a social reality characterized by problems of power, uncertainty, continuous negotiation, loose-endedness and local history (Miles and Ekholm, p. 62). Miles has developed a number of very useful insights which will help lighten the way along the complex and seldom smooth path towards effective educational change. These are discussed later in this chapter.

The Value of Collaborative Action Research

A sixth assumption, derived from the previous one, is that evaluative research, in order to be effective, can and should be collaborative, that is between researcher and school. While change imposed upon a school from outside is seldom effective, outside expertise can play a vital role in producing a more effective school. Indeed, the educational researcher's expertise is often a key ingredient in developing and implementing an effective programme design (Miles, 1987; Oldroyd and Tiller, 1987; and Holly and Whitehead, 1986). The researcher is able to be more, maybe even most, helpful when she or he is able to become an integral part of the school community and culture. In the St Mary's School Evaluation, one of the authors was the Deputy Principal who also made the evaluation the subject for his dissertation for an advanced university degree. The other author, from the university, was thoroughly familiar with the St Mary's community. From his experience as a parent, he had prior

knowledge of the school. He had been a teacher and had also served as a school board chairman for a school which is one of the primary feeder schools for St Mary's. Finally, while on study leave from the university, he had served as a full-time teaching member of St Mary's College. It was during this period that the St Mary's Evaluation was formulated and designed. This strong collaboration between research and school played a major role in the successful implementation of the St Mary's Project.

An Emphasis on Fundamental Values

A final assumption which we make in this chapter, is that educational change is about fundamental values. We are not concerned here about 'mere management' or cosmetic applications which go to the trappings rather than the essence of schooling. Nor are we concerned with the latest educational trend. Indeed, we agree with Holmes and Wynne (1989) that it is often the principal's responsibility to oppose such changes. Our concern here is with how to bring about, within a school, those educational changes which reassert fundamental and central values about human nature: moral and religious issues, development of self, personal and communal responsibility, meaningful relationships, concern for others, and so on — changes which should be at the top of every educational agenda.

Guidelines for the Effective Management of Change

'Read this Warning First!'

The remainder of this chapter describes the 'lessons', the policy implications, we have drawn from our experience with the St Mary's Project and from reading the extensive literature on educational change. This experience has made us both humble and wary of a 'ten commandment' approach to educational change. The guidelines discussed below are therefore not meant to be prescriptive, but suggestive and hopefully thought-provoking. For each school and context, change is to some extent unique. More than this, a school community is not a static entity; rather a school is comprised of people — students, teachers, parents — who will not see eye-to-eye on every issue. School communities must somehow cope with the dynamic tension of competing and often conflicting demands of excellence, equality, comprehensiveness, etc. Increasingly, too, schools are influenced by the social, economic and political forces which derive from the particular local, regional, national and international setting within which they are situated.

Accordingly, no 'formula' for change can fit all situations. For this

reason, although we find much to commend in the formulations such as Miles' (1987) fourteen 'causal' factors in producing effective school change, we reject a rigid approach which suggests certain factors are always 'pre-conditions' to others, or work in a certain, standardized way. Indeed, some organizational theorists would dispute whether we can determine cause from effect. As Clark *et al.* (1989) surmise:

> March, Weick and Peters and Waterman have argued that in effective organizations there is what they have termed a 'bias for action'. The peculiar characteristic of this bias is that it asserts that action in organizations frequently precedes intent. Organizations, these theorists contend, often discover preferences by acting . . . Do high expectations for student success 'cause' high pupil achievement or does high achievement result in high expectations for student performance? One only has to deal with this issue if it is assumed that linear causality is found frequently in organizations. Many organizational theorists would subscribe to Weick's argument that:

> When any two events are related interdependently, designating one of those two cause and the other effect is an arbitrary designation. . . In any causal loop no variable is any more or less important than any other variable. No variable in a loop controls other variables without itself being controlled by them. (p. 181)

Instead of a cause-effect model, we, in the spirit of Einstein, prefer a theory of relativity. In any given situation, various change factors, like molecules, will react in different ways. Factors such as leadership may combine with other elements in one situation, yet react differently in other contexts involving different combinations. At different times, factors may be a cause and an effect. The process of change itself also makes us hesitant to be prescriptive in offering guidelines for change. For a start, other than its pervasiveness, we do not yet know a great deal about change — a body of knowledge which remains both under-theorized and under-researched.

Introduction to the Guidelines for the Effective Management of Change

School improvement does not come about automatically. Schools and school leaders must prepare for change (Gyte, 1988). In a seminal work Miles (1987) has identified and analyzed sixteen 'causal' factors which serve as very practical, though general, guidelines regarding the effective implementation of change in a school setting. These factors are derived from the key findings of his study of urban high school improvement efforts in the USA (Miles, 1987). Miles' research focusses on the equally

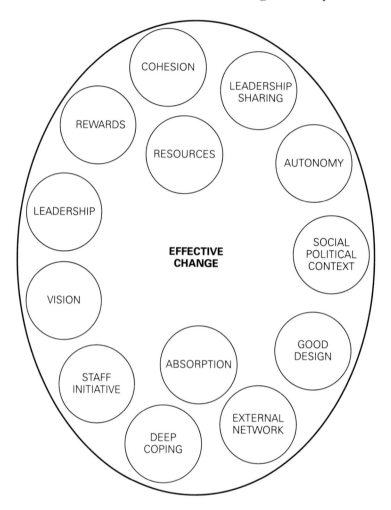

Figure 11   Factors involved in effective school change

important practical question of strategic pathways to a more effective school.

Shakespeare observed wisely in *King Lear* that 'ripeness is all'; and, four necessary preconditions, states Miles, must exist before a school is ripe to embark along the path of educational change.

a)   a principal with leadership and management skills;
b)   the existence of some school autonomy;
c)   a staff environment characterized by relatively low conflict and high trust — overall cohesiveness; and
d)   good programme design which matches the characteristics of the particular school. (Miles, 1987)

Whilst we agree that the following factors are often related to school improvement, we are reluctant, for the reasons stated above, to see them as necessarily causal, or operative in every case, or always in the same way. Though they will be discussed separately, it is important to realize that these guidelines are interrelated. The degree of interrelatedness, however, will vary depending upon the characteristics of the particular school (Margulies and Wallace 1973, pp. 154–7). Thus, these guidelines should be viewed as comprising bundles of different elements whose linkages in any particular context may be comparatively tight or loose (Weick, 1976).

Guideline 1: The Importance of Vision

Chapter 5 demonstrated the significance of school vision. Effective school change cannot be premised upon an amorphous, vague idea of school improvement. School effectiveness is brought about by the realization of a compelling vision of education (Starratt, 1986; Beare, Caldwell and Millikan, 1988). 'To lead, is fundamentally to show the way' (W. Greenfield, 1987, p. 16). While some change, good or bad, can eventuate through educational 'drift', planned and purposeful school change is most often driven by a vision incorporating the ideals, values, and concept of the educational good as defined by the particular school community.

Guideline 2: Leadership

The state-of-the-art

Just as we sounded a cautionary note in our discussion of Miles' factors relating to effective school improvement, we make two caveats before making generalizations about leadership. First, despite thousands of studies on the nature of leadership, very little is known about it (Yukl, 1989). Indeed, the proliferation of leadership theories from such diverse disciplines as psychology, sociology, social-psychology, political science, business, theology, anthropology, and so on, each employing its own schemata and vocabulary, is confusing at best. As Salancik *et al.* (1975) concluded:

> There is perhaps no area of study in organizational behavior which has more blind alleys and less critical knowledge than the area of leadership. Practitioners and researchers alike have groped for years with such questions as: What is leadership? How does it work? How does one become an effective leader? Yet after many years of investigation, it appears we have no ready, useful answers. (p. 81)

Second, is the difficulty of designing a theory which can account for the inherent complexity of our society coupled with a natural bias to want to attribute events to particular causes. As Yukl (1989) notes:

> Stereotypes, implicit theories, and simplified assumptions about causality aid people in making sense out of events that would otherwise be incomprehensible. (p. 265)

While acknowledging the confused state of knowledge about leadership and the inherent cultural biases in attributing leadership causes to organizational events, we nevertheless submit that people, like schools, can and do make a difference. Therefore, we find the following synthesis about what we do know to be both insightful and useful.

Leadership and vision

Speaking at the 1987 Victorian Catholic Education Conference in Melbourne, Sr Mary Ann Eckhoff, Superintendent of over forty Catholic schools in her St Louis diocese in the United States, observed that in her wide experience of schools she had never seen a poor school with a good principal or vice versa. A precondition of an excellent school is a principal with effective leadership and management skills. (See also Hoyle, 1988; Peters and Austin, 1985.)

Vision only becomes reality when, through effective leadership, it illuminates the ordinary events of school life with dramatic significance, is articulated in compelling ways by school leaders, is shared with colleagues, becomes implanted in the structures and processes of the organization, when day-to-day decisions are made in light of it, and when all members of an organization celebrate the vision in ritual, ceremonies and art forms (Starratt, 1986, p. 15). While the principal does not have to fulfil all these leadership functions, it is clear that school improvement assumes effective leadership. As W. Greenfield (1987) concludes 'others may lead, but the principal must lead'. To lead is also to communicate, to sell, to enthuse, to have a sense of mission (Hoyle, 1988). And, when a vision permeates the whole school community the result is cohesion. Furthermore, leadership is not a one-way process. Staff members, as they participate actively in the process of change, will themselves in turn be influential in shaping the school's vision. Finally, members of a school community, united around a clear and compelling vision, will encourage each other to work, slowly but surely, towards making the dream a reality.

A micro view of leadership

Beare, Caldwell and Millikan (1988) in their book, *Creating an Excellent School*, provide an excellent summary of the latest developments in leadership theory and its relevance to educational settings. In brief, leadership theory has evolved from an earlier micro view which empha-

sized a scientific approach and which focussed on a narrow range of factors affecting leadership. Examples of this earlier work were Stogdill's (1974) analysis of leadership traits (e.g., energy, persistence, sense of responsibility, self-confidence and so on) which generally characterized effective leaders; Hersey and Blanchard's (1982) work which focussed on the adaptation of leadership style to the maturity of followers; and Fiedler, Chemsers and Mahar's (1977) contingency leadership theory which suggests that different leaders have different styles and that effective leaders are those who find or create a leadership context which best matches their particular style.

The emerging macro view of leadership

While the empirically-based micro approaches to leadership are valuable, a macro or holistic, interdisciplinary approach to leadership has recently emerged which has great relevance not only to leadership, but also to the role of leaders in bringing about effective schools. This macro view is characterized by writers such as Thomas Greenfield (1986) and William Greenfield (1987) who see leadership in very broad terms as intricately involved with the culture and values of an organization. As William Greenfield (1987) argues:

> Because the school functions as a moral institution, the school principal has a special responsibility to be a conscientious moral actor, that is, to take actions and make decisions in a distinctly moral manner. Schools are normatively complex and present principals with daily considerations of a moral nature. (pp. 4–5)

Thomas Greenfield (1986) suggests that 'leaders will try to commit others to the values that they themselves believe are good. Organisations are built on the unification of people around values' (p. 166). Holt (1987) concludes that many educational leaders, taking a narrow view of leadership, have misunderstood both the nature of education and the way teachers solve curriculum problems. Teaching and learning cannot be reduced to procedures. Instead, leaders must realize that trying to improve schools involves the solution of problems which are essentially moral because they involve value judgments about the nature of the educational 'good' and about attendant practical problems concerning how to make that 'good' fit the reality of a particular school. This view of educational change requires that educational leadership be conceived in very broad terms, encompassing the whole culture of the organization — its values, beliefs, norms, myths, rituals, symbols and structures and how these relate to a wider community of which the school is but a part (Handy, 1988).

Beare, Caldwell and Millikan (1988, Chapter 6) posit the following generalizations about leadership which they see emerging from the latest literature:

a) outstanding leaders emphasize transforming leadership — appealing to higher order needs of people to be involved and committed to a cause which they perceive as significant and of great importance. Mother Teresa, Winston Churchill, Martin Luther King, Jr are examples of leaders who emphasized higher order needs. Transformational leadership is to be contrasted with transactional leadership which focusses on the simple exchange of one thing for another and more immediate, and generally lower order, needs;

b) outstanding leaders have a compelling vision — a desired future state for their organization;

c) the vision is communicated in a way which secures commitment and develops cohesion among members of the organization. To lead is to communicate;

d) communication of the vision conveys meaning and saturates every aspect of school life with significance;

e) schools, being moral institutions, and principals, being moral leaders — values are central to leadership;

f) leaders have a pivotal role to play in developing the organization's culture — shared values, beliefs, rituals, etc;

g) the research and literature strongly support a leadership approach which incorporates school-based management and collaborative decision making which reflect an enhanced view of teachers as professionals;

h) there are many kinds of leadership forces — technical management, human relations, educational expertise, shared symbols and cultural life — and these are usually diffused amongst the leaders of the school;

i) attention must be given to institutionalizing the vision if transforming leadership is to be successful;

j) both masculine (e.g., competitive, team approach) and feminine (e.g., nurturing, caring) leadership qualities are important regardless of the gender of the leader.

The above characteristics may be daunting to a school leader. Nevertheless an effective principal can communicate a compelling vision of excellence, develop staff cohesion, foster and coordinate external support networks, provide rewards for staff, share leadership with others, initiate deep coping strategies and guide the whole change process towards its eventual establishment as a natural positive element of the school's ethos.

Consistent with these concepts, Sr Barbara Amott, the Principal of St Mary's College, was and remains an example of an effective leader. Since coming to St Mary's in 1979, she has worked hard to build a

cohesive staff, united around a compelling vision which she frequently articulates at staff meetings, assemblies and school rituals, such as graduation ceremonies. Numerous staff development days have been devoted to building staff cohesion and to the staff's articulation of the unique role to be played by St Mary's as a Catholic school offering a Catholic education. The Principal has also developed an intricate and supportive network of parents, past scholars and parish members who collectively have played a key role in contributing to and fostering the school's vision of education. The Principal established a curriculum committee of teachers to help guide the school along the path toward improvement. Similarly, it was the Principal's initiative which led the outside research consultant to come to St Mary's to assist the staff in conducting a school evaluation. There is little doubt that, in the case of St Mary's, Sr Barbara's own sense of vision formed the foundation upon which are built the essential causal elements of effective school improvement.

Shared leadership

Earlier the characteristics of outstanding leaders were described. One aspect not drawn out was that such leadership implies that it be a shared quality. Educational change is likely to be most effective when it involves the whole school community, when leadership is shared. Leadership sharing is in part what Starratt refers to when discussing the communalizing of a school's vision so that it becomes a shared vision. It is what Sergiovanni means when noting that the leadership forces of a school do not usually reside in one person. Rather, most effective schools have many 'leaders' for the leadership must be shared to be effective. There must be what is termed in the literature — 'leadership density'. Leadership sharing also involves what Peters and Waterman describe as 'productivity through people'. Furthermore, it is what Caldwell, Spinks and others provide by their collaborative school management approach to educational decision making. Power sharing is inextricably linked with the moral leadership of the principal. As W. Greenfield contends:

> The exercise of interpersonal competence does not constitute manipulation of the teacher, or the 'using' of teachers to accomplish private ends because (1) principals, through dialogue, help teachers to articulate mutually held goals and ways to achieve them and (2) the idea of empowerment assumes a voluntary commitment by the teacher toward those goals. From one perspective however, the teacher *is* the means, because it is *only* through the teacher's adoption of and commitment to the principal's (or another's) vision that the desired ends-in-view can be realized. Such adoption and internalization underlies the probability of significant change in a school. (1987, pp. 14–15)

An effective principal has the attitude that people do not work *for* me; they work *with* me.

There seems little doubt that power or leadership sharing will become an increasingly important factor in creating effective schools. There are several reasons for this belief. First, more than ever before, educational issues are complex, multi-faceted and highly technical. As a result, no single person can be competent in every area. This means that leaders will have to delegate more in order to make full use of the specific expertise of various individuals within the organization and from external support networks. Second, there is also a general trend toward more democratic structures and more interdependence between various organizations and organizational structures. Consequently, a collaborative and participatory approach will become more necessary and common. Third, both the necessity for, and rate of, change will likely continue to accelerate. Thus, organizations, in order to be more flexible and facilitating of such change, will have to have more people involved in the management process so that the capacity to adjust becomes integral to the institution. Fourth, in order for educational innovations to keep pace with changes in society, it will be important for large organizations to maintain the benefits of smallness by giving greater autonomy to individual components of the system. This will of necessity mean greater power or leadership sharing (Godet, 1987). Finally, by encouraging more people to become involved in school leadership, not only will teachers be more committed, but they themselves will also grow and develop, thereby contributing more to the organization and being individually happier for it (Jones, 1987).

Such leadership or power sharing is an essential component of a school evaluation. The St Mary's College Evaluation found this to be so. Staff, present and past students and parents shared the directing of the process. Even though they were critical of particular school policies or practices, these groups were very positive about the fact that school leaders sought their opinions and their involvement.

Guideline 3: Cohesiveness

A corollary of shared leadership is group cohesion. Miles found that those schools which were successful in effecting educational change were characterized by relatively low conflict and high trust, that is, cohesiveness. In other words there must be a climate conducive to change. As Owens (1981) points out, schools which:

> emphasize supportiveness, open communication, and intellectuality, and reward achievement and success out-perform those that stress competition, constraint, restrictive rules, standards and operational procedures and reward conformity. (p. 226)

Owens' description, depicts some of the characteristics of a cohesive school, but ignores the more fundamental question of how that cohesion is created in the first place. The specific answer to this question will vary according to the unique circumstances of each school community. Nevertheless, a number of general overarching principles are involved, which may apply to all organizations.

First, it must be recognized that there is no quick, easy, instant formula for achieving group cohesion. Commitment, cohesion, trust — all are achieved with some 'cost'. They require a tremendous investment in time, effort and concern for staff, students and parents. Unfortunately, many school leaders devote almost all their time, resources and energy into making the 'right' decision, with virtually no investment in building commitment to the decision, which is part of the planning for change.

Second, cohesion is at once a necessary by-product of, and a precondition for, the effective adoption by the school community of a particular educational vision. Cohesion is about motivating others to adopt the communal vision as their own and to work towards its realization. Thus cohesion is something which must be developed and 'requires a high degree of interpersonal knowledge as well as skill' (W. Greenfield, 1987, pp. 13–14). This means that school leaders must 'treat people as partners, treat them as equals and treat them with respect' (Peters and Waterman, 1982, p. 238). It means that the leaders must exemplify in their own behaviour around the school the kind of relationship which the leaders expect between teachers and students, amongst teachers, and amongst all the school community (Starratt, 1986, p. 18). The process of developing cohesion will, in turn, have an impact upon other factors such as the willingness of the staff to become 'involved', the degree to which they will take initiative for the school's sake, and the extent to which staff may be reinforced in their efforts accordingly, upon the implementation of change itself.

Cohesion is thereby influenced by and in turn influences vision. However, it is helpful to realize that underlying a school's vision is a set of values. Any organization must be, in Peters and Waterman's terms, 'hands-on, value driven':

> We call the fifth attribute of the excellent companies 'hands-on, value-driven'. We are struck by the explicit attention they pay to values, and by the way in which their leaders have created exciting environments through personal attention, persistence, and direct intervention — far down the line. (1982, p. 279)

Such is the stuff of which school cohesion may be made!

Finally, although it is easy to say that staff cohesion is a necessary 'precondition' for effective educational change, it is not easy to achieve. Nevertheless, in order to bring about effective change, it is crucial that school leaders understand the group of the particular school community.

There is not scope in this chapter to discuss this fully. However, the work of Mead (1967), Cooley (1964), Becker (1960) and others provides many insights into the nature of human behaviour within social settings and how such realities as 'symbolic interaction', 'reference groups' and 'significant others' influence individual behaviour. In fact, much research is still needed regarding how the groupings which comprise the social setting of a school community may be instrumental in establishing and maintaining its shared values. Of course, such group pressures may also 'frustrate the negotiation of shared collegial norms. Reference groups used for the defence of one set of values can obstruct the open discussion of and agreement on others' (Nias, 1988, p. 302; Woods, 1979).

Returning again to the St Mary's College Evaluation Project, though it was formally initiated in 1986, the groundwork for the project had begun in 1979 when Sr Barbara became principal. School unity, around a unique Catholic vision of education has been a dominant theme on her agenda. Prefects have frequently been invited to report to and attend staff meetings. Staff are required to attend general Parents and Friends Association meetings each term. Parent-teacher nights each term include a general discussion with parents which usually involves an issue related to values inherent in the school. These are examples of the specific means by which a cohesion of all the personnel of the school might be formed and maintained. Without this earlier development in staff cohesion, an evaluation of St Mary's College may not have been achievable.

Guideline 4: Rewards — 'What about Me?'

The path to school improvement is seldom smooth. And the school's vision requires the commitment of the teachers. Nevertheless, teachers are not merely organizational units. If progress towards achievement of the school's vision is to be maintained the hard work and dedication of teachers must be rewarded (Burack and Torda, 1985, pp. 50–3). However, to be effective these rewards must fit the unique combination of needs which exist in a particular school. Rewards can take many forms: praise, recognition, attention, time, additional responsibility, etc. Accordingly, it is important for a principal to know his or her teachers well so that rewards may match the actual needs of the persons who are involved (Conner and Lake, 1988).

The literature on motivation can also provide some guidance here. Hoy and Miskel (1982) define motivation as:

> the complex forces, drives, needs, tension states, or other mechanisms that start and maintain voluntary activity directed toward the achievement of personal goals. (p. 137)

It is beyond the scope of this book to discuss motivation in depth, but mention of a few motivation theories will suggest their relevance. Though now a little dated and under attack by some writers, Maslow's need hierarchy theory suggests that people have a hierarchy of needs. Thus in rewarding staff, a principal will want to take into account not only basic 'security' needs, but also 'higher' needs such as the need for recognition and status and the need for self-actualization and development of the full person. Herzberg's two-factor theory postulates that one set of factors contributes to job satisfaction, while a second separate set of factors relates to job dissatisfaction. As such a principal can motivate staff by eliminating job dissatisfiers (described by Herzberg as 'hygienes') as well as building job satisfiers ('motivators') which enhance the achievement and recognition of staff (Hoy and Miskel, 1982, pp. 139–48).

Vroom's expectancy theory is especially relevant to staff commitment and motivation. Expectancy theory assumes that people evaluate 'the expected outcomes or personal payoffs resulting from their actions, and then they choose how to behave', and also that individual values and attitudes interact with environmental components (e.g., school climate, role expectations, etc) to influence behaviour. The three major components of this theory involve:

Valence: perceived positive or negative value, worth or attractiveness that an individual ascribes to potential outcomes, rewards, or incentives for working in an organization.

Instrumentality: perceived probability that an incentive with valence will be forthcoming after a given level of performance or achievement.

Expectancy: subjective probability that a given effort will yield a specified performance level (Hoy and Miskel, pp. 155–61).

According to Vroom's theory, motivation will be greatest when the outcomes have high personal value (valence), the behaviour will lead to reward (instrumentality) and the ability exists to perform at the desired level (expectancy). Vroom's theory is particularly insightful in explaining the linkages between programme design, staff empowerment, leadership and the consequent willingness, commitment and initiative of school staff.

Mention should also be made of Skinner's reinforcement theory. While not accounting for all learning behaviour, the basic concept of positive reinforcement is relevant for any successful implementation of change. The principal needs to structure the school's programme so that behaviour which facilitates the desired change can be rewarded. At the same time, it might be necessary to utilize non-reinforcement techniques

to discourage behaviour which is incompatible with planned school improvement efforts. The reality is that most school leaders devote too little attention to positive reinforcement. Even worse, many organizations are dominated by negative reinforcement characterized by the principal spending much of his or her time on the few staff who are unsupportive rather than nurturing, encouraging and positively rewarding the majority of staff who are supportive. In contrast, outstanding leaders spend most of their efforts positively rewarding the good behaviour of the majority rather than focussing most of their management and leadership energies on a few who are likely to remain negative in any event (Peters and Waterman, 1982, Chapter 3).

We consider that the St Mary's Project was characterized by adequate rewards and support given by the Principal, Sr Barbara, to staff who have been involved in the evaluation. The Principal has taken every opportunity to praise the efforts of all involved. Also, the ideas, recommendations and comments of staff, both individually and collectively, were listened to and weighed carefully. As with any group, however, there were a few staff members who felt threatened by change and evaluation. It was important to keep these staff members informed, to consider their opinions and to stress the evolutionary nature of school improvement. One teacher could have been described as hostile and cynical about the evaluation. With this teacher, the Principal utilized non-reinforcement in ignoring the cynical behaviour, while at the same time making sure that the staff member felt 'in on things' and was receiving full information.

Finally, in relation to rewards and motivation of staff, attention must be given to higher levels of motivation brought about by transforming leadership. As Burns (1978) characterizes it, transforming leadership:

> occurs when one or more persons *engage* with others in such a way that leaders and followers raise one another to higher levels of motivation and morality. Their purposes, which might have started out separate but related, in the case of transactional leadership, become fused. Power bases are linked not as counter-weights but as mutual support for common purpose. Various names are used for such leadership: elevating, mobilizing, inspiring, exalting, uplifting, exhorting, evangelizing. The relationship can be moralistic, of course. But transforming leadership ultimately becomes moral in that it raises the level of human conduct and ethical aspiration of both the leader and the led, and thus has a transforming effect on both ... Transforming leadership is dynamic in the sense that the leaders throw themselves into a relationship with followers who feel 'elevated' by it and often become more active themselves, thereby creating new cadres of leaders. (p. 20)

Guideline 5: The Need for 'Coping Strategies'

Even with adequate rewards and a great 'esprit de corps', school improvement programmes run into difficulties (Farrar, 1987, p. 4). Teachers resist, resources don't materialize, staff leave, the school parents don't attend meetings, students are apathetic, and so on. Moreover, human issues — resistance, scepticism, delays, lack of coordination, lack of time, shortage of staff — tend to be the most numerous and the most weighty (Miles, 1987, p. 16). So, dealing with the 'teething' problems of any significant school improvement programme requires productive coping skills.

Miles (1987, pp. 16–17) describes three broad types of coping: shallow, mild and deep. Unsuccessful school improvement programmes tend to employ shallow coping strategies (exemplified by 'doing nothing, delaying, people-shuffling,' etc) or mild coping strategies, like 'easing off, negotiating, or holding off somebody' or some programme. Deep coping, in contrast, is far more productive than mild or shallow coping. It involves 'adding new people, re-designing the system, empowering, team building, making it work'. Leaders skilled in the process of deep coping have the attitude which often characterized the nation-wide efforts of countries in World War II when peace time economies were converted to war economies almost overnight — 'If it is possible give us a day; if it is impossible, give us two days!' Effective school improvement programmes establish deep coping mechanisms which allow the programme to be adaptive, to evolve in such ways that it fits the specific characteristics of the particular school. As Farrar (1987) observed in her study of effective urban high schools in the USA:

> Leadership in the face of what often seemed an endless stream of new and chronic complications, called for the ability to be decisive and to act quickly to address problems that were particularly threatening to the programme. Principals who handled these situations effectively were those who maintained a certain 'psychological distance' from the problem. They were flexible and solved problems by making major programme changes or terminating programme projects or shifting resources from one project to another. Skills in forging consensus or in developing compromise positions in inter-faculty disputes, rather than announcing decisions by principal fiat, proved particularly effective in dealing with problems or conflicts that developed within the programme. (p. 5)

Caldwell and Spinks (1986 and 1988) and Beare, Caldwell and Millikan (1988) contend that a collaborative approach to school management can help to both minimize conflict and maximize consensus. In large part this is because consensus building and power sharing are inherent charac-

teristics of the approach. Caldwell and Spinks' book, *Policy-Making and Planning for School Effectiveness* (1986, Chapter 12) provides an excellent survey of the literature on conflict resolution and offers much useful advice for minimizing and resolving conflicts and building consensus.

Guideline 6: School Autonomy

In order for a school to exercise leadership and unite the school community around a common vision, it must have the necessary autonomy to make desired changes and offer appropriate rewards to those involved. As indicated earlier in this chapter, there is considerable support in the research for the belief that schools are the essential unit of change and that school-based management and collaborative decision making are especially effective in realizing school improvement. This emphasis on the smaller more responsive organizational unit of the school also finds considerable support from business management research (Godet, 1987). Peters and Waterman (1982), for example, in their influential book, *In Search of Excellence: Lessons from America's Best-run Companies*, indicate that a major factor in the success of large companies like IBM is the fact that they remain flexible and responsive because they maintain the features of being small. That is, the organizational structure gives considerable autonomy to smaller units within the organization. As a result of these developments and the realization that effective curriculum change cannot be imposed from the top down, there is increasing interest in many countries in giving schools a significant degree of control over their own resources. Miles, in his study of effective urban schools, also found school autonomy to be a necessary precondition for effective educational change. People in the 'organization' must feel sufficiently empowered to make a difference. If a school can have a significant control over its own resources, curriculum, timetable, staffing and so on, it can ensure that any programme design for change will fit the needs of that particular school community. Rudyard Kipling wrote in his poem, *The Elephant's Child*:

> I keep six honest serving men
> They taught me all I knew
> Their names are What and Why and When
> And How and Where and Who.

To realize improvement, the school community must be provided with the autonomy to determine for itself the what, why, when, how, where and who of educational change.

School autonomy is a feature of St Mary's College because it is a non-systemic Catholic school controlled solely by the Presentation Sisters of Tasmania. While some general policy guidelines and support services

are provided by the Tasmanian Catholic Education Office, the major decisions and day-to-day operation of the school are completely in the hands of the Principal and the School Board, together with other school leaders. The school has full control over staffing, resources, school organization, curriculum, enrolments, and school policies. The people who have the most direct stake in making the school work also have the power to set the school's educational course and make changes which direct the school toward the fulfilment of its unique vision of education.

Guideline 7: Control Over the Staffing and other Resources within a School

Another important factor in bringing about effective school improvement is the school's adequate control over its staffing. Such control is important for a number of reasons. First, with such control a principal can attract to the school teachers who will be committed to its vision. Second, if necessary, the principal can also assist uncommitted or hostile staff members to look for a school community to whose vision they can commit themselves. Third, there is staff control. This means that the principal has full power to channel rewards so that they are given to those staff who support and work towards the improvement of the school as it moves towards its vision. Finally, for all these reasons, such staff control enhances staff willingness and initiative.

As with control over staffing, the degree of control a school has over resources is directly influenced by the extent of a school's autonomy. For school improvement to occur it is vital that school leaders have access to, and ability to exert sufficient control over technical expertise, staffing, training, time allocations, administrative support, etc. Of the required resources, perhaps the most frequently overlooked are adequate staffing and time. As D. Clark *et al.* surmises:

> Good schools have a reasonable level of human resources and slack time. In the IES [instructionally effective schools] literature, this shows up in a high ration of adults to children in the building. In the SI [school improvement] literature, the importance of internal and external assisters is emphasized. Both literatures describe the necessity of time for teachers to participate in staff development activity and to incorporate new practices into their already crowded professional lives. Good practice is facilitated by a reasonable level of organizational redundancy and slack at the classroom level. Tolerance for failure, encouragement of experimentation, and the capacity to invent and adapt innovations are not achievable in organizational settings where effectiveness is regularly traded off for efficiency. (1989, p. 184)

School improvement has costs — and school leaders must have both the ability to pay the price required and the choice to obtain what resources they most need for improving their particular situation.

Guideline 8: The Teachers' Willingness and Initiative

Staff willingness and initiative of teachers to contribute to and carry out the difficult task of school improvement is a direct by-product of leadership sharing in particular, and of effective leadership in general. School improvement requires that people learn new skills. This cannot be done simply by explanation, reading or listening to guest speakers. Learning the skills of school improvement requires doing and regular feedback. Staff will only be willing to engage in this re-learning process if they are committed to the school's vision, if adequate support is provided from the external network of the school and if they are rewarded by and for their participation (Miles, 1987; Beare, Caldwell and Millikan, 1988; Miles and Ekholm, 1986).

Guideline 9: Good Programme Design

The adage that 'to fail to plan is to plan to fail' may apply to school improvement. Accordingly, the fourth factor (to Miles a 'precondition') for effective school improvement is that of a good programme design. Programme design means the essential elements required in a plan for effecting appropriate change in the school. It does not simply refer to the adequacy of the curriculum of the school. A good design entails the presence of training and technical support, adequate evaluation, planning and monitoring procedures, etc. It is also important that the design fits the particular characteristics of the school. This is why a programme imposed upon the school from outside and from the top down does not usually result in significant long-term improvement. It is also why a school must have a significant degree of autonomy to adapt or adjust the programme to meet its particular and local needs. The research on organizational change also suggests that a good programme design will involve 'power sharing'. Members of an organization will be provided with information as accurate and complete as possible. They will be considered and, as far as possible, involved in the planning and execution of the change project. Members will also be rewarded for their participation and assistance. A good programme design will also provide a linkage between the school and valuable support groups, such as university consultants, departmental experts and members of the community. Finally, a good programme design will be flexible and promote evolutionary or gradual change, rather than radical and therefore threatening change.

A major ingredient of the St Mary's College Evaluation was attention to its design, on the basis of efforts toward building staff cohesion and the school community's sharing of a vision for the school. In time a curriculum would be organized through which the need for a school evaluation and review would be crystalized. When that occurred, outside consultancy from the University was obtained. In this case an ideal plan ensued with the consultant actually becoming a member of staff for four months. Also, and consistent with Miles' research findings, the design was implemented through a collaborative process. The school staff were asked to to suggest the areas, and specific questions, which would be the focus for the school's evaluation. This was vital in three respects. First, it gave the staff and the whole St Mary's community a stake in the project. They knew what was going on, why, and how. Second, the project did not develop aimlessly; a special focus gave the project a sense of direction. Third, in getting teachers actively involved, the project exhibited some sense of anticipation, even urgency, which helped to get things done even when people were busy and tired from coping with the day-to-day school duties. Interestingly, this sense of anticipation extended to parents and especially to past students several of whom wrote to the authors expressing their delight at being asked to reflect and comment upon the quality of education experienced during their years at St Mary's.

Where does the St Mary's Project go from here? Following presentation of the findings of the evaluation to the school, the process of collaboration amongst parents, staff, students and administrators will continue. Among their tasks will be the setting of goals and priorities and the initiating of policies which might be implemented to further help the school community work towards its educational vision. Here, the zeal, enthusiasm and good will of the staff in responding to the evaluation results will be significant. It will be important for all to be aware that the process takes time. If change is going to be effective, it must proceed gradually and with great commitment from the whole school community.

Such procedures are consistent with the first stage of the Collaborative School Management Cycle as outlined in Chapter 7. Once the new changes have become 'institutionalized' in goals and policies, the school will then move through the remaining stages of the collaborative process. These cyclical stages provide a meta structure, the broad programme design, by which successful change can be managed at St Mary's as it moves toward making its educational vision a school reality.

Guideline 10: Supportive Networks Surrounding the School

Improvement in a school seldom works in isolation. This is because a school itself does not work or exist in a vacuum. The task of school

improvement often requires interaction with numerous forces outside as well as inside the school. For this reason, the effective leader will develop an external network of resources which will support and facilitate the change process. The exact composition of this network will depend upon the type of school, its location, size and other factors. However, often included in such networks are outside consultants (for example with expertise in evaluation, and research methodologies, programme design, etc), education department support groups (e.g., curriculum branch), school system policy makers and superintendents, and competent members of the community.

In the St Mary's Project, certain people in the Catholic Education Office, one or two local parishes, the university, guest speakers, etc were part of the external support network. Moreover, not only have network members come to the College, but St Mary's teachers have also attended seminars and courses from which they have learnt new skills and received support and encouragement to further develop themselves individually by contributing to the improvement of the St Mary's community. In addition to encouraging teacher willingness and initiative, this support network has helped staff to cope with the trouble spots which are part of any change process. They have enabled St Mary's to pursue a more orderly and gradual course of change.

Guideline 11: Evolutionary Not Revolutionary Change

Developing and implementing a programme of school improvement does not come about by some equivalent of a military coup. Effective educational change is not revolutionary, but evolutionary (Blake and Mouton, 1985, pp. 40–4). It is gradual, non-threatening, adaptive, flexible. It maintains the delicate balance between stability and change which characterizes all successful school organization (Popkewitz, 1983). It is not sudden, climactic and disruptive. Thus the best school improvement projects studied by Miles (1987) fostered:

> an evolutionary programme development process, which permitted the school to add, subtract, modify programme pieces as they went along, rather than starting out with a full-blown design which they tried to implement systematically. (p. 13)

Evolutionary programme development is a product of vision, control over resources, supportive external networks, staff willingness and initiative, and extensive use of deep coping strategies.

The St Mary's Project was required to make adjustments to its programme design. Its methodology, costs, the time-frame for reporting and many other aspects have undergone change and have evolved to fit the exigencies of the specific educational setting of this school. This

capacity to evolve and adjust has been another necessary element in successful school improvement.

Guideline 12: Implementation and Adoption

Plans for effective school improvement are also brought into fruition through effective implementation. Implementation itself, however, is influenced by the factors already discussed: compelling vision, sound programme design, gradual and evolutionary change, strong and shared leadership, willingness and initiative of teachers, and skills of deep coping, etc. If these other factors exist, the improvement programme is likely to be well implemented. In their first discussions of the final Report of the St Mary's College Evaluation, the teachers confirmed the view that such factors have been essential to a sensible implementation of the evaluation's findings.

Guideline 13: 'Institutionalization'

Perhaps the test of effective implementation is whether the plans for improvement are institutionalized or absorbed. Miles found that 'institutionalizing' the programme was another important factor in effective school improvement (Miles, 1987, pp. 7–8). This means that the programme pervaded what Starratt (1986) described as the school's standard operational procedures, policies, curriculum, day-to-day operating schedule — the very bones of the school. In other words, the school has absorbed it. The values inherent in the programme echoed the central values and meanings espoused in the school's vision and celebrated in its ceremonies (formal and informal), and ordinary daily and weekly activities (Starratt, 1986). Again, institutionalizing is greatly influenced by the nature of the school's leadership and vision. In order for this absorption to occur the teachers must feel a sense of ownership so that the programme for change becomes their programme (Conner and Patterson, 1985, pp. 57–8).

Conclusion

There is an interesting paradox in the discussion of change which has been largely ignored in the literature. It is that change and social order are in reality two parts of the same problem. Within the culture of the institution of the school are the seeds of change which bloom into the flower of school improvement. That new flower, in turn, will produce other seeds which bloom again into other flowers. Moreover, as in

nature, the make-up of the flower itself will continue to evolve as it is influenced by, and must adjust to, different environmental forces. Over the years the improving school will help shape society, and itself will be shaped by the social context in which it operates. Thus educational reform is characterized by dual and paradoxical qualities of change and stability (Popkewitz, 1983).

In this chapter we have suggested how a school's vision, revived through an evaluative experience, may be realized and some of the ways by which a school can get from what is to what should be. We have explored the necessary preconditions of, and causal factors related to, the successful management of educational change. The case of St Mary's College has been drawn in order to provide an actual illustration of the dynamics of school improvement. Emerging from the theoretical work of Miles, Caldwell, and others, is an educational map, which is validated by the St Mary's experience, and which other travellers may find useful in making their way towards more effective schools. Furthermore, it is a map which schools will need more than ever in the face of accelerating change, greater demands for accountability, uncertain futures and an increasingly complex society. In the face of these realities, common reactions of resignation or 'back to the basics' are no longer adequate. Rather, thinking before taking action, anticipating possible problems, adapting and undertaking present actions in light of a desired and en-visioned future — all performed in a spirit of enlightened optimism — these are the global pathways by which present and future educational visions may become school realities.

Chapter 9

Concluding Statement

As indicated in the introduction, the St Mary's College Project began with the intention to evaluate its curriculum and quality of school life. In the process, we became aware of the essential relevance of a number of contextual variables. In drawing the following conclusions we attempt to make reference to these variables and to their significance in bringing about school improvement.

Evaluation and school improvement
Another major conclusion of the St Mary's Study involves the role of evaluation in school improvement. Many schools have thought of evaluation as a luxury to be afforded only on rare and special occasions. The findings of the St Mary's Study support the contention that evaluation is essential both for purposes of school management and improvement. For it is through regular and continuous evaluation that a school can both monitor and measure the extent to which its vision has become reality.

Evaluation and school accountability
Evaluation, however, is not simply a vehicle for school management and improvement. Many schools are currently engaged in a struggle to maintain their unique ethos and autonomy at a time of general contraction and scarcity of educational resources. Constructive self-analysis by schools and their own clear sighted proposals for the management of change reflect more than a healthy sense of public image. By such a process schools will be accountable, but will be accountable with integrity. A higher aim is educational improvement.

Significance of ideological vision (with particular reference to Catholic schools)
Egan observes that the 'Second Vatican Council marked the end of the old order, and the birth of a new vision' for Catholic education (1988, p. 22). One of the hallmarks of this vision was the shift in emphasis which views parents, rather than the Church, as primarily responsible for

the Catholic education of children. A major finding of the St Mary's College Study 'validates' this vision by highlighting the overwhelming significant influence of parents upon students' personal and spiritual development.

Social capital
While parental influence is primary, that influence does not work in a vacuum. The St Mary's Study confirms the importance of the Catholic 'community' of parents, teachers and students in enhancing the quality of educational experience. Just how crucial this community support may be is reflected in evidence from a recent large-scale Carnegie study which found that half of students in grade 8 return from school to an empty home; and 40 per cent of the students surveyed said they wish they could spend more time with their mothers and fathers, and that they often felt lonely and lacked contact with adults. Other evidence shows that children are growing up largely in a world populated by other children and dominated by a the cultural values of the mass media. It is to be noted that the St Mary's evidence reveals some discordance in expectations between parents, students and teachers which should be a matter of concern and worthy of further investigation.

Validation of the influence of schooling
The St Mary's Study also supports the claim of Lesko, Coleman and Hoffer and others, that schools, in this case Catholic schools, can and do make a difference, especially in the lives of those students who are most at risk in terms of their lack of parental and community support. However, we note that this difference derives not only from the active support of the Catholic community network, but also from 'school effects', that is, the day-to-day interactions within the school itself.

Indications for further research
One of the intentions of the St Mary's Study was to gather evidence that could be the means to further probe specific categories of the school curriculum. This also implied that the evaluation was necessarily a continuing process, and not an end in itself. In our search of the literature it became clear that there is a paucity of research in terms of the contextual variables of this Study, particularly about Catholic schools. The St Mary's Study indicates that a more general investigation of Catholic schools, for instance in a particular region or diocese, is legitimate and promises benefit to the wider community.

Renewal of fundamental values in education
Pope John Paul II, in his recent apostolic exhortation on the *Family in the Modern World*, writes of education:

The great task that has to be faced today for the renewal of society is that of recapturing the ultimate meaning of life and its fundamental values.

Perhaps it is not too much of an assumption to suggest that the St Mary's Study, and all those involved in it, endorse the importance of such a commitment. In this respect, Neil Holm, Editor of the *Australian Journal of Christian Education*, makes the following comment on an article originating from this Study:

> If humans are to retain the image of God rather than the image of the machine, Christian educators must speak up when our educational institutions state their mission or vision. We must struggle for a dominance of humanity rather than technology.
>
> [The St Mary's College Study] serves us well as a model in this process. [The Study] reminds us that humanity involves moral and religious issues, partnership and participation, optimism and hope, overcoming and benefiting from adversity, developing and serving others, responsibility and self determination, conformity to conscience rather than others, intellectual and spiritual stimulation, and endearing and meaningful relationships. But these are not the issues that dominate education today. (p. 4)

Our hope is that this book will help in restoring such fundamental values to their rightful place at the top of the educational agenda.

Appendix 1:
Perceptions of School Questionnaire

ST MARY'S COLLEGE
PERCEPTIONS OF SCHOOL STUDY

In the attached questionnaire your opinions are sought about a number of aspects of school life. Firstly, please fill in the information questionnaire.

All the information will be kept absolutely confidential.

At the end of this questionnaire please add comments of your own if you think they will help. *Your opinion is valued.*

Thank you for your help.

Dr W. Ramsay
For St Mary's College

Strictly confidential   *No name required*

INFORMATION QUESTIONNAIRE

FOR GRADE 10 OR HSC STUDENTS: *Office use*
ALL ITEMS APPLY TO 1986

Questions		Ref No.	Code No.
1. Do you attend Mass (or service) regularly?	Yes	1	
If yes, at which Church?	No	2	
. . . .		3	
2. Which class or school responsibility have you held (e.g.,		4	
Prefect House Capt or Deputy, class representative, SVDP		5	
Committee etc)?		6	
. . . .			
3. Membership of school sporting team?		7	
. . . .		8	

4. Membership of school team; non-sporting (e.g., debating, Chess)?   9
                                                                              10

....

5. Other school representation (e.g., public speaking)?   11

....

6. Membership of non-school sporting team?   12

....

7. Membership of other school body (e.g., Church Youth Committee, Antioch)?   13
                                                                                     14

....

ID _____

INFORMATION QUESTIONNAIRE

FOR EX ST MARY'S COLLEGE   *Office Use*
STUDENTS GRADE 10 AND ABOVE

Questions	*Ref No.*	*Code No.*
1. How many years did you spend at SMC		
College?	15	
In what year did you leave?	16	
(For Questions 1–4 tick or circle appropriate answer)		
2. Did you leave school at grade 10	17	
grade 11	18	
grade 12	19	
3. What you did the year you left school?		
Full time study	20	
Part time study	21	
Full time work	22	
Part time work	23	
4. What are you doing this year?		
Full time study	24	
Part time study	25	
Full time work	26	
Part time work	27	
5. If 'Study' which institution?	28	
If 'Work' what occupation/profession	29	
Do you attend Mass regularly? Yes	30	
No	31	
If yes at which Church?	32	

234

(For Questions 6—8 Please give other years, as well as 1986, in which membership was held)	
6. Membership of any sporting team (give name of sport and	33
year(s))	34
7. Active membership of sporting body, as non-playing	35
member	36
....	37
8. Active membership of any non-sporting body (e.g., Social	38
Club, SVDP, Antioch)	39
....	40

Section 1 — What is the School for?

Here is a list of what some people think SCHOOLS should have taught you by the time you leave school. Some of these you may not see as the school's business and others you may see as important concerns of the school. In the left hand column rate how IMPORTANT you think each item on the list ought to be for your school. You do this by filling in the appropriate circle.

In the right hand column rate how well you think YOUR SCHOOL ACHIEVES each item on the list. Again, you do this by filling the appropriate circle. This is not a test. We want to know your opinion.

Use the following basis for rating:

LEFT COLUMN NUMBER	RIGHT COLUMN NUMBER
0 Of No Importance	0 Not Achieved
1 Of Slight Importance	1 Slightly Achieved
2 Moderately Important	2 Moderately Achieved
3 Important	3 Achieved
4 Very Important	4 Very Well Achieved

FOR EXAMPLE:

How IMPORTANT ought this goal be for schools?		How WELL does your school ACHIEVE this goal?
0 1 2 3 4	It is the School's task to make sure that you:	0 1 2 3 4
● 0 0 0 0	1. know a lot of facts about the world	0 0 0 0 ●

i.e., you would fill in this item in this way if:

(a) YOU think that it is OF NO IMPORTANCE for the school to make sure you know a lot of facts AND
(b) YOU think that your school ACHIEVES this goal VERY WELL.

HOW IMPORTANT ought this goal be for schools?		HOW WELL does your school ACHIEVE this goal?

Of No Imp. / Of Slight Imp. / Mod. Import. / Important. / Very Important.	IT IS THE SCHOOL'S TASK TO MAKE SURE THAT YOU:	Not Achieved. / Slightly Ach'd. / Mod. Ach'vd. / Achieved. / V. Well Achieved.	Ref No.	Code No.
0 1 2 3 4		0 1 2 3 4		
0 0 0 0 0	1. Know about a wide range of possible jobs.	1 0 0 0 0 0		
0 0 0 0 0	2. Understand in considerable *depth* one or more traditional academic subjects (e.g., English, chemistry).	2 0 0 0 0 0		
0 0 0 0 0	3. Have a reasonable understanding of yourself and the way others see you.	3 0 0 0 0 0		
0 0 0 0 0	4. Know and appreciate a number of the the major works of English Literature.	4 0 0 0 0 0		
0 0 0 0 0	5. Can organize your own time and work independently.	5 0 0 0 0 0		
0 0 0 0 0	6. Can listen sensitively and with understanding to others.	6 0 0 0 0 0		
0 0 0 0 0	7. Understand some of the abstract principles of mathematical reasoning (e.g., algebra, set theory).	7 0 0 0 0 0		
0 0 0 0 0	8. Are an individual developing as you wish.	8 0 0 0 0 0		
0 0 0 0 0	9. Are able to read with understanding.	9 0 0 0 0 0		
0 0 0 0 0	10. Accept those who think and act differently (e.g., those of different race, dress, life-style).	10 0 0 0 0 0		
0 0 0 0 0	11. Understand the world of work — its routines, demands, responsibilities.	11 0 0 0 0 0		
0 0 0 0 0	12. Have specific skills you need for a chosen field of work.	12 0 0 0 0 0		
0 0 0 0 0	13. Understand some of the basic ideas in sciences (e.g., biology, physics).	13 0 0 0 0 0		
0 0 0 0 0	14. Have some understanding of one or more of the fine arts (e.g., painting, classical music).	14 0 0 0 0 0		
0 0 0 0 0	15. Are generally obedient to parents, teachers and all in authority.	15 0 0 0 0 0		

0 0 0 0 0	16. Work hard at things you find difficult and do not like.	16 0 0 0 0 0
0 0 0 0 0	17. Are self-confident and possess self-respect.	17 0 0 0 0 0
0 0 0 0 0	18. Know of and are concerned to respond justly to major social issues (e.g., unemployment, the future of Aboriginal society).	18 0 0 0 0 0
0 0 0 0 0	19. Have developed an appreciation of beauty.	19 0 0 0 0 0
0 0 0 0 0	20. Can form a considered opinion and act on it even if this means going against what most people think.	20 0 0 0 0 0

Section 2 — Academic Category

In the following questions you are asked to give your opinion about choosing HSC subjects as it applies to your situation. We want you in each case to say whether you Definitely Agree, Mostly Agree, Mostly Disagree or Definitely Disagree, with the statements given. Please read each item carefully and tick the answer which best describes how you feel.

Remember in this section that you have to put 'You chose (or 'You would choose', for grade 10 students) particular HSC subjects because ...' in front of each item for it to make sense.

A. *YOU CHOSE (WOULD CHOOSE) PARTICULAR HSC SUBJECTS BE-CAUSE ...*

	Definitely Agree	Mostly Agree	Mostly Disagree	Definitely Disagree	Ref No.	Code No.
1. You needed particular subjects to qualify for entrance to university or some other educational institution.						
2. You understood that you needed particular subjects in order to gain the immediate employment of your choice.						
3. Your friend/friends was/were doing that subject.						
4. You were intrinsically interested in the subject.						

5. You had achieved good results in that subject in year 10.
6. You knew nothing of the subject and therefore wanted to fill a gap in your knowledge.
7. Your parents strongly influenced your choice of subject.
8. Choices were largely determined by the organization of subjects into various lines.
9. The Sciences (maths, science etc) appeared to be more important than the Humanities (English, social psychology, etc).
10. Appropriate information was readily available regarding prerequisite subjects for Tertiary study.
11. Appropriate information was readily available regarding the specific subjects required for specific fields of employment.

B. *YOUR CHOICE OF HSC SUBJECTS ASSISTED (IS LIKELY TO ASSIST) YOU . . .*

	Definitely Agree	Mostly Agree	Mostly Disagree	Definitely Disagree	Ref No.	Code No.
12. In gaining immediate employment.						
13. In gaining entrance to a tertiary institution.						
14. Providing a sound introduction and firm foundation for further study in any area or discipline.						
15. Providing a basis for a continuing personal						

interest in an area or
discipline.
16. Opening up new areas
of study for you.

Section 3 — Vocational Category

This section asks you to give your opinion on statements about vocational aspects of
school (such as leisure, home science, work experience). Again tick the box that best
describes how you feel about each statement.

	Definitely Agree	Mostly Agree	Mostly Disagree	Definitely Disagree	Ref No.	Code No.
1. The subjects I (study) studied at school suit (ed) my career choice.						
2. Leisure education was (is) useful in opening up to me a potential career.						
3. Because of my craft studies I am now able to do simple repairs at home.						
4. My skills in cooking, dressmaking have carried over into other areas.						
5. Work experience helped me in deciding upon my career.						
6. More vocational studies are required at HSC level if students are to be prepared for life after school.						
7. Work experience helped me understand the 'world of work'.						
8. Vocational Studies have proven beneficial in my life outside of school. Cooking Craft Dressmaking						

Section 4 — Personal/Spiritual Development Category

This section gives a number of statements about the contribution SMC might make
to students' personal or spiritual development.

Again tick each statement according to the way it best describes how you feel. Say whether you Definitely Agree, Mostly Agree, Mostly Disagree or Definitely Disagree.

	Definitely Agree	Mostly Agree	Mostly Disagree	Definitely Disagree	Ref. No.	Code No.
1. A respect for truth is a fundamental element in the stability of any society.						
2. At times I am afraid of losing my faith.						
3. The great world problems such as poverty and war don't worry me particularly.						
4. It is alright for people who are not married to live together.						
5. To drive a car when unsteady after drinking is not only foolish but morally wrong.						
6. Trying out drugs (e.g., marihuana), is alright so long as you don't go too far.						
7. I feel concerned that many people tell untruths lightly, that is, without serious reason.						
8. Religion helps me answer real questions about the meaning of life.						
9/10. My education at SMC (has) helped me in preparing for such things as marriage and pregnancy. Marriage Pregnancy						
11. Being a Catholic is very important to me.						

In your religious development, which includes your knowledge of Christian Doctrine, your appreciation of Christian values, your habits of Prayer, and your attendance at Mass (or Worship) and the Sacraments, *how important have been each of the following influences?*

Tick each statement according to the importance you place on each influence. Say whether you think it is *most important, very important, of some importance, of little importance or of no importance.*

	Most Imp.	Very Imp.	Some Imp.	Little Imp.	No Imp.	Ref No.	Code No.
12. The instruction of your parents and their example?							
13. The example and personal guidance of your teachers?							
14. Religious education provided by the school?							
15. The example of your friends at school?							
16. Religious instruction provided by your Parish or Church?							
17. The guidance and influence of some Religious, Priest or Minister?							

In the questions below circle the number which *most closely* refers to you — your belief or your practice.

Ref No.   Code No.

18. *Concerning GOD, I tend to think of GOD as:*
    1. Strictly just like a Judge in a Law Court. If I disobey Him I can expect a just, but severe punishment.
    2. The Creator of the Universe who keeps the planets in orbit and sees that the seasons follow one another in due order.
    3. One who will give anything I ask for, especially in times of crisis, provided I pray hard enough.
    4. A Spirit remote from the world who does not affect my everyday life in any way.
    5. A Loving Father who loves me very much and wants my love in return.
    6. If none of the above comes near to your idea of God, please write down how you think of God.

    . . . .

19. *Concerning your RELIGIOUS EDUCATION classes at school:*
    1. They strengthened my commitment to God.
    2. They were related to real life, and to my needs.
    3. I found them quite interesting.
    4. They were irrevelant to my life.
    5. I found them boring and uninteresting.

241

20. *Concerning the MASS. I normally attend Mass (Worship):*
    1. Daily or several times a week.
    2. At least on Sundays.
    3. About two or three times a month.
    4. About once a month.
    5. About four or five times a year.
    6. Very rarely or never.
21. *Concerning HOLY COMMUNION. I normally receive Holy Communion:*
    1. Daily or several times a week.
    2. At least on Sundays.
    3. About two or three times a month.
    4. About once a month.
    5. About four or five times a year.
    6. Very rarely or never.
22. *Concerning CONFESSION. I normally go to the Sacrament of Confession/Reconciliation:*
    1. Weekly.
    2. About once or twice a month.
    3. About once in two months.
    4. About once in three months.
    5. About once or twice a year.
    6. Practically never or never.
23. Observance of Christ's command to love our neighbour is shown by good deeds and charitable actions towards others. *I normally perform some APOSTOLIC ACTION or good deed for others:*
    1. Weekly.
    2. About once or twice a month.
    3. About once in two months.
    4. About once in three months.
    5. About once or twice a year.
    6. Practically never or never.
24. *Concerning PRAYER. I normally pray* (apart from school prayers and Sunday Mass/Worship):
    1. At least once or twice daily.
    2. Several times a week.
    3. Every week approximately.
    4. Every month approximately.
    5. Occasionally during the year.
    6. Practically never or never.

Section 5 — Leadership/Sporting

In this section you are asked to give your opinion about the aspects of leadership and sport that you experienced in school. Again say whether you Definitely Agree, Mostly Agree, Mostly Disagree or Definitely Disagree with the statements made. Tick the answer which best describes how you feel.

	Definitely Agree	Mostly Agree	Mostly Disagree	Definitely Disagree	Ref No.	Code No.

1. The teachers were good models of leadership.
2. School helped me to understand what leadership is.
3. The physical education classes at SMC provided a comprehensive and worthwhile programme.
4. Physical education and sport were directed mainly at the gifted and talented students.
5. Students were encouraged by teachers to join outside clubs etc, when they leave school.
6. The value of physical activity was emphasized at SMC sufficiently for me to continue sport and leisure activities after leaving school (or outside school).
7. I developed the ability to be a leader because of my experience at SMC.
8. I enjoyed activities at SMC other than study and sport, which I will continue (have continued) after leaving school.

9–11. At SMC there were (say what these are if you wish) sufficient opportunities for me to develop leadership qualities

in grade 10
           11
           12

. . . .

12. At SMC I feel (felt)
free to make
mistakes and learn
from them (in areas
other than class
subjects).

13. There is (was) a
sufficient number of
physical education
classes.

Section 6 — The Q-Line Category

If you have participated in our Q-Line please answer the following questions. If *not* we would still like your thoughts which could be written at the end.

1. *Which subjects did (would) you do for your Q-Line? Circle your answer (you may circle more than one).*

    Ref No.   Code No.

   a. photography (applied science)
   b. home management
   c. computer studies
   d. drama
   e. art

   f. health and recreation
   g. personal development
   h. private study
   i. legal studies
   j. other (please state the subject).

2. *Why did (would) you choose these subjects? (Circle as many as apply).*
   a. personal interest
   b. my friends enrolled in that subject
   c. I had to choose something
   d. It complemented another subject
   e. I liked the teacher
   f. I wanted a break from my academic subjects
   g. I received a level 2 for it
   h. Other reasons (please state briefly).

. . . .

In the questions 3 to 10
Please indicate the answer closest to how you feel

	Definitely Agree	Agree	Disagree	Definitely Disagree
3. The Q-Line should be continued (please state why, or why not).				

. . . .

4. The Q-Line should be compulsory:

in grade 11
in grade 12
(please state your
reasons)

. . . .

5. The Q-Line is best kept
to Friday afternoon (If
you *disagree* which day
would be best?).

. . . .

6. The Q-Line subjects are
(were) sufficiently
practical (that is not too
theoretical).
7. There is (was) sufficient
time given to the Q-Line
subjects.
8. It should be possible to
gain a level 2 award for
all Q-Line subjects.
9. Teachers treat our Q-
Line subjects informally
and not like other
academic subjects in
which there is pressure to
pass them.
10. The Q-Line is (was) well
organized (If you
disagree what
improvement do you
suggest?)

. . . .

11. Which subjects do you
think should be retained
on a Q-Line? (please
signify: as in a, b, c, etc
of question 1).

. . . .

12. Which subjects should be
added to our Q-Line?
(place your suggestions
in order of preference).

. . . .

Section 7 — Teachers Category

In this section please indicate how true each statement is (was) of your teachers at St Mary's.

	True of Most Teachers (75%)	True of Many Teachers (50%–75%)	True of Some Teachers (25%–50%)	True of Very Few Teachers (25%)	True of No Teachers (25%)	Ref No.	Code No.
1. Teachers clearly outline and organize their classwork.							
2. Teachers allow classroom discussion.							
3. Teachers try to make their teaching material relevant to current trends and students' needs.							
4. Teachers give friendly help to any student having problems with classwork.							
5. Teachers try to be sure that students understand the work that is done in class.							
6. Teachers cover a great deal of material in the time allowed.							
7. Teachers place too much emphasis on detailed facts and memorization.							
8. Teachers give students a broad, general understanding of their subjects.							
9. Teachers extend students to the limits of their abilities.							
10. Teachers encourage students to do independent work on their own.							
11. Teachers are understanding of students' study problems.							
12. Teachers stimulate students to think and be creative.							
13. Teachers succeed in making their classes interesting.							
14. Teachers try to make their classes							

entertaining rather
than useful.
15. Teachers set
homework regularly.
16. Teachers correct
students' work
regularly

Please note any additional question or comment you wish against the categories marked.

What is School For:

Academic:

Vocational:

Personal/Spiritual Development:

Leadership/Sporting:

The Q-Line:

Teachers:

PERCEPTION OF SCHOOL STUDY

ADDENDUM

ID _____

The questions below did not make themselves clear enough, so that some of the 'answers' weren't always complete. Would you please answer the following again so that we can be sure?

SECTION 3

	Definitely Agree	Mostly Agree	Mostly Disagree	Definitely Disagree
8. Vocational Studies have proven beneficial in my life outside school:				
cooking	☐	☐	☐	☐
craft	☐	☐	☐	☐
dressmaking	☐	☐	☐	☐

SECTION 5

9–11. At SMC there were (say what these are if you wish) sufficient opportunities for me to develop leadership qualities in:				
grade 10	☐	☐	☐	☐
grade 11	☐	☐	☐	☐
grade 12	☐	☐	☐	☐

Thank you for this additional help.
Your opinions are valued.

Appendix 2:
Quality of School Life Questionnaire

ST MARY'S COLLEGE
QUALITY OF SCHOOL LIFE STUDY

We would like you to fill in this questionnaire so that we can find out how St Mary's College students feel about school.

Each item on the next four pages says that School Is A Place Where some particular thing happens to you or you feel a particular way. We want you to say whether you Definitely Agree, Mostly Agree. Mostly Disagree or Definitely Disagree with the items.

Please read each item carefully and tick the answer which best describes how you feel most of the time. Don't forget that you have to put 'School Is A Place Where ...' in front of each item for it to make sense, e.g., 'School Is A Place Where I really like to go' (item 11).

All the answers you give are confidential

SCHOOL IS A PLACE WHERE ...

	Definitely Agree	Mostly Agree	Mostly Disagree	Definitely Disagree
1. I have good friends.	☐	☐	☐	☐
2. people know they can depend on me.	☐	☐	☐	☐
3. I know how to cope with the work.	☐	☐	☐	☐
4. teachers are genuinely interested in what I do.	☐	☐	☐	☐
5. I have learnt how to find whatever information I need.	☐	☐	☐	☐
6. I am thought of as a person who matters.	☐	☐	☐	☐
7. I feel bored.	☐	☐	☐	☐
8. I act in a responsible way.	☐	☐	☐	☐
9. teachers are fair and just.	☐	☐	☐	☐
10. I know what my strengths and weaknesses are.	☐	☐	☐	☐
11. I really like to go.	☐	☐	☐	☐

SCHOOL IS A PLACE WHERE ...

	Definitely Agree	Mostly Agree	Mostly Disagree	Definitely Disagree
12. teachers take a personal interest in helping me with my school work.	☐	☐	☐	☐
13. I feel I belong.	☐	☐	☐	☐
14. mixing with other people helps me to understand myself.	☐	☐	☐	☐
15. teachers recognize any extra effort I make in my work.	☐	☐	☐	☐
16. I have learnt things that will be useful to me.	☐	☐	☐	☐
17. I feel important.	☐	☐	☐	☐
18. I learn to get along with other people.	☐	☐	☐	☐
19. teachers help me to do my best.	☐	☐	☐	☐
20. people have confidence in me.	☐	☐	☐	☐
21. teachers treat me fairly in class.	☐	☐	☐	☐
22. I try to do what is expected of me.	☐	☐	☐	☐
23. I feel proud to be a student.	☐	☐	☐	☐
24. I like to do extra work in the subjects that interest me.	☐	☐	☐	☐
25. people come to me for help.	☐	☐	☐	☐
26. teachers encourage me to express my opinions.	☐	☐	☐	☐
27. I feel lonely.	☐	☐	☐	☐
28. learning is easy for me.	☐	☐	☐	☐
29. I am interested in the work we do in class.	☐	☐	☐	☐
30. I can learn whatever I need to know.	☐	☐	☐	☐
31. I feel successful.	☐	☐	☐	☐
32. other students are very friendly.	☐	☐	☐	☐
33. I like to learn new things.	☐	☐	☐	☐

SCHOOL IS A PLACE WHERE ...

	Definitely Agree	Mostly Agree	Mostly Disagree	Definitely Disagree
34. I feel restless.	☐	☐	☐	☐
35. I know that people think a lot of me.	☐	☐	☐	☐
36. I feel I have become a worthwhile person.	☐	☐	☐	☐
37. teachers take notice of me in class.	☐	☐	☐	☐
38. teachers give me the marks I deserve.	☐	☐	☐	☐
39. I feel I am a reliable person.	☐	☐	☐	☐
40. I feel proud of myself.	☐	☐	☐	☐
41. people look up to me.	☐	☐	☐	☐
42. I am trusted to work on my own.	☐	☐	☐	☐
43. I feel depressed.	☐	☐	☐	☐
44. I know I can reach a satisfactory standard in my work.	☐	☐	☐	☐
45. other students accept me as I am.	☐	☐	☐	☐
46. I feel good about things.	☐	☐	☐	☐

47. I know the sorts of things I can do well. □ □ □ □
48. I can talk to teachers about the way they mark my work. □ □ □ □
49. I get excited about things. □ □ □ □
50. I learn a lot about myself. □ □ □ □
51. teachers listen to what I say. □ □ □ □
52. I feel happy. □ □ □ □
53. I try to look after the interests of other students. □ □ □ □
54. I am known by a lot of people. □ □ □ □
55. I find that learning is a lot of fun. □ □ □ □

SCHOOL IS A PLACE WHERE . . .

	Definitely Agree	Mostly Agree	Mostly Disagree	Definitely Disagree
56. I get enjoyment from being there.	□	□	□	□
57. I have learnt to see other people's points of view.	□	□	□	□
58. other students listen to what I say.	□	□	□	□
59. I feel confident.	□	□	□	□
60. I get satisfaction from the school work I do.	□	□	□	□
61. I feel that things go my way.	□	□	□	□
62. teachers are friendly to me in class.	□	□	□	□
63. I get to know myself better.	□	□	□	□
64. I am treated with respect.	□	□	□	□
65. I know I can do well enough to be successful.	□	□	□	□
66. I get upset.	□	□	□	□
67. I can question the things that teachers say about my work.	□	□	□	□
68. I can learn what I need to get by in life.	□	□	□	□
69. I feel great.	□	□	□	□
70. I have learnt to accept other people as they are.	□	□	□	□
71. teachers treat all students equally.	□	□	□	□

Appendix 3:
Questionnaire to Teachers (1)

ST MARY'S COLLEGE
PERCEPTION OF SCHOOL
AND
QUALITY OF SCHOOL LIFE STUDY

QUESTIONNAIRE FOR TEACHERS

This Questionnaire aims to find out staff members' views about aspects of the school programme.

Please answer all questions. Your responses will of course be kept strictly confidential.

Thank you for your cooperation and assistance. Your opinions are valued.

Dr William Ramsay,
Research Consultant,
University of Tasmania
April, 1988

Section 1 — Staff Expectations of Catholic Schools

The following statements are often made about the GOALS which Catholic schools should have. Each question begins. 'CATHOLIC SCHOOLS SHOULD...'

In the left hand column we would like you to record the degree of importance each goal should have in a Catholic school and in the right hand column please circle the answer which best describes how well you feel the goal has been achieved.

| 1 No Importance: |
| this goal should not be emphasized |
| 2 Of Little Importance |
| 3 Of Some Importance |
| 4 Very Important |
| 5 Most Important: |
| this goal should be strongly emphasized |

| 1 Not Achieved |
| 2 Slightly Achieved |
| 3 Moderately Achieved |
| 4 Achieved |
| 5 Very Well Achieved |

251

1 2 3 4 5	1. Help students to discover and fulfil themselves as human persons.	1 2 3 4 5
1 2 3 4 5	2. Develop students' knowledge and skills in specific areas.	1 2 3 4 5
1 2 3 4 5	3. Give students experience in the main areas of human knowledge (Arts, Science, Humanities).	1 2 3 4 5
1 2 3 4 5	4. Help students to understand their society.	1 2 3 4 5
1 2 3 4 5	5. Provide an atmosphere of Christian community where people are genuinely concerned for one another.	1 2 3 4 5
1 2 3 4 5	6. Develop in students personal qualities of independence and initiative so that they can stand on their own two feet.	1 2 3 4 5
1 2 3 4 5	7. Prepare their students for university study (e.g., by developing good study habits etc).	1 2 3 4 5
1 2 3 4 5	8. Provide students with opportunities for creative work.	1 2 3 4 5
1 2 3 4 5	9. Give adequate sex education to their students.	1 2 3 4 5
1 2 3 4 5	10. Teach Religious Education at a level comparable to other subjects.	1 2 3 4 5
1 2 3 4 5	11. Respect each student individually irrespective of ability or appearance.	1 2 3 4 5
1 2 3 4 5	12. Prepare their students for the HSC as well as possible.	1 2 3 4 5
1 2 3 4 5	13. Create friendly relations with other Church schools and groups.	1 2 3 4 5
1 2 3 4 5	14. Encourage a love of learning for its own sake.	1 2 3 4 5
1 2 3 4 5	15. Provide opportunities for students to participate intelligently in the liturgy (e.g., through Class Masses, etc).	1 2 3 4 5
1 2 3 4 5	16. Give all students a chance of success in some aspects of school life.	1 2 3 4 5
1 2 3 4 5	19. Make students aware of the great religions other than Christianity.	1 2 3 4 5
1 2 3 4 5	20. Give an example of dedicated Christian life through its religious teachers.	1 2 3 4 5
1 2 3 4 5	21. Help students to develop their personality and character.	1 2 3 4 5
1 2 3 4 5	22. Help students cope with life after leaving school.	1 2 3 4 5
1 2 3 4 5	23. Encourage a love of literature, art and music.	1 2 3 4 5
1 2 3 4 5	24. Encourage students to take part in local community and civic affairs.	1 2 3 4 5
1 2 3 4 5	25. Integrate Religious Education and other subjects where possible.	1 2 3 4 5
1 2 3 4 5	26. Help students to learn how to get on with other people.	1 2 3 4 5
1 2 3 4 5	27. Develop in students skills which will enable them to get as good a job as possible on leaving school.	1 2 3 4 5
1 2 3 4 5	28. Develop in students an awareness of pressing social problems (such as poverty, hunger and injustice).	1 2 3 4 5
1 2 3 4 5	29. Develop in students habits of independent and critical thought.	1 2 3 4 5
1 2 3 4 5	30. Provide an experience of life based on the values of Christ and the Gospel.	1 2 3 4 5

1 2 3 4 5	31. Provide counselling help to students in their problems.	1 2 3 4 5
1 2 3 4 5	32. Teach students about different careers and jobs so that they can decide what they want to do.	1 2 3 4 5
1 2 3 4 5	33. Prepare students to become good citizens.	1 2 3 4 5
1 2 3 4 5	34. Provide an environment in which students' faith can grow and develop.	1 2 3 4 5
1 2 3 4 5	35. Emphasize self-discipline rather than external conformity to rules.	1 2 3 4 5
1 2 3 4 5	36. Teach students things which will be of direct importance to them in their future jobs.	1 2 3 4 5
1 2 3 4 5	37. Encourage students to be concerned for the needs of others.	1 2 3 4 5
1 2 3 4 5	38. Develop in students an understanding of what is right and wrong.	1 2 3 4 5
1 2 3 4 5	39. Help students discover and develop their creative abilities.	1 2 3 4 5
1 2 3 4 5	40. Develop Christian values and the place of God in students' lives.	1 2 3 4 5
1 2 3 4 5	41. Develop students' intellectual abilities.	1 2 3 4 5
1 2 3 4 5	42. Encourage students' to be obedient to parents, teachers and all in authority.	1 2 3 4 5
1 2 3 4 5	43. Develop in students an appreciation of beauty.	1 2 3 4 5
1 2 3 4 5	44. Develop in students the ability to form a considered opinion and act on it even if this means going against what people think.	1 2 3 4 5

Section 2 — School Life

This section refers to the Quality of School Life Provided at St Mary's College.
Note that each question begins with: For St Mary's College students, School is a place where ...

Please circle the answer which best describes your view:

> 1 Certainly false; I strongly disagree
> 2 Probably false; I'm inclined to disagree
> 3 Uncertain
> 4 Probably true; I'm inclined to agree
> 5 Certainly true; I strongly agree

For St Mary's College students, SCHOOL IS A PLACE WHERE ...

1. They know how to cope with the work.	1 2 3 4 5
2. Their teachers are fair and just.	1 2 3 4 5
3. They really like to go.	1 2 3 4 5
4. They feel frustrated.	1 2 3 4 5
5. They find mixing with other people helps them to understand themselves.	1 2 3 4 5

6. They feel important.	1 2 3 4 5
7. They learn to get along with other people.	1 2 3 4 5
8. Their teachers help them to do their best.	1 2 3 4 5
9. People have confidence in them.	1 2 3 4 5
10. Teachers treat them fairly in class.	1 2 3 4 5
11. People come to them for help.	1 2 3 4 5
12. They feel lonely.	1 2 3 4 5
13. They feel restless.	1 2 3 4 5
14. They know that people think a lot of them.	1 2 3 4 5
15. Teachers give them the marks they deserve.	1 2 3 4 5
16. People look up to them.	1 2 3 4 5
17. They feel depressed.	1 2 3 4 5
18. They know they can reach a satisfactory standard in their work.	1 2 3 4 5
19. They know the sorts of things they can do well.	1 2 3 4 5
20. They learn a lot about themselves.	1 2 3 4 5
21. Their teachers listen to what they say.	1 2 3 4 5
22. They feel happy.	1 2 3 4 5
23. They find that learning is a lot of fun.	1 2 3 4 5
24. They get enjoyment from being there.	1 2 3 4 5
25. They get satisfaction from the school work they do.	1 2 3 4 5
26. They get to know themselves better.	1 2 3 4 5
27. They know they can do well enough to be successful.	1 2 3 4 5
28. They get upset.	1 2 3 4 5
29. They feel great.	1 2 3 4 5
30. They have learnt to accept other people as they are.	1 2 3 4 5

Section 3 — Academic Category

In the following questions you are asked to give your opinion as to the reason/s why students chose or would choose various HSC subjects. In each case say whether you Definitely Disagree, Mostly Disagree, Mostly Agree or Definitely Agree, with the statements given.

Remember in this section that you have to put 'Students chose (or "would choose", for grade 10 students) particular HSC subjects because ...' in front of each item for it to make sense.

Students chose (would choose) particular HSC subjects because ...

1 Definitely Disagree
2 Mostly Disagree
3 Mostly Agree
4 Definitely Agree

1. Students needed particular subjects to qualify for entrance to university or some other educational institution.	1 2 3 4
2. Students understood that they needed particular subjects in order to gain the immediate employment of your choice.	1 2 3 4
3. Their friends were doing that subject.	1 2 3 4
4. They were intrinsically interested in the subject.	1 2 3 4
5. They had achieved good results in that subject in year 10.	1 2 3 4
6. They knew nothing of the subject and therefore wanted to fill a gap in their knowledge.	1 2 3 4

7. Their parents strongly influenced their choice of subject. 1 2 3 4
8. Choices were largely determined by the organization of subjects into various lines. 1 2 3 4
9. The Sciences (maths, science etc) appeared to be more important than the Humanities (English, social psychology etc). 1 2 3 4

Section 4 — Vocational Category

This section asks you go give your opinion on statements about vocational aspects of school (such as leisure, home science, work experience). Again circle the number that best describes your situation.

> 1 Definitely Disagree
> 2 Most Disagree
> 3 Mostly Agree
> 4 Definitely Agree

1. The subjects which students (study) (studied) at school suit(ed) their career choice. 1 2 3 4
2. Leisure education was (is) useful in opening up a potential career. 1 2 3 4
3. Because of their craft studies they are now able to do simple repairs at home. 1 2 3 4
4. Their skills in cooking, dressmaking have carried over into other areas. 1 2 3 4
5. Work experience helped students in deciding upon their careers. 1 2 3 4
6. More vocational studies are required at HSC level if students are to be prepared for life after school. 1 2 3 4
7. Work experience helped students understand the 'world of work'. 1 2 3 4
8. Vocational studies have proven beneficial in students' lives outside of school.
   a) Cooking 1 2 3 4
   b) Craft 1 2 3 4
   c) Dressmaking 1 2 3 4

Section 5 — Spiritual Development Category

In students' religious development, which includes their knowledge of Christian Doctrine, their appreciation of Christian values, their habits of Prayer, and their attendance at Mass (or Worship) and the Sacraments, how important have been each of the following influences?

Circle each statement according to the importance you place on each influence. Say whether you think it is of No Importance, of Little Importance, of Some Importance, Very Important or Most Important.

> 1 No Importance
> 2 Little Importance
> 3 Some Importance
> 4 Very Important
> 5 Most Important

1. The instruction of parents and their example? 1 2 3 4 5
2. The example and personal guidance of teachers? 1 2 3 4 5
3. Religious education provided by the school? 1 2 3 4 5
4. The example of friends at school? 1 2 3 4 5
5. Religious instruction provided by the Parish or Church? 1 2 3 4 5
6. The guidance and influence of some Religious, Priest, or Minister? 1 2 3 4 5

Please indicate your opinion of the teaching of Religious Education (RE) -

7. I am very concerned about the teaching of RE in this school. 1 2 3 4 5
8. I am concerned about the teaching of RE in this school. 1 2 3 4 5
9. I am satisfied about how RE is taught in this school. 1 2 3 4 5
10. I am happy with the teaching of RE in this school. 1 2 3 4 5
11. I am very happy about the teaching of RE in this school. 1 2 3 4 5

Section 6 — Leadership/Sport

In this section you are asked to give your opinion about the aspects of leadership and sport that are experienced by students at St Mary's. Again say whether you Definitely Disagree, Mostly Disagree, Mostly Agree or Definitely Agree with the statements made.

> 1 Definitely Disagree
> 2 Mostly Disagree
> 3 Mostly Agree
> 4 Definitely Agree

1. The teachers are good models of leadership. 1 2 3 4
2. School helps students to understand what leadership is. 1 2 3 4
3. The physical education classes at SMC provide a comprehensive and worthwhile programme. 1 2 3 4
4. Physical education and sport are directed mainly at the gifted and talented students. 1 2 3 4
5. Students are encouraged by teachers to join outside clubs etc. when they leave school. 1 2 3 4
6. The value of physical activity is emphasized at SMC sufficiently for students to want to continue sport and leisure activities after leaving school (or outside school). 1 2 3 4
7. Students have developed the ability to be leaders because of their experience at SMC. 1 2 3 4
8. Students enjoy activities at SMC other than study and sport, which they will probably continue (have continued) after leaving school. 1 2 3 4
9–11. At SMC there are/were sufficient opportunities for students to develop leadership qualities in 1 2 3 4
                               grade 10 1 2 3 4
                               grade 11 1 2 3 4
                               grade 12

. . . .

12. At SMC students feel (felt) free to make mistakes and learn from them (in areas other than class subjects). 1 2 3 4
13. There is (was) a sufficient number of physical education classes. 1 2 3 4

Section 7 — Teachers Category

In this section please indicate how true each statement is (was) of teachers at St Mary's.

> 1 True of No Teachers (25%)
> 2 True of Very Few Teachers (25%)
> 3 True of Some Teachers (25%−50%)
> 4 True of Many Teachers (50%−75%)
> 5 True of Most Teachers (75%)

1. Teachers clearly outline and organize their classwork.   1 2 3 4 5
2. Teachers allow classroom discussion.   1 2 3 4 5
3. Teachers try to make their teaching material relevant to current trends and student's needs.   1 2 3 4 5
4. Teachers give friendly help to any student having problems with classwork.   1 2 3 4 5
5. Teachers try to be sure that students understand the work that is done in class.   1 2 3 4 5
6. Teachers cover a great deal of material in the time allowed.   1 2 3 4 5
7. Teachers place too much emphasis on detailed facts and memorization.   1 2 3 4 5
8. Teachers give students a broad, general understanding of their subjects.   1 2 3 4 5
9. Teachers extend students to the limits of their abilities.   1 2 3 4 5
10. Teachers encourage students to do independent work on their own.   1 2 3 4 5
11. Teachers are understanding of students' study problems.   1 2 3 4 5
12. Teachers stimulate students to think and be creative.   1 2 3 4 5
13. Teachers succeed in making their classes interesting.   1 2 3 4 5
14. Teachers try to make their classes entertaining rather than useful.   1 2 3 4 5
15. Teachers set homework regularly.   1 2 3 4 5
16. Teachers correct students' work regularly.   1 2 3 4 5

Section 8 — School Administration/Organization

This section gives a number of statements about the administration/organization of St Mary's College.

Again, please circle the answer which best describes how you feel. Say whether you Definitely Disagree, Mostly Disagree, are Uncertain, Mostly Agree or Definitely Agree.

> 1 Definitely Disagree
> 2 Mostly Disagree
> 3 Uncertain
> 4 Mostly Agree
> 5 Definitely Agree

1. There is effective communication between administration and parents.   1 2 3 4 5
2. School attendance is regularly checked.   1 2 3 4 5
3. The Parents & Friends Association is effective.   1 2 3 4 5
4. The School Newsletter is informative and positive.   1 2 3 4 5
5. The School Yearbook — The Santa Maria, is an excellent publication and record of the year's activities.   1 2 3 4 5
6. St Mary's enjoys an excellent reputation in the local community.   1 2 3 4 5
7. The school has been successful in its efforts to involve parents in its activities.   1 2 3 4 5
8. There is adequate teacher involvement in sport and other extra-curricular activities.   1 2 3 4 5
9. Reports on your child's progress are informative, timely and positive.   1 2 3 4 5
10. The school rules are reasonable.   1 2 3 4 5
11. Student discipline is well maintained.   1 2 3 4 5
12. The quality of food offered in the tuck shop is nutritiously sound and appealing.   1 2 3 4 5
13. The quality of service in the tuck shop is friendly and helpful.   1 2 3 4 5
14. The quality and variety of goods provided by the Book Store is good.   1 2 3 4 5
15. The service in the Book Store is helpful and friendly.   1 2 3 4 5
16. Ample opportunities are provided for participation in extra-curricular activities, e.g., music, sport, drama, debating etc.   1 2 3 4 5
17. There is adequate guidance about subject selection.   1 2 3 4 5
18. Office staff are helpful and friendly.   1 2 3 4 5
19. The quality of communication between parents and teachers is excellent.   1 2 3 4 5
20. The cleanliness and appearance of the school are well maintained.   1 2 3 4 5
21. The morale of the teachers is high.   1 2 3 4 5
22. The morale and spirit of students is high.   1 2 3 4 5

Thank you for you cooperation

Appendix 4:
Questionnaire to Teachers (2)

ST MARY'S COLLEGE
PERCEPTION OF SCHOOL
AND
QUALITY OF SCHOOL LIFE STUDY

ADDITIONAL QUESTIONNAIRE FOR TEACHERS

In order to make better sense out of the data we have so far it has become necessary to gather teachers' opinions more precisely in relation to questions asked of both students and parents. Would you please assist the study by filling in this additional questionnaire?

There are no necessarily right or wrong answers, but it is essential that you answer all questions. Your responses will be kept strictly confidential.

Again, I do apologise for the extra work asked of you at this time of the year.

Bill Ramsay
University of Tasmania
October, 1988

Section 1 — Curriculum

This section refers to issues related to the CURRICULUM of your school (e.g., subjects taught, learning activities etc.).

For each statement below please indicate how strongly you agree, or disagree, with it as follows:

```
1 Certainly false; I strongly disagree
2 Probably false; I'm inclined to disagree
3 Uncertain
4 Probably true; I'm inclined to agree
5 Certainly true; I strongly agree
```

1. In general, the curriculum of this school is meeting students' needs.   1 2 3 4 5
2. There are opportunities for students to get to know and work with teachers outside the classroom.   1 2 3 4 5
3. The out-of-school activities of the school have sufficient variety, scope and quality.   1 2 3 4 5
4. There is a good sports programme in the school.   1 2 3 4 5
5. This school offers a good range and variety of subjects in years 11 and 12.   1 2 3 4 5
6. The subjects offered at this school develop in students a capacity for independent and critical thinking.   1 2 3 4 5
7. The subjects taught in this school offer useful knowledge or develop useful skills.   1 2 3 4 5
8. The Religious Education programme is an important part of the curriculum of the school.   1 2 3 4 5
9. The subjects taught in this school are relevant to life and to students' needs.   1 2 3 4 5
10. The subjects taught in this school prepare students adequately for their future employment and careers.   1 2 3 4 5
11. The curriculum of this school is dominated too much by the HSC examination.   1 2 3 4 5
12. The sports programme in the school helps students' personal and physical development.   1 2 3 4 5
13. The subjects which students study in the school help to give meaning and purpose to their lives.   1 2 3 4 5
14. The school helps to educate students towards a proper approach to the Sacraments.   1 2 3 4 5
15. The subjects taught in this school assist students' human and personal development.   1 2 3 4 5

Section 2 — School Administration and Organization

In the following questions you are asked to give your opinion about the school's administration. In each case please say whether you Definitely Disagree, Mostly Disagree, are Uncertain, Mostly Agree or Definitely Agree.

1 Definitely Disagree
2 Mostly Disagree
3 Uncertain
4 Mostly Agree
5 Definitely Agree

1. All staff have opportunities to participate in decision making in appropriate areas.   1 2 3 4 5
2. Decisions that are made are implemented quickly and effectively.   1 2 3 4 5
3. Staff are kept well informed in matters of importance to them.   1 2 3 4 5
4. Communication between staff and Principal is effective.   1 2 3 4 5
5. Communication between staff and Registrar is effective.   1 2 3 4 5
6. Communication between staff and other office personnel is effective.   1 2 3 4 5

  7. Cooperation among staff is effective.   1 2 3 4 5

  8. Communication between staff and Form Coordinators is effective.   1 2 3 4 5

  9. Morale of staff is high.   1 2 3 4 5

10. Morale of students is high.   1 2 3 4 5

11. The school adapts well to change.   1 2 3 4 5

12. There is a positive and balanced approach to innovation.   1 2 3 4 5

13. The duties and responsibilities of all school personnel are clearly defined.   1 2 3 4 5

14. Effective use is made of skills of staff.   1 2 3 4 5

15. Teachers are consulted regarding their assignment to classes.   1 2 3 4 5

16. Teachers are encouraged to develop themselves professionally.   1 2 3 4 5

17. Timetables within the school lead to well coordinated activities.   1 2 3 4 5

18. There is adequate student supervision.   1 2 3 4 5

19. Active teacher participation at staff meetings is encouraged.   1 2 3 4 5

20. Opportunities are provided for in-service activities related to teachers' needs.   1 2 3 4 5

21. The school has an effective policy on the maintenance of pupil discipline.   1 2 3 4 5

22. The teaching in the school is consistent with the school's aims.   1 2 3 4 5

23. Staff are involved in the curriculum development process.   1 2 3 4 5

24. The school shows an active concern for others in the community.   1 2 3 4 5

25. Relations between the school and clergy are harmonious.   1 2 3 4 5

26. Relations between the school and parents are harmonious.   1 2 3 4 5

27. The quality of my relationships with students is positive.   1 2 3 4 5

28. I am satisfied with the quality of the realtionships between staff and students generally.   1 2 3 4 5

29. There are sufficient materials, equipment, facilities etc, for effective teaching.   1 2 3 4 5

30. The school has a consistent and coherent vision which determines the focus of its activities.   1 2 3 4 5

31. What do you regard as the College's greatest strengths?

. . . .

. . . .

. . . .

32. What aspects of the College causes you the greatest concern?

. . . .

. . . .

. . . .

Thank you for your cooperation

Appendix 5:
Questionnaire to Parents

ST MARY'S COLLEGE
PERCEPTION OF SCHOOL
AND
QUALITY OF SCHOOL LIFE STUDY

QUESTIONNAIRE FOR PARENTS

This questionnaire is designed to find out from parents, in questions similar to those previously asked of the students, what you think about various issues related to the School.

There are no necessarily right or wrong answers, but it is essential that you answer all questions. Your responses will be kept strictly confidential.

Thank you for your cooperation and assistance. Your opinions are valued.

Dr William Ramsay,
Research Consultant,
University of Tasmania
April, 1988.

Section 1 — Parents' Expectations of Catholic Schools

The following statements are often made about the GOALS which Catholic schools should have. Each question begins: 'CATHOLIC SCHOOLS SHOULD ...'

In the left hand column we would like you to record the degree of importance each goal should have in a Catholic school and in the right hand column please circle the answer which best describes how well you feel the goal has been achieved.

1 Of No Importance 2 Of Slight Importance 3 Moderately Important 4 Important 5 Very Important	1 Not Achieved 2 Slightly Achieved 3 Moderately Achieved 4 Achieved 5 Very Well Achieved

1 2 3 4 5	1. Help students to discover and fulfil themselves as human persons.	1 2 3 4 5
1 2 3 4 5	2. Develop students' knowledge and skills in specific areas.	1 2 3 4 5
1 2 3 4 5	3. Give students experience in the main areas of human knowledge (Arts, Science, Humanities).	1 2 3 4 5
1 2 3 4 5	4. Help students to understand their society.	1 2 3 4 5
1 2 3 4 5	5. Provide an atmosphere of Christian community where people are genuinely concerned for one another.	1 2 3 4 5
1 2 3 4 5	6. Develop in students personal qualities of independence and initiative so that they can stand on their own two feet.	1 2 3 4 5
1 2 3 4 5	7. Prepare their students for university study (e.g., by developing good study habits etc).	1 2 3 4 5
1 2 3 4 5	8. Provide students with opportunities for creative work.	1 2 3 4 5
1 2 3 4 5	9. Give adequate sex education to their students.	1 2 3 4 5
1 2 3 4 5	10. Teach Religious Education at a level comparable to other subjects.	1 2 3 4 5
1 2 3 4 5	11. Respect each student individually irrespective of ability or appearance.	1 2 3 4 5
1 2 3 4 5	12. Prepare their students for the HSC as well as possible.	1 2 3 4 5
1 2 3 4 5	13. Create friendly relations with other Church schools and groups.	1 2 3 4 5
1 2 3 4 5	14. Encourage a love of learning for its own sake.	1 2 3 4 5
1 2 3 4 5	15. Provide opportunities for students to participate intelligently in the liturgy (e.g., through Class Masses, etc).	1 2 3 4 5
1 2 3 4 5	16. Give all students a chance of success in some aspects of school life.	1 2 3 4 5
1 2 3 4 5	17. Help students to prepare for future employment.	1 2 3 4 5
1 2 3 4 5	18. Provide opportunities for students to discuss	1 2 3 4 5
1 2 3 4 5	19. Make students aware of the great religions other than Christianity.	1 2 3 4 5
1 2 3 4 5	20. Give an example of dedicated Christian life through its religious teachers.	1 2 3 4 5
1 2 3 4 5	21. Help students to develop their personality and character.	1 2 3 4 5
1 2 3 4 5	22. Help students cope with life after leaving school.	1 2 3 4 5
1 2 3 4 5	23. Encourage a love of literature, art and music.	1 2 3 4 5
1 2 3 4 5	24. Encourage students to take part in local community and civic affairs.	1 2 3 4 5
1 2 3 4 5	25. Integrate Religious Education and other subjects where possible.	1 2 3 4 5
1 2 3 4 5	26. Help students to learn how to get on with other people.	1 2 3 4 5
1 2 3 4 5	27. Develop in students skills which will enable them to get as good a job as possible on leaving school.	1 2 3 4 5
1 2 3 4 5	28. Develop in students an awareness of pressing social problems (such as poverty, hunger and injustice).	1 2 3 4 5

1 2 3 4 5	29. Develop in students habits of independent and critical thought.	1 2 3 4 5
1 2 3 4 5	30. Provide an experience of life based on the values of Christ and the Gospel.	1 2 3 4 5
1 2 3 4 5	31. Provide counselling help to students in their problems.	1 2 3 4 5
1 2 3 4 5	32. Teach students about different careers and jobs so that they can decide what they want to do.	1 2 3 4 5
1 2 3 4 5	33. Prepare students to become good citizens.	1 2 3 4 5
1 2 3 4 5	34. Provide an environment in which students' faith can grow and develop.	1 2 3 4 5
1 2 3 4 5	35. Emphasize self-discipline rather than external confirmity to rules.	1 2 3 4 5
1 2 3 4 5	36. Teach students things which will be of direct importance to them in their future jobs.	1 2 3 4 5
1 2 3 4 5	37. Encourage students to be concerned for the needs of others.	1 2 3 4 5
1 2 3 4 5	38. Develop in students an understanding of what is right and wrong.	1 2 3 4 5
1 2 3 4 5	39. Help students discover and develop their creative abilities.	1 2 3 4 5
1 2 3 4 5	40. Develop Christian values and the place of God in students' lives.	1 2 3 4 5
1 2 3 4 5	41. Develop students' intellectual abilities.	1 2 3 4 5
1 2 3 4 5	42. Encourage students' to be obedient to parents, teachers and all in authority.	1 2 3 4 5
1 2 3 4 5	43. Develop in students an appreciation of beauty.	1 2 3 4 5
1 2 3 4 5	44. Develop in students the ability to form a considered opinion and act on it even if this means going against what people think.	1 2 3 4 5

Section 2 — School Life

This section refers to the Quality of School Life provided at St Mary's College.
Each question begins with: For my daughter, school is a place where ...
Please circle the answer which best describes how you feel:

> 1 Certainly false; I strongly disagree
> 2 Probably false; I'm inclined to disagree
> 3 Uncertain
> 4 Probably true; I'm inclined to agree
> 5 Certainly true; I strongly agree

For my daughter, SCHOOL IS A PLACE WHERE ...

1. She knows how to cope with the work.		1 2 3 4 5
2. Her teachers are fair and just.		1 2 3 4 5
3. She really likes to go.		1 2 3 4 5
4. She feels frustrated.		1 2 3 4 5

5.	She finds mixing with other people helps her to understand herself.	1 2 3 4 5
6.	She feels important.	1 2 3 4 5
7.	She learns to get along with other people.	1 2 3 4 5
8.	Her teachers help her to do her best.	1 2 3 4 5
9.	People have confidence in her.	1 2 3 4 5
10.	Teachers treat her fairly in class.	1 2 3 4 5
11.	People come to her for help.	1 2 3 4 5
12.	She feels lonely.	1 2 3 4 5
13.	She feels restless.	1 2 3 4 5
14.	She knows that people think a lot of her.	1 2 3 4 5
15.	Teachers give her the marks she deserves.	1 2 3 4 5
16.	People look up to her.	1 2 3 4 5
17.	She feels depressed.	1 2 3 4 5
18.	She knows she can reach a satisfactory standard in her work.	1 2 3 4 5
19.	She knows the sorts of things she can do well.	1 2 3 4 5
20.	She learns a lot about herself.	1 2 3 4 5
21.	Her teachers listen to what she says.	1 2 3 4 5
22.	She feels happy.	1 2 3 4 5
23.	She finds that learning is a lot of fun.	1 2 3 4 5
24.	She gets enjoyment from being there.	1 2 3 4 5
25.	She gets satisfaction from the school work she does.	1 2 3 4 5
26.	She gets to know herself better.	1 2 3 4 5
27.	She knows she can do well enough to be successful.	1 2 3 4 5
28.	She gets upset.	1 2 3 4 5
29.	She feels great.	1 2 3 4 5
30.	She has learnt to accept other people as they are.	1 2 3 4 5

Section 3 — Academic Category

In the following questions you are asked to give your opinion about the reason/s why your daughter chose or would choose various HSC subjects. We want you in each case to say whether you Definitely Disagree, Mostly Disagree, Mostly Agree or Definitely Agree, with the statements given. Please read each item carefully and circle the answer which best describes your situation.

Remember in this section that you have to put 'Your daughter chose (or 'Your daughter would choose', for grade 10 students) particular HSC subjects because ...' in front of each item for it to make sense.

My daughter chose (would choose) particular HSC subjects because ...

> 1 Definitely Disagree
> 2 Mostly Disagree
> 3 Mostly Agree
> 4 Definitely Agree

1.	She needed particular subjects to qualify for entrance to university or some other educational institution.	1 2 3 4
2.	She understood that she needed particular subjects in order to gain the immediate employment of your choice.	1 2 3 4
3.	Her friend/friends was/were doing that subject.	1 2 3 4

4. She was intrinsically interested in the subject.   1 2 3 4
5. She had achieved good results in that subject in year 10.   1 2 3 4
6. She knew nothing of the subject and therefore wanted to fill a gap in   1 2 3 4
her knowledge.
7. Her parents strongly influenced her choice of subject.   1 2 3 4
8. Choices were largely determined by the organization of subjects into   1 2 3 4
various lines.
9. The Sciences (maths, science etc.) appeared to be more important than   1 2 3 4
the Humanities (English, social psychology etc.).

Section 4 — Vocational Category

This section asks you go give your opinion on statements about vocational aspects of
school (such as leisure, home science, work experience). Again circle the number that
best describes your situation.

> 1 Definitely Disagree
> 2 Mostly Disagree
> 3 Mostly Agree
> 4 Definitely Agree

1. The subjects my daughter (studies) studied at school suits(ed) her   1 2 3 4
career choice.
2. Leisure education was (is) useful in opening up a potential career.   1 2 3 4
3. Because of her craft studies she is now able to do simple repairs at   1 2 3 4
home.
4. Her skills in cooking, dressmaking have carried over into other areas.   1 2 3 4
5. Work experience helped her in deciding upon her career.   1 2 3 4
6. More vocational studies are required at HSC level if students are to be   1 2 3 4
prepared for life after school.
7. Work experience helped her understand the 'world of work'.   1 2 3 4
8. Vocational studies have proven beneficial in her life outside of school.
    a) Cooking   1 2 3 4
    b) Craft   1 2 3 4
    c) Dressmaking   1 2 3 4
9. HSC students should have Wednesday and Friday afternoons devoted   1 2 3 4
to the pursuit of a less academic, more leisure oriented subjects.
10. Such a programme as described above in (9) should be compulsory for   1 2 3 4
HSC students.

Section 5 — Spiritual Development Category

In your daughter's religious development, which includes her knowledge of Christian
Doctrine, her appreciation of Christian values, her habits of Prayer, and her attendance at Mass (or Worship) and the Sacraments, how important have been each of the
following influences?
    Circle each statement according to the importance you place on each influence.

Say whether you think it is of No Importance, of Little Importance, of Some Importance, Very Important or Most Important.

```
1  No Importance
2  Little Importance
3  Some Importance
4  Very Important
5  Most Important
```

1. The instruction of parents and their example?   1 2 3 4 5
2. The example and personal guidance of teachers?   1 2 3 4 5
3. Religious education provided by the school?   1 2 3 4 5
4. The example of friends at school?   1 2 3 4 5
5. Religious instruction provided by the Parish or Church?   1 2 3 4 5
6. The guidance and influence of some Religious, Priest, or Minister?   1 2 3 4 5
7. We would like you to tell us your attitude towards the teaching of
    Religious Education (RE) —
    a) I am very concerned or alarmed about the teaching of RE in this   1 2 3 4 5
        school.
    b) I am concerned about the teaching of RE in this school.   1 2 3 4 5
    c) I am satisfied about how RE is taught in this school.   1 2 3 4 5
    d) I am happy with the teaching of RE in this school.   1 2 3 4 5
    e) I am very happy about the teaching of RE in this school.   1 2 3 4 5
8. Are there some things about St Mary's that you have come to
    appreciate and value?

    . . . .
9. As a parent trying to bring up your children in the faith, what causes
    you greatest concern or anxiety today?

    . . . .

Section 6 — Leadership/Sport

In this section you are asked to give your opinion about the aspects of leadership and sport that your daughter experienced in school. Again say whether you Definitely Disagree, Mostly Disagree, Mostly Agree or Definitely Agree with the statements made.

```
1  Definitely Disagree
2  Mostly Disagree
3  Mostly Agree
4  Definitely Agree
```

1. The teachers are good models of leadership.   1 2 3 4
2. School helped your daughter to understand what leadership is.   1 2 3 4
3. The physical education classes at SMC provide a comprehensive and   1 2 3 4
    worthwhile programme.
4. Physical education and sport are directed mainly at the gifted and   1 2 3 4
    talented students.

5. Students are encouraged by teachers to join outside clubs etc. when they leave school.   1 2 3 4
6. The value of physical activity is emphasized at SMC sufficiently for your daughter to want to continue sport and leisure activities after leaving school (or outside school).   1 2 3 4
7. Your daughter developed the ability to be a leader because of her experience at SMC.   1 2 3 4
8. Your daughter enjoys activities at SMC other than study and sport, which she will continue (has continued) after leaving school.   1 2 3 4

9–11. At SMC there are/were (say what these are if you wish) sufficient opportunities for your daughter leadership qualities in

      grade 10   1 2 3 4
      grade 11   1 2 3 4
      grade 12   1 2 3 4

. . . .

12. At SMC your daughter feels (felt) free to make mistakes and learn from them (in areas other than class subjects).   1 2 3 4
13. There is (was) a sufficient number of physical education classes.   1 2 3 4

Section 7 — Teachers Category

In this section please indicate how true each statements is (was) of your daughter's teachers at St Mary's.

> 1 True of No Teachers (25%)
> 2 True of Very Few Teachers (25%)
> 3 True of Some Teachers (25%−50%)
> 4 True of Many Teachers (50%−75%)
> 5 True of Most Teachers (75%)

1. Teachers clearly outline and organize their classwork.   1 2 3 4 5
2. Teachers allow classroom discussion.   1 2 3 4 5
3. Teachers try to make their teaching material relevant to current trends and student's needs.   1 2 3 4 5
4. Teachers give friendly help to any student having problems with classwork.   1 2 3 4 5
5. Teachers try to be sure that students understand the work that is done in class.   1 2 3 4 5
6. Teachers cover a great deal of material in the time allowed.   1 2 3 4 5
7. Teachers place too much emphasis on detailed facts and memorization.   1 2 3 4 5
8. Teachers give students a broad, general understanding of their subjects.   1 2 3 4 5
9. Teachers extend students to the limits of their abilities.   1 2 3 4 5
10. Teachers encourage students to do independent work on their own.   1 2 3 4 5
11. Teachers are understanding of students' study problems.   1 2 3 4 5
12. Teachers stimulate students to think and be creative.   1 2 3 4 5
13. Teachers succeed in making their classes interesting.   1 2 3 4 5
14. Teachers try to make their classes entertaining rather than useful.   1 2 3 4 5

15. Teachers set homework regularly.   1 2 3 4 5
16. Teachers correct students' work regularly.   1 2 3 4 5

Section 8 — School Administration/Organization

This section gives a number of statements about the administration/organization of St Mary's College.

Again, please circle the answer which best describes how you feel. Say whether you Definitely Disagree, Mostly Disagree, are Uncertain, Mostly Agree or Definitely Agree.

> 1 Definitely Disagree
> 2 Mostly Disagree
> 3 Uncertain
> 4 Mostly Agree
> 5 Definitely Agree

1. There is effective communication between administration and   1 2 3 4 5
   parents.
2. School attendance is regularly checked.   1 2 3 4 5
3. The Parents & Friends Association is effective.   1 2 3 4 5
4. The School Newsletter is informative and positive.   1 2 3 4 5
5. The School Yearbook, the Santa Maria, is an excellent publication   1 2 3 4 5
   and record of the year's activities.
6. St Mary's enjoys an excellent reputation in the local community.   1 2 3 4 5
7. The school has been successful in its efforts to involve parents in 1 2 3 4 5
   its activities.
8. There is adequate teacher involement in sport and other extra-   1 2 3 4 5
   curricular activities.
9. Reports on your child's progress are informative, timely and   1 2 3 4 5
   positive.
10. The school rules are reasonable.   1 2 3 4 5
11. Student discipline is well maintained.   1 2 3 4 5
12. The quality of food offered in the tuck shop is nutritiously sound 1 2 3 4 5
    and appealing.
13. The quality of service in the tuck shop is friendly and helpful.   1 2 3 4 5
14. The quality and variety of goods provided by the Book Store is   1 2 3 4 5
    good.
15. The service in the Book Store is helpful and friendly.   1 2 3 4 5
16. Ample opportunities are provided for participation in extra-   1 2 3 4 5
    curricular activities, e.g., music, sport, drama, debating etc.
17. There is adequate guidance about subject selection.   1 2 3 4 5
18. Office staff are helpful and friendly.   1 2 3 4 5
19. The quality of communication between parents and teachers is   1 2 3 4 5
    excellent.
20. The cleanliness and appearance of the school are well maintained. 1 2 3 4 5
21. The morale of the teachers is high.   1 2 3 4 5
22. The morale and spirit of students is high.   1 2 3 4 5

Thank you for your cooperation

Appendix 6: Student Interviews

ST MARY'S COLLEGE
PERCEPTION OF SCHOOL STUDY
INTERVIEW SCHEDULE — PAGE 1

Thank you (name (s) of student interviewee (s), e.g., Mary) for agreeing to come to this short interview. The interviews, with a number of students and ex—students, are being held simply to add to our picture of students' perceptions of school life at St Mary's College.

As your interviewer, I shall ask a few questions and get you just to talk about them as you see them. Please feel quite free to say what you think in response to each question.

The interview is being recorded but is strictly confidential. No record of your full name will be attached, nor any connection made to your ID or responses on the questionnaire you completed. Also the whole thing will last only about 15 minutes.

May I stress that there are no necessarily right or wrong answers to the questions; just answer them as you feel.

Initially, do you remember the Categories in the Questionnaire?
Academic/Vocational/Personal/Spiritual/Leadership/Sporting?
These categories are all we'll refer to in the questions.

Shall we try the first question?

ST MARY'S COLLEGE
PERCEPTION OF SCHOOL STUDY
INTERVIEW SCHEDULE — PAGE 2

Questions
1. What do you mean by the word 'academic'?
2. What has St Mary's College done for you academically?
3. What do you mean by the word 'vocational'?
4. What has St Mary's College done for you vocationally?
5. What do you mean by the words 'personal development' and 'spiritual development'?
6. What has St Mary's College done for you in terms of personal and spiritual development?
7. What do you mean by the words 'leadership' and 'sport'?
8. What has St Mary's College done for you in terms of leadership and sport?

Thank you for answering these questions. Your opinions are valued.

Bibliography

ACKOFF, R.L. (1981) *Creating the Corporate Future: Plan Or Be Planned For*, New York: John Wiley and Sons.

ADELMAN, C., JENKINS, D. and KEMMIS, S. (1985) Re-Thinking the Case Study: Notes from the Second Cambridge Conference, Unpublished.

ARGYRIS, C. (1982) *Reasoning, Learning and Action: Individual and Organizational*, San Francisco, Jossey-Bass.

AINLEY, J., BATTEN, M. and MILLER, H. (1984) 'Staying at high school in Victoria', *ACER Research Monograph No. 237*, Hawthorn, Vic: ACER.

ALKIN, M.C. (1969) 'Evaluation theory development', *Evaluation Comment*, 2(1), pp. 2–7.

ALKIN, M.C. (1973) 'Evaluating "curriculum" and "instruction"', *Curriculum Theory Network*, 4, pp. 43–51.

ALKIN, M.C. (1975) 'Evaluation: Who needs it? Who cares?' *Studies in Educational Evaluation*, 1, pp. 201–12.

ALKIN, M.C. (1980) 'Naturalistic study of evaluation utilization', in BRASKAMP, L.A. and BROWN, R.D. (Eds) *Utilization of Evaluative Information*. New Directions for Program Evaluation No. 5, San Francisco: Josey Bass.

ALKIN, M.C. and DAILLAK, R.H. (1979) 'A study of evaluation utilization', *Educational Evaluation and Policy Analysis*, 1(4), pp. 41–9.

ALKIN, M.C., DAILLAK, R. and WHITE, P. (1979) *Using Evaluations: Does Evaluation Make a Difference?* Beverly Hills, Calif.: Sage.

ALLISON, D.J. (1983) 'Toward an improved understanding of the organizational nature of schools', *Educational Administration Quarterly*, 19(4), pp. 7–34.

ALVESSON, M.A. (1987) 'Organizations: Culture, and ideology', *International Studies of Management & Organization*, vol xvii (3), pp. 4–18.

ANDERSON, S.B. and BALL, S. (1978) *The Profession and Practice of Program Evaluation*, San Francisco: Jossey Bass.

ANDERSON, S.B., BALL, S. and MURPHY, T. (1975) *Encyclopedia of Educational Research*, San Francisco: Jossey-Bass.

ANGUS, L.B. (1988) *Continuity and Change in Catholic Schooling*, Lewes: Falmer Press.

ANTONOPLOS, D.P. (1977) Evaluation reconsidered: Pied pipers of pedagogy. Paper presented at Annual Meeting of American Educational Research Association, New York City.

APPLE, M.W., SUBKOVIAK, M.J. and LUFLER, H.S. Jr. (Eds) (1974) *Educational Evaluation: Analysis and Responsibility*, Berkeley: McCutchan.

APPLE, M.W. (1975) 'Scientific interests and the nature of educational institutions', in PINAR, W., *Curriculum Theorizing: The Reconceptualists*, Berkeley, CA: McCutchan.

ARGYRIS, C. and SCHON, D.A. (1974) *Theory in Practice: Increasing Professional Effectiveness*, San Francisco: Jossey-Bass.

ARMSTRONG, A.F. (1983) *Developments in Australian Research and Practice*, Melbourne: University of Melbourne Press.

ASTLEY, W.G. and VAN DE VEN, A.H. (1983) 'Central perspectives and debates in organizational theory', *Administrative Science Quarterly*, 28, pp. 245–73.

Australian Council for Educational Research (ACER) (1980) School Life Questionnaire, Hawthorn: Victoria: ACER.

BAIRD, J.R. and MITCHELL, I.J. (Eds) (1986) *Improving the Quality of Teaching and Learning — An Australian Case Study — The Peel Project*, Melbourne: Monash University Press.

BALL, S.J. (1989) 'Micro-politics versus management: Towards a sociology of school organization', in WALKER, S. and BARTON, L. (Eds) *Politics and the Processes of Schooling*, Milton Keynes: Open University Press, pp. 218–38.

BAKER, G., DOYLE, M., FITZPATRICK, M., STAFFORD, G. and WOOD, B. (1983) Shaping the Curriculum in Catholic High Schools in Victoria. Paper presented at the biennial conference of the Australian Curriculum Studies Association, Adelaide.

BASTIANI, J. (Ed.) (1987) *Parents and Teachers: Perspectives on Home-School Relations*, Windsor, Berkshire: NFER-Nelson.

BATES, R.J. (1978) The new sociology of education: Directions for theory and research, *New Zealand Journal of Educational Studies*, 13(1), pp. 3–22.

BATES, R.J. (1980a) 'New developments in the new sociology of education', *British Journal of Sociology of Education*, 1(1), pp. 67–79.

BATES, R.J. (1980b) 'Educational administration, the sociology of science and the management of knowledge', *Educational Administration Quarterly*, 16(2), pp. 1–20.

BATES, R.J. (1982) Towards a critical practice of educational administration. Paper prepared for Annual Conference of American Educational Research Association, New York.

BATES, R.J. (1983) *Educational Administration and the Management of Knowledge*, Geelong: Deakin University Press.

BATES, R.J. (1988) *Evaluating Schools: A Critical Approach*, Geelong: Deakin University Press.

BEARE, H. (1974) 'Is your school achieving? Why not an independent review of its accomplishments?', *Developing Education*, August, pp. 1–7.

BEARE, H. (1987) 'Metaphors about schools: The principal as cultural leader', in SIMPKINS, W.S., THOMAS, A.R. and THOMAS, E.B. (Eds) *Principal and Change: The Australian Experience*, Armidale, NSW: University of New England Press, pp. 275–96.

BEARE, H., CALDWELL, B. and MILLIKAN, R. (1988) *Creating an Excellent School*, Sydney: Croom Helm.

BECKER, H. (1960) 'Notes on the concept of commitment', *American Journal of Sociology*, 66, pp. 32–40.

BELL, D. (1984) *The Third Technological Revolution*, New York: Basic Books.

BENNETT, W. (1988) Address delivered to National Catholic Educational Association's 85th annual convention in New York on 7 April.

BENNIS, W. and NANUS, B. (1985) *Leaders: The Strategies for Taking Charge*, New York: Harper and Row.

BENNIS, W.G., BENNE, K.D. and CHIN, R. (Eds) (1961) *The Planning of Change*, New York: Holt, Rinehart and Winston.

BERGER, P. and LUCKMANN, T. (1967) *The Social Construction of Reality: A Treatise in the Sociology of Knowledge*, Garden City, NY: Doubleday Anchor.

BERNSTEIN, I.N., BOHRNSTEDT, C.W. and BORGATTA, E.F. (1975) 'External validity and evaluation research: A codification of problems', *Sociological Methods and Research*, 4, pp. 101–28.

BERNSTEIN, R. (1978) *The Restructuring of Social and Political Theory*, Philadelphia: University of Pennsylvania Press.

BLAKE, R. and MOUTON, J.S. (1985) 'Establishing acceptable norms', in KIRPATRICK, D.L. (Ed.) *How to Manage Change Effectively*, San Francisco: Jossey-Bass, pp. 40–4.

BLOOM, A. (1987) 'The Closing of the American Mind', *Australian Weekend Magazine*, 25–26 July.

BLOOM, B.S., MADARIS, G.F. and HASTINGS, J.T. (1981) *Evaluating to Improve Learning*, McGraw Hill, Inc.

BLUMBERG, A. and GREENFIELD, W. (1980) *The Effective Principal: Perspectives on School Leadership*, (Second edn) Boston: Allyn and Bacon.

BOLAM, R. (1982) *Strategies for School Improvement*, Paris: OECD/CERI.

BOUD, D. (Ed.) (1988) *Developing Student Autonomy in Learning*, 2nd edn., London, Kogan Page.

BOURDIEU, P. and PASSERON, J.C. (1977) *Reproduction in Education, Society and Culture*, London: Sage.

BOWLES, S. and GINTIS, H. (1976) *Schooling in Capitalist America*, London: Routledge and Kegan Paul.

BOYER, E. (1989) *Times Educational Supplement*, Number 3817, Friday, 25 August, p. 11.

BREDO, E. and FEINBERG, W. (1982) 'The Critical approach to educational research', in BREDO, E. and FEINBERG, W. (Eds) *Knowledge and Values in Social and Educational Research*, Philadelphia, Temple University Press.

BRENNAN, M. and HOADLEY, R. (1984) *School Self Evaluation*, Education Department of Victoria.

BRINKERHOFF, R.O., BRETHOWER, D.M., HLUCHYI, T. and NOWAKOWSKI, J.R. (1983) *Program Evaluation*, Boston: Kluwer-Nijhoff.

BROOKOVER, W., BEADY, C., FLOOD, P., SCHWEITZER, P. and WISENBAKER, J. (1979) *School Social Systems and Student Achievement: Schools Can Make a Difference*, New York: Praeger Publisher.

BROWN, J.K. (1984) 'Corporate soul-searching: The power of mission statement', *Across the Board*, March, pp. 44–52.

BRUNER, J. (1983) *In Search of Mind*, New York: Harper and Row.

BUETOW, H.A. (1988) *The Catholic School: Its Roots, Identity and Future*, New York: Crossroad.

BURACK, E.H. and TORDA, F. (1985) 'Rewards and punishment related to change', in KIRPATRICK, D.L. (Ed.) *How to Manage Change Effectively*, San Francisco: Jossey-Bass, pp. 50–3.

BURDIN, J.L. (Ed.) (1989) *School Leadership: A Contemporary Reader*, Newbury Park: Sage Publications.

BURGESS, T. (Ed.) (1986) *Education for Capability*, Windsor, Berkshire: NFER-Nelson.

BURNS, J.M. (1978) *Leadership*, New York: Harper and Row.

BURRELL, G. and MORGAN, G. (1979) *Sociological Paradigms and Organizational Analysis*, Exeter, NH: Heinemann.

CALDWELL, B.J. and SPINKS, J. (1986) *Policy-Making and Planning for School Effectiveness*, Hobart: Education Department, Tasmania.

CALDWELL, B.J. and SPINKS, J. (1988) *The Self-Managing School*, Lewes: Falmer Press.

CALDWELL, B.J. (1988) Emerging issues in leadership: Some points of view. Presented at seminar on senior staff development. Tasmanian Education Department, 7 October.

CALIFORNIA STATE DEPARTMENT OF EDUCATION (1979) *Program Evaluator's Guide* (2nd ed.) Manual developed as part of Evaluation Improvement Program, Princeton: Educational Testing Service.

CALLAHAN, R. (1962) *Education and the Cult of Efficiency*, Chicago: University of Chicago Press.

CAMERON, D. (1985) *Feminism and Linguistic Theory*, London: MacMillan.

CARO, F.G. (1971) 'Issues in the evaluation of social programs', *Review of Educational Research*, 41, pp. 87–114.

CARO, F.G. (Ed.) (1977) *Readings in Educational Research*, New York: Russell Sage Foundation.

CARROLL, J.B. (Ed.) (1956) *Language, Thought and Reality: Selected Writings of Benjamin Lee Whorf*, Cambridge, Mass: MIT Press.

CASE, C.M. (1969) 'The application of PERT to large-scale educational research and evaluation studies', *Educational Technology*, 9, pp. 79–83.

Catholic Education Council (1965) *Evidence to the Central Advisory Council on Primary Education*, London: Catholic Education Council.

CIRIELLO, M.J. (1988) The relationship between the commitment of Catholic school teachers and their personal instructional goals. Paper presented to the Annual Meeting of the American Educational Research Association, New Orleans, LA, 6 April.

CLARK, D., MCKIBBIN, S. and MALKAS, M. (Eds) (1981) *Alternative Perspectives Form Educational Organizations*, San Francisco: Far West Laboratory for Educational Research and Development.

CLARK, D.L., LOTTO, L.S. and ASTUTO, T.A. (1989) 'Effective school and school improvement: A comparative analysis of two lines of inquiry', in BURDIN, J.L. (Ed.) *School Leadership: A Contemporary Reader*, Newbury Park: Sage Publications, pp. 159–86.

CLARK, E.E. and RAMSAY, W. (1988) 'The role of schools and society in preserving and nurturing social capital', *Youth Studies and Abstracts: The Bulletin for the National Clearing House for Youth Studies*, vol 7 (3), pp. 11–17.

CLARK, E.E. and RAMSAY, W. (1989) 'Catholic schools, Catholic communities, and social capital', *Australasian Catholic Record,* IXVI (3), July, pp. 334–46.

CLARK, P. (1987) Anglo-American Innovation, Berlin/New York: de Gruyter.

CLIFT, P., NUTTAL, D. and McCORMICK, R. (1987) *Studies in School Self-evaluation*, Lewes: Falmer Press.

COLEMAN, J.S. *et al.* (1966) *Report on Equality of Educational Opportunity*, Washington: US Government Printing Office.

COLEMAN, J.S., HOFFER, T. and KILGORE, S. (1981) *High School Achievement: Public Catholic, and Private Schools Compared*, Chicago: University of Chicago Press.

COLEMAN, J.S. and HOFFER, T. (1987) *Public and Private High Schools: The Impact of Communities*, New York: Basic Books.

COLEMAN, J. (1987) 'Families and schools', *Educational Researcher* vol 16, Aug–Sept, 6.

COLLINS, C.W. and HUGHES, P.W. (1978) Expectations of secondary schools. Report to Australian Commonwealth Government Committee Enquiry into Education and Training. Canberra: College of Advanced Education.

COLLINS, C.W. and HUGHES, P.W. (1982) 'Where Junior Secondary Schools are Heading', *Australian Education Review*, 16, ACER Hawthorne, Victoria.

CONNELL, R.W. *et al.* (1982) *Making the Difference: Schools, Families and Social Division*, Sydney: Allen and Unwin.

CONNELL, R.W. (1983) *Which Way is Up: Essays on Class, Sex and Culture*, Sydney, Allen and Unwin.

CONNELL, R.W. (1985) *Teachers' Work*, Sydney, Allen and Unwin.

CONNER, D.R. and PATTERSON, R. (1985) 'Obtaining commitment to change', in KIRPATRICK, D.L. (Ed.) *How to Manage Change Effectively*, San Francisco: Jossey-Bass, pp. 54–62.

CONWAY, R.W. (1978) *Land of the Long Weekend*, South Melbourne: Sun Books.

COOK, T.D. and REICHARDT, S.S. (Eds) (1979) *Qualitative and Quantitative Methods in Evaluation Research*, Beverly Hills, Calif.: Sage.

COOLEY, C.H. (1964) *Human Nature in the Social Order*, New York: Schocken Books.

COOLEY, W.W. and LOHNES, P.R. (1976) *Evaluation Research in Education*, New York: Irvington.

COOMER, D.L. (1986) 'Reforming the evaluation process', in SIROTNIK, K.A. and OAKES, J. (Eds) *Critical Perspectives on the Organization and Improvement of Schooling*, Boston: Kluwer-Nijhoff.

Cooperative Review and Development: A Resource Manual, Melbourne: Catholic Education Office, undated.

Cooperative School Evaluations (Vols 1–4), Department of Education Queensland, 1982.

CORNSTEIN, A.C. and HUNKINS, F.P. (1988) *Curriculum Foundations, Principles and Issues*, Englewood Cliffs, NJ: Prentice Hall.

COX, P.L. (1983) 'Complimentary roles and successful change', *Educational Leadership*, 41, p. 3.

CRITTENDEN, B. (1978) 'Product or process in curriculum evaluation?' *Australian Educational Researcher*, 5(1), pp. 29–52.

CRONBACH, L.J. (1963) Course improvement through evaluation', *Teacher College Record*, 64, pp. 672–83.

CRONBACH, L.J. (1975) 'Beyond the two disciplines of scientific psychology', *American Psychologist*, 30, pp. 116–27.

Bibliography

CRONBACH, L.J., AMBRON, S., DORNBUSCH, S.M., HESS, R.D., HORNICK, R.C., PHILLIPS, D.C., WALKER, D.F. and WEINER, S.P. (1980) *Toward Reform of Program Evaluation: Aims, Methods, and Institutional Arrangements*, San Francisco: Jossey Bass.

CROZIER, M. *et al.* (1975) *The Crisis of Democracy: Report on Governability of Democracies to the Trilateral Commission*, New York: University Press.

CUBAN, L. (1984) 'Transforming the frog into a prince: Effective schools research, policy and practice at the district level', *Harvard Educational Review*, 54(2), p. 132.

CUBAN, L. (1988) *The Managerial Imperative and the Practice of Leadership in Schools*, Albany, NY: State University of New York Press.

CUBAN, L. (1987) *The Managerial Imperative and the Practice of Leadership in Schools*, Albany: State University of New York Press.

CULBERTSON, J. (1981) 'Three epistemologies and the study of educational administration', *Review*, 22(1), pp. 1–6.

CULBERTSON, J. (1982) 'Reflections on the administration of education, an interview by R.S. Podemskii', *Phi Delta Kappan*, 63, pp. 473–6.

CULBERTSON, J. (1983) 'Theory in educational administration: Echoes from critical thinkers', *Educational Researcher*, 12 (10), pp. 15–22.

CUMMING, J. (1985) School-focused evaluation: A question of balance. Unpublished paper, Victorian Institute of Secondary Edcuation.

CURRICULUM DEVELOPMENT CENTRE (1977) *Curriculum Evaluation*, Canberra.

CURRICULUM DEVELOPMENT CENTRE (1982) *Curriculum Evaluation: How it can be done*, Canberra.

DALE, R. (1989) *The Role of the State in Education*, Milton Keynes: Open University Press.

DALIN, P. and RUST, V.D. (1983) *Can Schools Learn?*, Windsor: NFER-Nelson.

DAVIS, E. (1980) *Teachers as Curriculum Evaluators*, Sydney: George Allen and Unwin.

D'CRUZ, J. (1975) 'Accountability in education', in D'CRUZ, J.V. and SHEEHAN, P.J. (Eds) *The Renewal of Australian schools: Essays on Educational Planning in Australia after the Karmel Report*, Melbourne: Primary Education.

DEAL, T. and KENNEDY, A. (1982) *Corporate cultures: The Rites and Rituals of Corporate Life*, Reading, MA: Addison-Wesley.

DEAL, T.E. (1985) 'The symbolism of effective schools', *The Elementary School Journal*, Volume 85(5), pp. 601–20.

DEAL, T.E. (1987) 'The culture of schools', in SHEIVE, L.T. and SCHOENHEIT, M.B. (Eds) *Leadership: Examing the Elusive*, Alexandria, VA, American Association for Curriculum Development.

DEBLOIS, C. (1979) 'Challenge to administrative theory', *The Canadian Administrator*, 18(8), pp. 1–6.

DELLA-PIANA, G.M. (1979) Poetry criticism as a perspective for educational evaluation criticism. Research on Evaluation Program Paper and Report Series, No. 13, Northwest Regional Educational Laboratory, January.

DENNY, T. (1978) In defense of story telling as a first step in educational evaluation. Paper presented to the International Reading Association, Houston, May.

DERNELLEY, R.W. and HERBERT, J.P. (1983) *Guidelines for School Evaluation*. National Council of Independent Schools.

DOBBERT, M.L. and DOBBERT, D.J. (1976) A general model for complete ethnographic evaluations. Paper presented at Annual Meeting of American Educational Research Association, San Francisco, April.

DONMOYER, R. (1976) The evaluator as artist: A discussion of premises and problems with examples from two aesthetically based evaluations. Paper presented at Annual Meeting of American Educational Research Association, San Francisco, April.

DRESSEL, P.L. (1976) *Handbook of Academic Evaluation*, San Francisco: Jossey Bass.

DUBOS, R. (1981) *Celebrations of Life*, New York: McGraw-Hill.

DUIGNAN, P. (1986) 'Research on effective schooling: Some implications for school improvement', *Journal of Educational Administration*, 24(1), pp. 59–73.

DUIGNAN, P. (1988) 'Who controls curriculum development in Australia?' *In the Nation's Interest*, Seventh National Conference of National Council for Independent Schools, Brisbane, 29 September–2 October, pp. 61–73.

DUNN, E. (1982) *Support for Review and Development: The Role of the Facilitator*, Education Department of Tasmania.

DUNN, J.G. (1986) 'Realising a classroom asset', *Curriculum Perspectives* 7, 2.

DURSTON, B. (1987) 'New federal priorities to threaten education', *Educare Digest*, Spring, No. 1, pp. 1–2.

ECKHOFF, M.A. (1987) Catholic schools towards 2000. Paper presented at 12th Annual Conference of Association of Victorian Catholic Secondary Schools, 27–29 May.

EDMONDS, R.R. (1979) 'Effective schools for the urban poor', *Educational Leadership*, 37, pp. 15–24.

EGAN, J. (1988) *Opting Out: Catholic Schools Today*, Herefordshire: Fowler Wright Books, Ltd.

EGGLESTON, J. and GALTON, M. (1976) 'Curriculum evaluation and interaction analysis', *British Journal of Teacher Education*, 2, pp. 189–99.

EISNER, E.W. (1967) 'Educational objectives: Help or hindrance?' *School Review*, 75, pp. 250–60.

EISNER, E.W. (1969) 'Instructional and expressive objectives: Their formulation and use in curriculum', in POPHAM, W.J., EISNER, E.W., SULLIVAN H.J. and TYLER, L.L. (Eds) *Instructional Objectives*, AERA Monograph Series on Curriculum Evaluations, No 3, Chicago: Rand McNally.

EISNER, E.W. (1972) 'Emerging models for educational evaluation,' *School Review*, 80, pp. 573–90.

EISNER, E.W. (1976) 'Educational connoisseurship and criticism: Their form and functions in educational evaluation', *Journal of Aesthetic Education*, 10, pp. 135–50.

EISNER, E.W. (1977) 'On the uses of educational connoisseurship and criticism for evaluating classroom life', *Teachers College Record*, 78, pp. 345–58.

EISNER, E.W. (1979a) 'The use of qualitative forms of evaluation for improving educational practice', *Educational Evaluation and Policy Analysis*, 1, pp. 11–19.

EISNER, E.W. (1979b) *The Educational Imagination: On the Design and Evaluation of School Progams*. New York: Macmillan.

EISNER, E.W. (1981) 'On the differences between scientific and artistic approaches to qualitative research', *Educational Researcher*, 10(4), pp. 5–9.

ELLIOTT, J. (1978) 'What is action-research in schools?' *Journal of Curriculum Studies*, 10, pp. 355–7.

ELLIOTT, J. and ADELMAN, C. (1975) Classroom action research. Unit 2 of Ford Teaching Project, Norwich: Centre for Applied Research in Education, University of East Anglia.

ENGLAND, G. (1985) 'Three approaches to understanding educational administration', *Study Guide 2: Thinking about Educational Administration*, Victoria: Deakin University.

EPSTEIN, J.L. (1981) *The Quality of School Life*, Lexington, Mass: D.C. Heath.

EPSTEIN, J.L. and McPARTLAND, J.M. (1976) 'The concept and measurement of the Quality of School Life', *American Educational Research Journal*, 13 (1), pp. 15–30.

ERICKSON, D.A. (1977) 'An overdue paradigm shift in educational administration, or how can we get that idiot off the freeway?', in CUNNINGHAM, L.L., HACK, W.G. and NYSTRAND, R.O. (Eds) *Educational Administration: The Developing Decades*, Berkeley, CA: McCutchan.

ETZIONI, A. (1988) *The Moral Dimension: Toward a New Economics*, New York: The Free Press.

FARRAR, E. (1987) Improving the urban high school: The role of leadership in the school district and state. Paper presented at American Educational Research Association Meeting, Washington D.C., 23 April.

FARLEY, T. (1985) *et al.*, *Reconceptualization of Vocational Education Program Evaluation*, Columbus, OH: National Center for Research in Vocational Education, Ohio State University.

FAY, B. (1975) *Social Theory and Political Practice*, London: George Allen & Unwin Ltd.

FAY, B. (1977) 'How people change themselves: The relationship between critical theory and its audiences', in BALL, T. (Ed.) *Political Theory and Praxis: New Perspectives*, Minneapolis: University of Minnesota Press, pp. 200–33.

FEHRENBACHER, H.L., OWENS, T.R. and HAENN, J.F. (1976) The use of student case study methodology in program evaluation. Paper in Research, Evaluation, Development Series, Northwest Regional Educational Laboratory, October.

FETTERMAN, D.M. and PITMAN, A.M. (1986) *Educational Evaluation: Ethnography in Theory, Practice, and Politics*, London: Sage Publications.

FIEDLER, F.E., CHEMERS, M.M. and MAHAR, L. (1977) *Improving Leadership Effectiveness: The Leader Match Concept*, New York: John Wiley & Sons.

FIEDLER, F.E. (1967) *A Theory of Leadership Effectiveness*, New York: McGraw Hill.

FINN, C.E. (1984) 'Towards strategic independence: Nine commandments for enhancing school effectiveness', *Phi Delta Kappan*, February, pp. 518–24.

FISHER, R. and URY, W. (1983) *Getting to Yes: Negotiating Agreement Without Giving In*, London: Hutchinson, (Second edn, 1986).

FLYNN, M. (1975) *Some Catholic Schools in Action*, Sydney: Catholic Education Office.

FLYNN, M. (1985) *The Effectiveness of Catholic Schools*, Homebush, NSW: St Paul Publications.

FOON, A.E. (1986) 'Evaluative procedures and accountability in Australian schools: A review of practice 1980–1985 and a prelude to the future', *NCIS Newsletter*, 4(3), pp. 1–4.

FOSTER, L.E. (1981) *Australian Education: A Sociological Perspective*, Sydney: Prentice-Hall of Australia, Ltd.

FOSTER, W. (1980) 'Administration and the crisis of legitimacy: A review of Habermasian thought', *Harvard Educational Review*, 50, pp. 496–505.

FOSTER, W. (1984) 'Toward a critical theory of educational administration', in SERGIOVANN, T.J. and CORBALLY, J.E. (Eds) *Leadership and Organizational Culture: New Perspectives on Administrative Theory and Practice*, Urbana, IL: University of Illinois Press, pp. 240–59.

FOSTER, W. (1986) 'A critical perspective on administration and organization in education', in SIROTNIK, K.A. and OAKES, J. (Eds) *Critical Perspectives on the Organization and Improvement of Schooling*, Boston: Kluwer-Nijhoff, pp. 95–129.

FRASER, B.J. (1977) 'Evaluating the intrinsic worth of the curricular goals: A discussion and an example', *Journal of Curriculum Studies*, 9, pp. 125–32.

FRASER, B.J. (1981) *Learning Environment in Curriculum Evaluation: A Review*, Monograph in Evaluation in Education series, London: Pergamon.

FRASER, B.J. (1982) *Annotated Bibliography of Curriculum Evaluation Literature*, Israel Curriculum Centre.

FRASER, B.J. (1984) 'Directions in curriculum evaluation', *Studies in Educational Evaluation*, 10, pp. 125–34.

FREIRE, P. (1972) *Pedagogy of the Oppressed*, Harmondsworth: Penguin Books.

GARDNER, D.E. (1977) 'Five evaluation Frameworks: Implications for decision making in higher eduation', *Journal of Higher education*, 48, pp. 571–93.

GARDNER, H. (1987) 'Symposium on the theory of multiple intelligence' in PERKINS, D., LOCKHEAD, J. and BISHOP, J. (Eds) *Thinking: The Second International Conference*, New Jersey: Lawrence Erlbaum Associates.

GEPHART, W.J. (1977) Evaluation reconsidered: Do we need a synthesis? Definitely! Paper presented at Annual Meeting of American Educational Research Association, New York City, April.

GEPHART, W.J. (1978) The facets of the evaluation process: A starter set. Paper presented at Annual Meeting of American Educational Research Association, Toronto, April.

GEPHART, W.J. (1979) Painting as an evaluation metaphor. Research on Evaluation Program Paper and Report Series, No. 19, Northwest Regional Educational Laboratory, April.

GIDDENS, A. (1976) *New Rules of Sociological Method*, New York: Basic Books.

GIROUX, H. (1981) *Ideology, Culture and the Process of Schooling*, Lewes: Falmer Press.

GIROUX, H. (1983) *Critical Theory and Educational Practice*, Geelong: Deakin University Press.

GLASS, G.V. (1972) 'Two generations of evaluation models', in TAYLOR, P.A. and COWLEY, D.M. (Eds) *Readings in Curriculum Evaluation*, Dubuque, Iowa: Brown.

GLASSMAN, N.S. (1986) *Evaluation-based Leadership: School Administration in Contemporary Perspective*, NY: State University of NY Press.

GLASSMAN, R.B. (1973) 'Persistence and loose coupling in living systems', *Behavioural Science*, 18, pp. 83–98.

GODET, M. (1987) *Scenarios and Strategic Management*, (trans. GREEN, D. and RODNEY, A.) London: Butterworths.

GOETZ, J.P. and LECOMPTE, M.D. (1980) Data collection and analysis in qualitative curriculum evaluation. Paper presented at Annual Meeting of American Educational Association, Boston, April.

GOFFMAN, E. (1959) *The Presentation of Self in Everyday Life*, Garden City, NY: Doubleday/Anchor.

GOLDBERG, M.L. (1971) 'Evaluation of Innovations', LAWLER, M.R. (Ed.) *Strategies for Planned Curricular Innovation*, New York: Teachers College Press.

GOOD, T.L. and BROPHY, J.E. (1987) *Looking in Classrooms*, 4th edn., New York, Harper and Row.

GOODMAN, N. and MARX, G.T. (1978) *Society Today* (Third edn) New York: Random House.

GREENFIELD, T.B. (1973) 'Organizations as social inventions: Rethinking assumptions about change', *Journal of Applied Behavioral Science*, 9(55), pp. 551–74.

GREENFIELD, T.B. (1975) 'Theory about organization: A new perspective and its implications for schools', in HOUGHTON, V., McHUGH, R. and MORGAN, C. (Eds) *Management in Education*, London: Ward Lock Educational.

GREENFIELD, T.B. (1978) 'Reflections on organization theory and the truths of irreconcilable realities', *Educational Administrative Quarterly*, 14(2), pp. 1–23.

GREENFIELD, T.B. (1980) 'The man who comes back through the door in the wall: Discovering truth, discovering self, discovering organizations', *Educational Quarterly*, 16(3), pp. 26–59.

GREENFIELD, T.B. (1982) 'Against group mind: On anarchistic theory of education', *McGill Journal of Education*, 17(1), pp. 3–11.

GREENFIELD, T.B. (1985) 'Theories of educational organization: A critical perspective', *International Encyclopedia of Education: Research and Studies*, Oxford: Pergamon Press.

GREENFIELD, T.B. (1986) 'Leaders and schools: Willfulness and nonnatural order in organizations', in SERGIOVANI, T.J. and CORBALLY, J. (Eds) *Leadership and Organizational Culture: New Perspectives on Administration Theory and Practice*, Urbana and Chicago: University of Chicago Press, pp. 142–69.

GREENFIELD, W. (1987) Moral imagination and value leadership in schools. Paper presented at the annual meeting of American Educational Research Association, Washington, D.C., 20 April.

GRIFFITHS, D.E. (1977) 'The individual in organization: A theoretical perspective,' *Educational Administration Quarterly*, 13(2), pp. 1–18.

GRIFFITHS, D.E. (1978) 'Contemporary theory development and educational administration', *Educational Administration*, 6(2), pp. 80–93.

GRIFFITHS, D.E. (1979) 'Intellectual turmoil in educational administration', *Educational Administration Quarterly*, 15(3), pp. 43–65.

GRONN, P. and GREENWAY, P. (1982) Beadles, bearers or bureaucrats? Life-histories of state school administrators. Paper presented at the annual conference of the Australian Association for Research in Education, Brisbane.

GUBA, E.G. (1975) 'Problems in utilizing the results of evaluation', *Journal of Research and Development in Education*, 8, pp. 42–54.

GUBA, E.G. (1978) *Towards a Methodology of Naturalistic Inquiry in Educational*

Evaluation, CSE Monograph Series in Evaluation, No. 8, Los Angeles: Center for Study of Evaluation, University of California.

GUBA, E.G. (1979) Investigative reporting. Research in Evaluation Program Paper and Report Series, Northwest Regional Laboratory, January.

GUESS, R. (1981) *The Idea of a critical theory: Habermas and the Frankfurt School*, New York: Cambridge University Press.

GUTMANN, A. (1987) *Democratic Education*, New Jersey: Princeton University Press.

GYTE, G. (1988) 'Changing the curriculum in a school', in FIRTH, D. (Ed.) *School Management in Practice*, Essex: Longman, pp. 171–84.

HABERMAS, J. (1971) *Knowledge and Human Interest*, Boston: Beacon Press.

HABERMAS, J. (1973) *Theory and Practice*, Boston: Beacon Press.

HABERMAS, J. (1975) *Legitimation Crisis*, Boston: Beacon Press.

HABERMAS, J. (1979) *Communication and the Evolution of Society*, (McCARTHY, T., Trans.) Boston: Beacon Press.

HABERMAS, J. (1984) *Reason and the Rationalization of Society (Vol 1 of The Theory of Communicative Action)* (McCARTHY, T., Trans) Boston: Beacon Press.

HABERMAS, J. (1987) *Lifeworld and System: A Critique of Functionalist Reason (Vol 2 of The Theory of Communicative Action)* (McCARTHY, T., Trans), Cambridge: Polity Press.

HALL, M.E. (1979) Portrayal as a way of addressing problems in communicating evaluation findings. Paper presented at Annual Meeting of American Educational Research Association, San Francisco, April.

HALPIN, D. (1981) 'Accountability, answerability and the reporting of active learning time', *Organizational Evaluation in Schools (Reader 2)*, Victoria: Deakin University.

HALSEY, A.H. (1978) *Change in British Society*, Oxford: Oxford University Press.

HAMILTON, D. (1976) *Curriculum Evaluation*, London: Open Books.

HAMILTON, D. (1977) 'Making sense of curriculum evaluation: Continuities and discontinuities in an educational idea', *Review of Research in Education*, 5, pp. 318–47.

HAMILTON, D., JENKINS, D., KING, C., MACDONALD, B. and PARLETT, M. (Eds) (1977) *Beyond the Numbers Game: A Reader in Educational Evaluation*, London: Macmillan.

HAMMOND, R.L. (1972) 'Evaluation at the local level', in TAYLOR, P.A. and COWLEY, D.M. (Eds) *Readings in Curriculum Evaluation*, Dubuque, Iowa: Brown.

HANDY, C. (1988) 'Cultural forces in schools', in GLATTER, R. *et al.* (Eds) *Understanding School Management*, Stratford: Open University Press, pp. 107–16.

HARGREAVES, D. (1988) Keynote address. Presented at Bicentennial Principals' Conference held in Hobart, Tasmania on 10 August.

HARKER, R.K. (1984) 'On reproduction, habitus and education', *British Journal of Sociology of Education*, Vol 5 (2), pp. 117–27.

HARLEN, W.A. (1973) 'Formulating objectives — problems and approaches', *British Journal of Educational Technology*, 3(3), October.

HARLEN, W.A. (1975) 'A critical look at the classical strategy applied to formative curriculum evaluation', *Studies in Educational Evaluation*, 1, pp. 37–53.

HARLEN, W.A. (1976) 'Change and development in evaluation strategy', in TAW-

NEY, D. (Ed.) *Curriculum Evaluation Today: Trends and Implications*, Schools Council Research Studies, London: Macmillan.

HARLAN, W. (Ed.) (1978) *Evaluation and the Teacher's Role*, Schools Council Research Studies, London: Macmillan.

HARMON, W.W. (1976) 'Sizing up the social revolution', *Phi Delta Kappan*, p. 58.

HAVELOCK, R.G. (1973) *The Change Agent's Guide to Innovation in Education*, New Jersey: Educational Technology Publications.

HAWKBRIDGE, D.G. (1978) 'British and American approaches to evaluative studies in education', *Studies in Educational Evaluation*, 4, pp. 55–70.

HELD, D. (1980) *Introduction to Critical Theory*, Berkeley: University of California Press.

HERON, J. (1981) 'Philosophical basis for a new paradigm', in REASON, P. and ROWAN, J. (Eds) *Human Inquiry: A Sourcebook of New Paradigm Research*, Chichester: John Wiley and Sons.

HERSEY, P. and BLANCHARD, K. (1982) *Management of Organizational Behavior: Utilizing Human Resources*, (Fourth edn) Englewood Cliffs, NJ: Prentice-Hall.

HODGKINSON, C. (1978) *Towards a Philosophy of Administration*, Oxford: Basil Blackwell.

HOGBEN, D. (1977) Curriculum evaluation: By whom, for whom? Paper presented at Annual Conference of Australian Association for Research in Education, Canberra, November.

HOLLY, P. and WHITEHEAD, D. (Eds) (1986) *Collaborative Action Research*, Cambridge: Carn Publications, Bulletin No 7.

HOLMES, M. and WYNNE, E.A. (1989) *Making the School an Effective Community*, Lewes: Falmer Press.

HOLT, M. (1981) *Evaluating the Evaluators*, London: Hodder and Stoughton.

HOLT, M. (1987) *Judgement, Planning and Educational Change*, London: Harper and Row.

HOPKINS, D. and WIDEEN, M. (Eds) (1984) *Alternative Perspectives on School Improvement*, Lewes: Falmer Press.

HOSPERS, J. (1982) *Human conduct: Problems of ethics*, New York: Harcourt Brace Jovanovich, Inc.

HOUSE, E.R. (1976) 'Justice in evaluation,' in GLASS, G.V. (Ed.) *Evaluation Studies Review Annual*, Vol. 1. Beverly Hills, Calif.: Sage.

HOUSE, E.R. (Ed.) (1973) *School Evaluation: The Politics and Process*, Berkeley: McCutchan.

HOUSE, E.R. (1977) *The Logic of Evaluative Argument*, CSE Monograph Series in Evaluation, No. 7, Los Angeles: Center for Study of Evaluation, University of California.

HOUSE, E.R. (1978) 'Assumptions underlying evaluation models', *Educational Researcher*, 7(3), pp. 4–12.

HOUSE, E.R. (1979) 'Coherence and credibility: The aesthetics of evaluation', *Educational Evaluation and Policy Analysis*, 1(5), pp. 5–17.

HOUSE, E.R. (1979) (in collaboration with CASE, N.S.) 'Fair evaluation agreement', *Educational Theory*, 29, pp. 159–69.

HOUSE, E.R. (1980) *Evaluating with Validity*, Beverly Hills, Calif.: Sage.

HOUSE, E.R., RIVERS, W. and STUFFLEBEAM, D. (1974) 'An assessment of the Michigan accountability system', *Phi Delta Kappan*, 55, pp. 663–9.

HOY, W.K. and MISKEL, C.G. (1982) *Educational Administration: Theory, Research and Practice.* (2nd ed.) New York: Random House.

HOYLE, E. (1988) 'Leadership and mission', in GLATTER, R. *et al.* (Eds) *Understanding School Management,* Stratford: Open University Press, pp. 28–43.

HUBERMAN, A.M. and MILES, M.B. (1984) *Innovations Up Close,* New York: Plenum.

HUBERMAN, A.M. and MILES, M.B. (1986) 'Rethinking the quest for school improvement: Some findings from the DESSI study', in LIEBERMAN, A. (Ed.) *Rethinking School Improvement: Research, Craft and Concept,* New York: Teachers College Press.

HUGHES, P.W. (1985) *Changing Patterns of Secondary Education,* Hobart, University of Tasmania.

HUGHES, P., RUSSELL, N., MCCONACHY, D. and HARLEN, W. (1982) *Teachers as Evaluators Project: A Guide to Evaluation,* Canberra: Curriculum Development Centre.

HUNT, J. and FORDHAM, A. (1983) Year 10 students' and present high school leavers' views of ACT high schooling. Research Report, ACT Schools Authority.

HUNT, T. and KUNKEL, N. (1984) 'Catholic schools: The nation's largest alternative school system', in CASPER, J. and HUNT, T. (Eds) *Religious Schooling in America,* Birmingham, Alabama: Religious Education Press.

HUNTER, C. (1980) 'The politics of participation — with specific reference to teacher, pupil relationships', in WOODS, P. (Ed.) *Teacher Strategies,* London: Croom Helm.

JENCKS, C.S. *et al.* (1972) *Inequality: A Reassessment of the Effect of Family and Schooling in America,* New York: Basic Books.

JENKINS, D., KEMMIS, S., MACDONALD, B. and VERMA, C. (1979) 'Racism and educational evaluation', in VERMA, G.K. and BAGLEY, C. (Eds) *Race, Education and Identity,* London: Macmillan.

JENKINS, D. (1976) 'Six alternative models of curriculum evaluation', *Curriculum Design and Development Unit 20,* Milton Keynes: Open University Press.

JOINT COMMITTEE ON STANDARDS FOR EDUCATIONAL EVALUATION (1980) *Standards for Evaluations of Educational Programs, Projects and Materials,* New York: McGraw Hill.

JONES, A. (1987) *Leadership for Tomorrow's Schools,* Oxford: Basil Blackwell.

JONES, B.L. and MALOY, R.W. (1988) *Partnerships for Improving Schools,* New York: Greenwood Press.

JOYCE, B.R. and SHOWERS, B.K. (1980) 'Improving in-service training: The message of research', *Educational Leadership,* 37, pp. 379–85.

KATZ, J. and HENRY, M. (1989) *Turning Professors into Teachers: A New Approach to Faculty Development and Student Learning,* New York, Macmillan.

KEEVES, J.P. (Ed.) (1988) *Educational Research, Methodology, and Measurement: An International Handbook,* Oxford: Pergamon Press.

KELLEY, B.E. and BREDESON, P.V. (1987) Principals as symbol managers: Measure of meaning in schools. Paper prepared for Annual Meeting of the American Educational Research Association, Washington, D.C., April.

KELLY, E.F. (1975) 'Curriculum evaluation and literary criticism: Comments on the analogy', *Curriculum Theory Network,* 5, pp. 87–106.

KEMMIS, S. (1977) 'Telling it like it is: The problem of making a portrayal of an

educational program', in RUBIN, L. (Ed.) *Curriculum handbook: Administration and theory* Boston: Allyn and Bacon.

KEMMIS, S. (1980) Program evaluation in distance education: Against the technologisation of reason. Paper presented at National Workshop on Distance Teaching, Townsville, May.

KEMMIS, S. and HUGHES, P. (1979) Curriculum evaluation in higher education: Self reflection in a critical community. Paper presented at Annual Conference of Higher Education Research and Development Society of Australia, Brisbane, May.

KEMMIS, S. (1981) *A Guide to Evaluation Design*, Victoria, Deakin University.

KING, J.A. and THOMPSON, B. (1983) 'Research on school use of program evaluation: A Literature review and research agenda', *Studies in Educational Evaluation*, 9, pp. 5–21.

KIRPATRICK, D.L. (Ed.) (1985) *How to Manage Change Effectively*, San Francisco: Jossey Bass.

KRATHWOHL, D.R. (1980) 'The myth of value-free evaluation', *Educational Evaluation and Policy Analysis*, 2(1), pp. 37–45.

LAKOMSKI, G. (1987) 'Critical theory and educational administration', *The Journal of Educational Administration*, 25(1), pp. 84–100.

LESKO, N. (1988) *Symbolizing Society*, Lewes: Falmer Press.

LEVITON, L.C. and HUGHES, E.F. (1981) 'Research on the utilization of evaluations: A review and synthesis', *Evaluation Review*, 5, pp. 525–48.

LEWY, A. (1973) 'The practice of curriculum evaluation', *Curriculum Theory Network*, 11, pp. 6–33.

LEWY, A. (Ed.) (1977a) *Handbook of Curriculum Evaluation*, Paris: Unesco.

LEWY, A. (1977b) 'Responsive evaluation: An interpretation', *Studies in Educational Evaluation*, 3, pp. 143–8.

LIEBERMAN, A. and MILLER, L. (1984) *Teachers, Their World and Their Work; Implications for School Improvement*, Alexandria, VA, Association for Supervision and Curriculum Development.

LIEBERMAN, A. (Ed.) (1986) *Rethinking School Improvement: Research, Craft and Concept*, NY: Teachers College Press.

LIERMAN, W. (1987) 'Adult education: Movement and discipline between the golden sixties and the iron eighties', in LIERMAN, W. and KULICH, J. (Eds) *Adult Education and the Challenges of the 1990's*, London: Croom Helm.

LIGHTFOOT, S.L. (1978) *Worlds Apart: Relationships Between Families and Schools*, New York: Basic Books.

LIGHTFOOT, S.L. (1983) *The Good High School*, New York: Basic Books.

LONG, R. (1986) *Developing Parental Involvement in Primary Schools*, London: Macmillan.

LORTIE, D.C. (1975) *Schoolteacher: A Sociological Study*, Chicago: University of Chicago Press.

LOVEGROVE, et al. (1982) *Open Education and the Secondary School: A Book of Readings*, Adelaide, Education Department of South Australia.

MACDONALD, B. (1976) 'Evaluation and the control of educaton', in TAWNEY, D. (Ed.) *Curriculum Evaluation Today: Trends and Implications*, Schools Council Research Studies, London: Macmillan.

MACDONALD, B. and WALKER, R. (1975) 'Case-study and the social philosophy of educational research', *Cambridge Journal of Education*, 5(1), pp. 2–11.

MACKENZIE, DvE. (1983) 'Research for school improvement; An appraisal of some recent trends', *Educational Researcher*, 12(4).

MARGULIES, N. and WALLACE, J. (1973) *Organization Change: Techniques and Application*, Glenview, Illinois, Scott, Foresman.

McCARTHY, T. (1978) *The Critical Theory of Jurgen Habermas*, Cambridge: MIT Press.

McCONACHY, D. (1981) *Teachers as Evaluators Project: Bibliography*, ACT: Curriculum Development Centre.

McDANIEL, M.A. (1982) 'Tomorrow's curriculum today' in Toffler, A. (Ed.) *Learning for Tomorrow; The Role of the Future in Education*, New York: Vintage Books, pp. 29–40.

McPECK, J.E. (1981) *Crictical Thinking and Education*, Oxford, Martin Robertson.

MADAUS, G.F. SCRIVEN, M. and STUFFLEBEAM, D.L. (Eds) (1983) *Viewpoints on Educational and Human Services Evaluation*, Boston: Kluwer-Nijhoff.

MADEY, D.L. (1982) 'Some benefits of integrating qualitative and quantitative methods in program evaluation, with illustrations', *Educational Evaluation and Policy Analysis*, 4, pp. 223–236.

MADIGAN, J. (1986) *Evaluation of the Impact of the ELIC In-service Course in Western Australia*, Perth: Education Department of Western Australia.

MALING-KEEPES, J. (1976) *Educational Evaluation: Key Characteristics*, Melbourne: Australian Council for Educational Research.

MARCH, J.G. and OLSEN, J.P. (Eds) (1976) *Ambiguity and Choice in Organizations*, Bergen: Universitepsfarbaget.

MARSH, C. (1988) *Spotlight on School Improvement*, Sydney: Allen and Unwin.

MARSH, C. and STAFFORD, K. (1988) *Curriculum Practices and Issues*, (Second edn) Sydney: McGraw-Hill.

MEAD, G.H. (1967) *Mind, Self and Society*, Chicago: University of Chicago Press.

MILES, M.B. (1987) Practical guidelines for school administrators: How to get there. Paper read at Symposium on Effective Schools Programs and the Urban High School: The Management of Large Scale Change at the Annual Meeting of the American Educational Research Association, Washington, D.C., 23 April.

MILES, M.B. and EKHOLM, M. (1986) 'School Improvement at the school level', in VAN VELZEN, W.G., MILES, M.B., EKHOLM, M.B., HAMEYER, U. and ROBIN, D. (Eds) *Making School Improvement Work*, ISIP, pp. 123–80.

MITCHELL, T.R., DOWLING, P.J., KABANOFF, B.V. and LARSON, J.R. (1988) *People in Organizations: An Introduction to Organizational Behaviour in Australia*, Sydney: McGraw-Hill.

MORRELL, F. (1989) *Children of the Future*, London: Hogarth Press.

MORRISON, J. (1978) 'Social change and Catholic education', *Education*, 98, pp. 279–94.

MURPHY, J., WELL, M., HALLINGER, P. and MITMAN, A. (1985) 'School effectiveness: A Conceptual framework', *Educational Forum*, 12, 3.

MURPHY, R. and TORRANCE, H. (Eds) (1987) *Evaluating Education: Issues and Methods*, London: Harper and Row.

MUSGRAVE, P.W. (1988) *Socialising Contexts: The Subject in Society*, Sydney: Allen and Unwin.

NAISBITT, J. (1982) *Megatrends*, New York: Warner Books.

National Conference of Catholic Bishops (1972) *To Teach as Jesus Did*, Washington, D.C., United States Catholic Conference.

NIAS, J. (1988) 'Reference groups in primary teaching: Talking, listening and identity', in GLATTER, R. *et al.* (Eds) *Understanding School Management*, Stratford: Open University Press, pp. 294–303.

NISBET, J. (1974) Innovation — Bandwagon or hearse? Unpublished Frank Tate memorial lecture, Monash University, Melbourne, July.

OLDROYD, D. and TILLER, T. (1987) 'Change from within: An account of school-based collaborative action research in an English secondary school', *Journal of Education for Teaching*, 12(3), pp. 13–27.

OWENS, ROBERT G. (1981) *Organizational Behavior in Education*, (Second edn) Englewood Cliffs, NJ: Prentice-Hall.

OWENS, T.R. (1973) 'Educational evaluation by adversary proceedings', in HOUSE E.R. (Ed.) *School Evaluation: The Politics and the Process*, Berkeley: McCutchan.

OWENS, T.R. and EVANS, W.D. (1977) *Program Evaluation Skills for Busy Administrators*, Portland: Northwest Regional Educational Laboratory.

PARLETT, M. (1977) 'A study of two experimental programmes at MIT', in HAMILTON, D., JENKINS, D., KING, C., MacDONALD, B. and PARLETT, M. (Eds) *Beyond the Numbers Game: A Reader in Educational Evaluation*, London: Macmillan.

PARLETT, M. and DEARDEN, G. (Eds) (1977) *Introduction to Illuminative Evaluation: Studies in Higher Education*, Cardiff-by-the-Sea, Calif.: Pacific Soundings Press.

PARLETT, M. and HAMILTON, D. (1972) Evaluation as illumination: A new approach to the study of innovatory programmes. Occasional Paper No. 9, Centre for Research in the Educational Sciences, University of Edinburgh.

PARSONS, C. (1976) 'The new evaluation: A cautionary note', *Journal of Curriculum Studies*, 8, pp. 125–38.

PARSONS, T. (1949) *The Structure of Social Action*, Glencoe, IL: The Free Press.

PATTON, M.Q. (1980) *Qualitative Evaluation Methods*, Beverly Hills, Calif: Sage.

PAYNE, D.A. (Ed.) (1974) *Curriculum Evaluation: Commentaries on Purpose, Process, Product*, Lexington, Mass.: Heath.

PERROW, C. (1978) 'Demystifying organizations', in SCARVI, R.C. and HASENFELD, Y. (Eds) *The Management of Human Services*, New York: Columbia University Press.

PERROW, C. (1982) 'Disintegrating social sciences', *Phi Delta Kappan*, 63(10), pp. 684–8.

PETERS, T.J. and WATERMAN, R.H. JR. (1982) *In Search of Excellence: Lessons from America's Best-run Companies*, New York: Harper and Row.

PETERS, T.J. and AUSTIN, N. (1985) *A Passion for Excellence*, New York: Warner Books.

POPE JOHN PAUL II, (1982) *The Pope Teaches* (The Pope in Britain: Collected Homilies and Speeches), Slough: St Paul Publications.

POPHAM, W.J. (1975) *Educational Evaluation*, Englewood Cliffs, New Jersey: Prentice Hall. (second edition, 1988).

POPHAM, W.J. and CARLSON, D. (1977) 'Deep dark deficits of the adversary evaluation model, *Educational Researcher*, 6(6), pp. 3–6.

POPKEWITZ, T. (1980) 'Paradigms in educational science: Different Meanings and purpose to theory,' *The Journal of Education*, 162(1), pp. 28–46.

POPKEWITZ, T. (1983) *Change and Stability in Schooling: The Dual Quality of Educational Reform*, Victoria, Australia: Deakin University Press.

POSTMAN, N. (1987) *Amusing Ourselves to Death*, London: Methuen.

PROVUS, M.M. (1969) 'Evaluation of ongoing programs in the public school system', in TYLER, R.W. (Ed.) *Educational Evaluation: New Roles, New Means*, 68th yearbook of the National Society for Study of Education, Part 2, Chicago: University of Chicago Press.

PURKEY, S.C. and SMITH, M.S. (1985) 'School reform: The distict policy implications of the effective schools literatue', *Elementary School Journal*, 85, pp. 353–89.

PURSELL, C.H. and COOKSON, P.W. (1982) 'The effective principal in action', *The Effective Principal: A Research Summary*, Reston, Va: National Assoiation of Secondary Principals.

PUSEY, M.R. (1979) 'The legitimacy of state eduction systems', in PUSEY, M.R. and YOUNG, R.E. (Eds) *Control and Knowledge: The Mediation of Power in Institutional and Educational Settings*, Canberra: Australia National University.

QUALITY OF EDUCATION IN AUSTRALIA: REPORT OF THE REVIEW COMMITTEE (1985) Canberra: Australian Government Publishing Service.

QUALITY AND EQUALITY: COMMONWEALTH SPECIFIC PURPOSE PROGRAMS FOR AUSTRALIAN SCHOOLS (1985) Canberra: Canberra Publishing and Printing Company.

RAMSAY, W. and CLARK, E.E. (1988) 'From educational vision to school reality: The role of evaluation', *Catholic School Studies*, 61(2), pp. 47–50.

RAMSAY, W. and CLARK, E.E. (1988) 'The impact of new developments in school improvment: Vision, evaluation, effective change', *Unicorn*, 14(3), pp. 132–7.

RAMSAY, W. and CLARK, E.E. (1988) The role of school evaluation in preserving educational independence. Proceedings of Seventh National Conference of National Conference of National Council of Independent Schools September 29–October 2, pp. 122–134.

RAMARY, W. and CLARK, E.E. (1988) 'From education vision to school reality: The role of school evaluation', *Journal of Christian Education*, Papers, 93, December 7–17.

RAMSAY, W. and CLARK, E.E. (1989) *St Mary's College School Improvement Project: A Twofold Longitudinal Study Incorporating Students', Teachers' and Parents' Perceptions of School and Quality of School Life*, Hobart: University of Tasmania.

RAMARY, W. and RANSLEY, W. (1986) 'A method of analysis for determining dimensions of teching style', *Teaching and Teacher Education*, 2(1), pp. 69–79.

RATTRAY-WOOD, L. and PARROTT, J. (1985) 'Crises in society and educational administration', *Study Guide 1: Tradition and Turmoil in Education Administration*, Victoria: Deakin University, pp. 14–57.

RIPPEY, R.M. (Ed.) (1973) *Studies in Transactional Evaluation*, Berkeley: McCutchan.

RIST, R.C. (1977) 'On the relations among educational research paradigms: From disdain to detente', *Anthropology and Education Quarterly*, 8, pp. 42–9.

ROBINSON, R. (1984) 'Different approaches to the evaluation of programs and services', *Australian Psychologist*, 19, pp. 147–61.

ROSE, C. and NYRE, G.F. (1977) *The Practie of Evaluation*, ERIC/TM Report 65, Princeton: ERIC Clearinghouse on Tests, Measurement, and Evaluation, Educational Testing Service.

ROSSI, P.H. and WRIGHT, S.R. (1977) 'Evaluation research: An assessment of theory, practice, and politics', *Evaluation Quarterly*, 1, pp. 5–51.

ROUECHE, J.E. and BAKER, G.A. (1986) *Profiling Excellence in America's Schools*, Arlington, Va: American Assoication of School Administrators.

RUTTER, M., MAUGHAN, M., MORTIMORE, P. and OUSTON, J. (1979) *Fifteen Thousand Hours: Secondary Schools and Their Effects on Children*, London: Open Books.

SACRED CONGREGATION FOR CATHOLIC EDUCATIONS (1977) *The Catholic School*, Sydney: St Paul Publications.

SACRED CONGREGATION FOR CATHOLIC EDUCATION (1982) *Lay Catholics in Schools: Witnesses to Faith*, Sydney: St Paul Publications.

SALANCIK, G.R., CALDER, B.J., ROLAND, K.M., LEBLEBICI, H. and CONWAY, M. (1975) 'Leadership as an outcome of social structure and processes: A multidimensional analysis', in HUNT, J.C. and LARSON, L.L. (Eds) *Leadership Frontiers*, Kent, OH: Kent State University Press.

SARASON, S.B. (1982) *The Culture of the School and the Problem of Change*, (Second edn) Boston: Allyn and Bacon.

SCHEIN, E.H. (1985) *Organizational Culture and Leadership*, San Francisco: Jossey-Bass.

SCHEYER, P. and STAKE, R.E. (1976) 'A program's self-evaluation portfolio', *Studies in Educational Evaluation*, 2, pp. 37–40.

SCHEYER, P., (1978) Still photography: Can it provide program portrayal? Paper presented at Annual Meeting of American Educational Research Association, Tornoto, March.

SCHON, D. (1983) *The Reflective Practitioner*, New York: Basic Book.

SCHON, D. (1987) *Educating the Reflective Practitioner*, New York: Basic Books.

Department of Education School Based Evaluation (Vols 1–10), Queensland, 1982.

SCHOOL BASED EVALUATION IN ACT GOVERNMENT SCHOOLS (1981) ACT Schools Authority.

SCHOOL CONTROLLED EVALUATION: SUPPORT PROJECT FOR SCHOOL CONTROLLED EVALUATION IN SOUTH AUSTRALIA (1980) Education Department of South Australia.

SCHOOL EVALUATION (1985) Commonwealth Schools Commission.

SCHOOL EVALUATION MANUAL FOR AUSTRALIAN SCHOOLS (1980) National School Evaluation Committee.

SCRIVEN, M. (1967) 'The methodology of evaluation', in TYLER, R., GAGNE, R. and SCRIVEN, M. (Eds) *Perspectives of Curriculum Evaluation*, AERA Monograph Series on Curriculum Evalution, No. 1, Chicago: Rand McNally.

SCRIVEN, M. (1972) 'Pros and cons about goal free evaluation', *Evaluation Comment*, 3(4), pp. 1–4.

SCRIVEN, M. (1973) 'Goal-free evaluation', in HOUSE, E.R. (Ed.) *School Evaluation: The Politics and the Process*, Berkeley: McCutchan.

SCRIVEN, M. (1974) 'Maximizing the power of causal investigations: The modus

operandi method', in POPHAM, W.J. (Ed.) *Evaluation in Education — Current Applications*, Berkeley: McCutchan.

SCRIVEN, M. (1980) *Evaluation Thesaurus*, Point Reyes, Calif.: Edgepress.

SERGIOVANNI, T.J. (1984) 'Leadership and excellence in schooling', *Educational Leadership*, February.

SERGIOVANNI, T.J. and STARRATT, R.J. (1983) *Supervision: Human perspectives* (Third edn), New York: McGraw-Hill.

SHEIVE, L.T. and SCHOENHEIT, M.B. (1987) 'Vision and the work life of eduational leaders', in SHEIVE, L.T. and SCHOENHEIT, M.B. (Eds) *Leadership: Examining the Elusive*, 1987 Yearbook of the Association for Supervision and Curriculum Development. Alexandria, Va: ASCA.

SIMONS, H. (Ed.) (1980) *Towards a Science of the Singular*, Occasional Paper No. 10, Nordwich: Centre for Applied Research in Education, University of East Anglia.

SIMMONS, R.J. (Ed.) (1985) *Religious Education in Catholic Schools*, Sydney: Catholic Education Office.

SMITH, D.L. and FRASER, B.J. (1980) 'Towards a confluence of quantitative and qualitative approaches to curriculum evaluation', *Journal of Curriculum Stuides*, 12, pp. 367–70.

SMITH, L.M. (1978) 'An evolving logic of participant observation, educational ethnography, and other case studies', *Review of Research in Education*, 6, pp. 316–77.

SMITH, L.M., PRUNTY, J.J., DWYER, D.C. and KLEIN, P.F. (1988) *Innovation and Change in Schooling: History, Politics and Agency*, Lewes: Falmer Press.

SMITH, M.L. (1978) *The Development of New Evaluation Methodologies*, Research on Evaluation Program Paper and Report Series, Northwest Regional Educational Laboratory, September.

SMITH, M.L. (1987) *Research and Evaluation in Education and the Social Sciences*, New Jersey: Prentice Hall, Inc.

SMITH, M.L. and MURRAY, S.L. (1974) *The Status of Research Models of Product Development and Evaluation*, Research, Evaluation and Development Paper Series, Northwest Regional Educational Laboratory, August.

SMITH, N. (1981) *Metaphors for Evaluation*, Beverly Hills: Sage Publications.

SMYTH, W.J. (1985) 'Educational administration: A critique of the tradition', *Study Guide 1: Tradition and Turmoil in Educational Administration*, Victoria, Deakin University Press, pp. 1–11.

SPADY, W. and MITCHELL, P.E. (1977) The uses of authority and power in the organization and control of school task performances. Unpublished AERA symposium paper.

STAKE, R.E. (1967) 'The countenance of educational evaluation', *Teachers College Record*, 68, pp. 523–40.

STAKE, R.E. (1972) Responsive evaluation. Unpublished paper, Center for Instructional Research and Curriculum Evaluation, University of Illinois at Urbana-Champaign.

STAKE, R.E. (1975a) 'To evaluate an arts program', in STAKE, R.E. (Ed.) *Evaluatory the Arts in Education: A Responsive Approach*, Columbus, Ohio, Merrill.

STAKE, R.E. (Ed.) (1975b) *Evaluating the Arts in Education: A Responsible Approach*, Columbus: Merrill.

STAKE, R.E. (1976) 'A theoretical statement of responsive evaluation', *Studies in Educational Evaluation*, 2, pp. 19–22.

STAKE, R.E. (1979) Portrayal of programs through evaluation studies. Unpublished paper presented at CIRCE-IOE Spring Evaluation Conference, Urbana, April.

STAKE, R.E. and EASLEY, J.A. Jr. (1978) *Case Studies in Science Education*, Urbana, Ill.: Centre for Instructional Research and Curriculum Evaluation, University of Illinois.

STAKE, R.E. and GJERDE, C. (1974) 'An evaluation of TCITY', in KRAFT, R.H.P., SMITH, L.M., POHLAND, P.A., BRAUNER, C.J. and GJERDE, C. (Eds) *Four Evaluation Examples: Anthropological, Economic, Narrative, Portrayal*, AERA Monograph Series on Curriculum Evaluation, No. 7, Chicago: Rand McNally.

STANFORD EVALUATION CONSORTIUM (1976) 'Review of "Handbook of evaluation Research"', *Educational Researcher*, 9(11), pp. 9–19.

STARRATT, R.J. (1986) Excellence in education and quality of leadership. Occasional Paper No 1 of the Southern Tasmania Council for Educational Administration.

STARRATT, R.J. (1988) Dimensions of the principal's leadership: Vision and Dramatic consciousness. Paper presented to Southern Tasmania Council for Educational Administration, 15 August.

STEHNOUSE, L.(1975) *An Introduction to Curriculum Research and Development*, London: Heinemann, (Chapter X).

STENZIL, N. (1979) Committee hearings as an evaluation format. Research on Evaluation Program Paper and Report Series, No. 22, Northwest Regional Educational Laboratory, August.

STERNE, M. (1979) 'What makes a good school?' *Education*, 24 August, 198.

STOEL, W.G.R. and SCHEERENS, J. (1988) The validity of characteristics of effective schools across contexts and nations. Paper presented at annual meeting of the American Educational Research Association, April, New Orleans.

STOGDILL, R.M. (1974) *Handbook of Leadership: A Survey of Theory and Research*, New York: The Free Press.

STRATON, R.G. (1977) 'Ethical issues in evaluating educational programs', *Studies in Educational Evaluation*, 3, pp. 57–66.

STUFFLEBEAM, D.L. (1969) 'Evaluation as enlightenment for decision making', in BEATTY, W.H. (Ed.) *Improving Educational Assessment and an Inventory of Measures of Affective Behavior*, Washington: Association for Supervision and Curriculum Development

STUFFLEBEAM, D.L. (1971) 'The relevance of the CIPP evaluation model for educational accountability', *Journal of Research and Development in Education*, 5, pp. 19–25.

STUFFLEBEAM, D.L. (1974) Meta-evaluation. Paper 3 in unpublished Occasional Paper Series, Evaluation Center, Western Michigan University.

STUFFLEBEAM, D.L., FOLEY, W.J., GEPHART, W.J., GUBA, E.G., HAMMOND, R.L., MERRIMAN, H.O. and PROVUS, M.M. (1971) *Educational Evaluation and Decision Making*, Itasca, Ill.: Peacock.

STUFFLEBEAM, D.L. and WEBSTER, W.J. (1980) 'An analysis of alternative

approaches to evaluation', *Educational Evaluation and Policy Analysis*, 2(3), pp. 5–20.

STUFFLEBEAM, D.L. and SHINKFIELD, A.J. (1985) *Systematic Evaluation*, Boston: Kluwer-Nijhoff.

TAMIR, P. (1981) 'The potential of evaluation in curriculum implementation', in LEWY, A. (Ed.) *Evaluation Roles*, London: Pergamon.

TAWNEY, D. (Ed.) (1976) *Curriculum Evaluation Today: Trends and Implications*, Schools Council Research Studies, London: Macmillan.

TAYLOR, F. (1972) *Scientific Management*, Westport: Greenwood Press.

TAYLOR, P.A. and COWLEY, D.M. (1972) *Readings in Curriculum Evaluation*, Dubuque, Iowa: Brown.

TAYLOR, P.A. and MAGUIRE, T.O. (1966) 'A theoretical evaluation model', *Manitoba Journal of Educational Research*, 1(2), pp. 12–17.

TEMPLIN, P. (1979) Photography in evaluation. Paper presented at Annual Meeting of American Educational Research Association, San Francisco, April.

THOMAS, E.B. (1987) 'Matters of concern', in SIMPKINS, W.S., THOMAS, A.R. and THOMAS, E.B. (Eds) *Principal and Change: The Australian Experience*, Armidale, NSW: University of New England Press, pp. 29–40.

THOMAS, J.B. and HELD, D. (1982) *Habermas Critical Debates*, Cambridge: MIT Press.

THURSTON, P. (1978) 'Revitalizing adversary evaluation: Deep dark deficits or muddled mistaken musings', *Educational Research*, 7(7), pp. 3–8.

TIMAR, T. and KIRP, D.L. (1988) *Managing Educational Excellence*, Lewes: Falmer Press.

TOFFLER, A. (1970) *Future Shock*, London: Pan Books.

TOFFLER, A. (1981) *The Third Wave*, London: Pan Books.

TOFFLER, A. (1982) *Learning for Tomorrow: The Role of the Future in Education*, New York: Vintage Books.

TYLER, R.W. (1942) 'General statement on evaluation', *Journal of Educational Research*, pp. 492–501.

TYLER, R.W. (1949) *Basic Principles of Curriculum and Instruction*, Illinois: University of Chicago Press.

TYMKO, J.L. (1984) *Making Sense of the Literature on Effective Schools*, Edmonton, Alberta: The Alberta Academy for Educational Leadership.

VAN MANEN, M. (1977) 'Linking ways of knowing with ways of being practical', *Curriculum Inquiry*, 6(3), pp. 205–28.

VAN VELZEN, W.G., MILES, M.B., EKHOLM, M., HAMEYER, U. and ROBIN, D. (1986) *Making School Improvement Work*, Paris: OECD.

Victorian Minister of Education, *Ministerial Papers 1–4*, Melbourne: Minister of Education.

WALKER, J.C. and EVERS, C.W. (1988) 'The epistemological unity of educational research', in KEEVES, J.P. (Ed.) *Educational Research, Methodology, and Measurement: An International Handbook*, Oxford: Pergamon, pp. 28–36.

WALKER, S. and BARTON, L. (Eds) (1989) *Politics and the Processes of Schooling*, Milton Keynes: Open University Press.

WATKINS, P.E. (1983) 'Scientific management and critical theory in educational administration', in BATES, R. (Ed.) *Educational Administration and the Manage-*

ment of Knowledge, (ESA 841: Theory and Practice in Educational Administration) Victoria, Australia: Deakin University, pp. 119–35.

WEHLAGE, G.G., RUTTER, R.A., SMITH, G.A., LESKO, N. and FERNANDEZ, R.R.
(1989) *Reducing the Risk: Schools as Communities of Support*, Philadelphia,
Falmer Press.

WEHLAGE, G.G. and LIPMAN, P. (1988) Integrating school and community: The
Annie, E. Casey Foundation's new futures initiatiave for at-risk youth,
Madison, Wisconsin, National Center on Effective Secondary Schools.

WEICK, K. (1976) 'Educational organizations as loosely coupled systems', *Administrative Science Quarterly*, 21(1), pp. 1–19.

WELCH, W.W. (1969) 'Curriculum evaluation', *Review of Educational Research*, 39,
pp. 429–43.

WELCH, W.W. (1974) 'The process of evaluation', *Journal of Research in Science
Teaching*, 11, pp. 175–84.

WELCH, W.W. (1976) 'Evaluating the impact of national curriculum projects',
Science Education, pp. 475–83.

WEXLER, P. (1987) *Social Analysis of Education: After the New Sociology*, London:
Routledge and Kegan Paul.

WHORF, B.L. (1956) 'Language thought and reality', in CARROLL, J.B. (Ed.)
Selected Writings of Benjamin Lee Whorf, Cambridge, Mass., MIT Press.

WILLIAMS, T. and BATTEN, M. (1981) The Quality of School Life. ACER Research Monograph No. 12. Hawthorn, Vic: Australian Council for Educational Research.

WILLIAMS, T. and BATTEN, M. (1983) The Quality of School Life. Unpublished
paper, Hawthorn, Vic: Australian Council for Educational Research.

WILLIS, G.L. (Ed.) (1978) *Qualitative Evaluation: Concepts and Cases in Curriculum
Criticism*, Berkeley, McCutchan.

WILLMOT, G.M. (1988) Factors influencing the quality of school life in South
Australian Secondary Schools. Unpublished PhD Thesis, Flinders University, SA.

WISSLER, D.F. and ORITIZ, F.I. (1987) *The Superintendent's Leadership in School
Reform*, Lewes: Falmer Press.

WOLF, R.L. (1975) 'Trial by jury: A new evaluation method', *Phi Delta Kappan*,
57, pp. 185–7.

WOLF, R.L. (1979a) 'The use of judicial evaluation methods in the formulation of
educational policy', *Educational Evaluation and Policy Analysis*, 1(3), pp. 19–
28.

WOLF, R.L. (1979b) Strategies for conducting naturalistic evaluation in socio-
educational settings: The naturalistic interview. Occasional Paper Series.
Evaluation Center, Western Michigan University.

WOLF, R.L. and TYKMITZ, B.L. (1978) Whatever happened to the giant wombat:
A naturalistic investigation of the impact of the ice age mammals and
emergence of man exhibit. National Museum of Natural History, Smithso-
nian Institution.

WORLD COMMISSION ON ENVIRONMENT AND DEVELOPMENT (1987) *Our Common
Future*, Oxford: Oxford University Press.

WORTHEN, B.R. (1977a) 'Characteristics of good evaluation studies', *Journal of
Research and Development in Education*, 10, pp. 3–20.

WORTHEN, B. (1977b) Eclecticism and evaluation models: Snapshots of an

elephant's anatomy. Paper presented at Annual Meeting of American Educational Research Association, New York City, April.

WORTHEN, B.R. (1978a) 'Some thoughts about current models for evaluating curricula', *Australian Educational Researcher*, 5(3), pp. 9–19.

WORTHEN, B.R. (1978b) Metaphors and methodologies for evaluation. Paper presented at Annual Meeting of American Educational Research Association, Toronto, March.

WORTHEN, B.R. (1978c) 'Expertise needed in curriculum evaluation', *Australian Education Researcher*, 5(2), pp. 5–27.

WORTHEN, B.R. and ROGERS, W.T. (1977) Uses and abuses of adversary evaluation: A consumer's guide. Paper presented to Annual Meeting of American Educational Research Association, New York City, April.

WORTHEN, B.R. and SANDERS, J.R. (1978) *Educational Evaluation: Theory and Practice*, Worthington: Jones.

YUKL, G.A. (1989) Leadership in Organizations (Second edn), Englewood Cliffs, NJ: Prentice Hall.

Index